OCEANSIDE PUBLIC LIBRARY
330 N. Coast Highway
Oceanside, CA 92054

Gogol

PLAYS AND SELECTED WRITINGS

D0038795

CIVIC CENTER

891.723
GOG

Gogol

PLAYS AND SELECTED WRITINGS

(Nikolai)

Nikolay Gogol

Edited and with an Introduction and Notes by Milton Ehre

Translated by Milton Ehre and Fruma Gottschalk

Northwestern University Press

Evanston, Illinois

Northwestern University Press
Evanston, Illinois 60208-4210

Licensed by The University of Chicago Press, Chicago,
Illinois. © 1980 by The University of Chicago. All rights
reserved, including performance rights.

Originally published as *The Theater of Nikolay Gogol: Plays
and Selected Writings.*

Northwestern University Press edition published 1994
Printed in the United States of America

ISBN: 0-8101-1159-4

Library of Congress Cataloging-in-Publication Data

Gogol', Nikolaĭ Vasil'evich, 1809–1852.
    [Plays. English. Selections]
    Gogol—plays and selected writings / Nikolay Gogol ;
edited with an introduction and notes by Milton Ehre ;
translated by Milton Ehre and Fruma Gottschalk.
        p. cm. — (European drama classics)
    Originally published: The theater of Nikolay Gogol.
Chicago : University of Chicago Press, 1980.
    Includes bibliographical references.
    Contents: Marriage — The government inspector —
The gamblers.
    ISBN 0-8101-1159-4 (pbk.)
    1. Gogol', Nikolaĭ Vasil'evich, 1809–1852—Translations
into English. I. Ehre, Milton, 1933– . II. Gottschalk,
Fruma, 1900–   . III. Gogol', Nikolaĭ Vasil'evich, 1809–
1852. Theater of Nikolay Gogol. IV. Title. V. Series.
PG3333.A6 1994A
891.72'3–dc20   94-22811
                                                      CIP

The paper used in this publication meets the minimum
requirements of the American National Standard for
Information Sciences—Permanence of Paper for Printed
Library Materials, ANSI Z39.48-1984.

3 1232 00889 0727

16

FOR JOELLE AND JULIEANNE

Contents

Introduction

A number of Russian writers of the nineteenth century known to us through their prose fiction—Tolstoy, Turgenev, Pisemsky, Saltykov-Shchedrin—also wrote plays. Nikolay Gogol (1809–52) pursued a career more like that of Chekhov. He was not a full-time novelist making an occasional foray into another medium, bringing along the esthetic imperatives of his major concern. From his school years, when he directed and acted in plays of the classical repertoire (he was by all accounts an impressive comic actor and a superb reader), the theater was an absorbing interest. He saw himself as both dramatist and writer of prose fiction, and to each he brought the full resources of his considerable creative powers. His plays were as innovative as his fiction, and have proved as durable.

If he wrote little for the theater, only three complete plays, he also wrote relatively little prose fiction, a score of short stories and an incomplete novel, *Dead Souls*. A common metaphor for Gogol's career has been that of a comet, bursting suddenly upon the landscape, burning itself out quickly, but transforming the configuration of Russian literary culture. If we discount juvenilia and a later volume of essays in the form of letters expounding his views on Russian society, religion, art, and literature (*Selected Passages from a Correspondence with Friends*), then except for *The Overcoat* (1842) Gogol's essential corpus was conceived, written, or begun in an eight-year period (1829–36), and even *The Overcoat* may have been on his mind from the early thirties.

Though many of his writings resulted from bursts of inspiration, Gogol was also a meticulous craftsman. He advised writers to dash off their projects hastily, even carelessly, and then go back to them at periodic intervals (ideally eight times!), and his manuscripts attest numerous revisions. The plays underwent more extensive reworkings than any of his short stories.

Gogol's first try at comedy was *The Order of Vladimir, Third Class*, begun in 1832 and later abandoned. It was to be the story of an opportunistic bureaucrat who schemes to attain the decoration of the title—the cross of St. Vladimir conferred noble status—and eventually goes mad, imagining he has metamorphosed into his coveted medal. If this sounds like vintage Gogol, the surviving manuscripts suggest it wasn't. They show a complicated plot with several intrigues going on at once, a secondary love story, scenes that seem to hold only ethnographic interest, including pictures of life among the upper aristocracy—procedures and topics that are all untypical of Gogol. He attributed his hesitation in continuing to fear of the censors, but a friend's judgment that the novice at drama "wanted to include too much and continually encountered difficulties" is more plausible.[1]

Whatever the reason, *Marriage,* which he started the following year, might have served a double purpose: There was little the censors could object to in this hilarious farce, and working on a play designed largely for laughs (though it also has a serious dimension) forced Gogol to take into account what he had neglected in his previous venture—quickness of pace, rhythm, performability. The play is a marvel of construction, a perfect play in a minor vein. Though it attained final form only in 1841, well after the writing of the first version of *The Government Inspector,* a complete draft was ready by 1835, and the efforts that went into it were a proving ground for his most significant achievement in comedy.

On October 7, 1835, Gogol implored Pushkin to send him "an authentically Russian anecdote" upon which he would, he promised, knock off a comedy "funnier than hell." In less than two months perhaps Russia's greatest play and one of the great comedies of the world repertoire was completed. Studies of the original manuscript of *The Government Inspector* have led scholars to believe that it was written in several days of feverish activity. The play was carefully edited for publication and production in 1836, and revised once again for a second edition of 1841. April 19, 1836, the date of its premiere, is a landmark in the history of the Russian theater. Because the play depicted the endemic corruption and incompetence of Russian officialdom, production required the extraordinary intervention of the emperor. We may guess that Nicholas I, who had little confidence in his subordinates, consented in order to have an opportunity to see them squirm. The performance became a cause célèbre, provoking comparisons to the tumultuous reception of Beaumarchais' *Marriage of Figaro* in the pre-Revolutionary France of Louis XVI. The tsar's presence at opening night brought out the important dignitaries of state and the beau monde of the capital, who were scandalized by what they took as an affront to good taste (it was called a dirty play!) and a slander of Holy Russia. The reaction in Moscow was similar, leading someone to ask the actor Shchepkin, who played the mayor, what else he expected when half the audience was on the take and the other half was greasing palms. The play also had its defenders, and many—most likely, the majority—simply had a good laugh and went home. For those disaffected with the status quo, the work crystallized everything they hated in Russia ("contemporary Russia's terrible confession," Herzen called it), and they claimed Gogol as their own.[2] However, Gogol's age was one of burgeoning criticism of society from a conservative as well as a radical position, and in time it became clear that he was closer to the nostalgic Slavophiles than the forward-looking Westerners. It is difficult to tell what disturbed the soon-to-be apologist of patriarchal Russia more: the censure of the right or the embraces of the left. On June 6, 1836, in the midst of the uproar, he scurried away from Russia to spend most of the next twelve years of his life in exile, much of it in his beloved Rome.

The Gamblers, the third play in Gogol's trilogy, was also begun in the Petersburg period but was not finished until 1842. It is less perfect than the other two. The characters are well-drawn but not memorable; the manner is constrained, aiming at wry humor and irony rather than broad comedy. Nevertheless, this "comic scene," as Gogol called it,[3] is a subtle and thoughtful play, which for all its flaws, merits more attention than it has received.

A historical drama on Alfred the Great remained incomplete. It was apparently intended as an apotheosis of enlightened monarchy —a frequent aim of previous Russian tragedy. The characters speak in the turgid rhetoric Gogol slipped into whenever he allowed himself to be deflected from his comic vision. He did complete a draft of a play on the Ukrainian Cossacks of the seventeenth century, but burned the manuscript when the poet Zhukovsky fell asleep at a reading. It was to have been a romantic evocation of the heroic Ukrainian past (Gogol was Ukrainian by birth)—a kind of *Taras Bulba* for the stage.

Two fragments dating to 1832 may be remainders of his first abortive attempts at plays. One is terribly melodramatic; the other seems headed in a sentimental-didactic direction. A benevolent fate kept Gogol from completing anything but comedies for the theater.

In 1842 Gogol's literary career more or less ground to a halt. It had lasted slightly over a decade. The first half of that marvelous decade was one of intense conception and creation. The second was spent in wrapping up: some works were finished, others rewritten. Subsequent years formed a troubled and sometimes grim epilogue. Labor on the sequel to *Dead Souls* turned into uncharacteristic drudgery (the first volume had come out in 1842). Intellectual activity, such as it was, shifted from art to a desperate search for salvation—both for himself and for the Russia he loved and yet spent over half his adult life fleeing.

The great books of Russian literature have often appeared to us as isolated monuments arising mysteriously in a forbidding landscape. In truth they grew out of an atmosphere of excited, even heated, intellectual debate and artistic endeavor. Gogol's plays were the culmination of nearly a century of lively theatrical activity, from the inception of the modern Russian theater, conventionally dated to the institution, in 1756 in Petersburg, of the first regular theater, by official decree of the Empress Elizabeth. Before Gogol, Russians produced few plays that have survived in the contemporary repertoire—only two (Fonvizin's *The Minor* and Griboyedov's *Woe from Wit*), if we exclude Pushkin's brilliant poetic dramas (the *Little Tragedies*), which are rarely performed, and his experiment in

Shakespearean tragedy, *Boris Godunov*, which has achieved theatrical prominence only in Musorgsky's great opera. Nevertheless, by the 1830s Russians had adapted and produced hundreds of foreign plays (mostly French), created a considerable corpus of original drama, organized acting companies and founded theaters, in the provinces as well as in Moscow and Petersburg, and developed a vigorous criticism. Without the sustenance of this theatrical culture, Gogol's plays would have been inconceivable.

The Russian tradition, still alive in Gogol's youth, was neoclassical in manner, aristocratic in temper, and pedagogical in purpose. Russians of the eighteenth century took their models from the French classical theater of Corneille, Racine, and Molière; later from Voltaire and other figures of the French Enlightenment. Their plays were often only schematic and mechanical applications of the classical method, provoking the Romantics of the 1830s to dismiss the century as derivative and imitative—a tendency that has persisted. Even the eighteenth century heard complaints and calls for a more national art. But for the classicist, art *was* imitation—of models of excellence and universal patterns. Besides, Russians had little choice. The native tradition of folk drama was too raw for the tastes of educated audiences and too narrow for their complex experience; the older "school plays," so called because of their association with the theological academies, had little to say to a society in the process of secularization. The classical repertoire furnished a school in which dramatists without a usable tradition could master the complex techniques of writing plays. The Russian eighteenth century, often depicted as static and sterile, was an age of intense experimentation in form, and in the forging of a literary language.

Indeed the eighteenth century was a century when all Russia went to school—in the reign of Peter the Great (1682–1725) to acquire the technological and administrative skills prerequisite to the creation of a modern power; in the age of Catherine (1762–96), also "the Great," to attain the cultural urbanity of a ruling elite. Russians were passionately responsive to the European Enlightenment for the simple reason that there was so much enlightening to be done. Peter had made a heroic effort to pull Russia out of its medieval rigidity, and the project continued through the century. Literature was to entertain, but its first function was to educate. Drama, the most social of the arts, was the most exposed to the pedagogical impulse. "The theater is a national school...," Catherine wrote, as did Gogol a half century later, "and I am the senior teacher."[4]

What Catherine, who wrote a number of plays herself, and the dramatists of her age tried to instill in their fellow Russians were the Enlightenment virtues of reason and reasonableness, of civic duty and patriotism. Teaching might take the form of moralistic interpolations in a text, or the negative form of satire—after the ode, the most cultivated of the neoclassical genres. "Comedy's nature is to correct manners through ridicule/ Its rule—to amuse and serve," reads a famous couplet of Alexander Sumarokov, the founder of the modern Russian drama and the leading exponent of Russian neoclassicism. Sumarokov's lines, paraphrasing, through Boileau, Horace's blend of the *utile* and *dulce,* might stand as a motto of Russian comedy before Gogol. The view of literature as socially useful, correcting manners through satire, or providing exemplary models in tragedy, fell on fertile ground in Russia. The nobility had a long tradition of service to the state and continued to take positions in the military or the bureaucracy even after the compulsory service introduced by Peter was abolished. Though the government's desire to have advancement in the service depend on education was resisted by the tradition bound, a significant minority came to see enlightenment, more than birth or wealth, as the mark of nobility: "If the master's mind is not more enlightened than the peasant's/ I see no difference whatsoever," reads another couplet of Sumarokov.[5] The theater offered lessons in true nobility, and in the pitfalls of a spurious nobility: "A nobleman unworthy of being a nobleman! I know nothing in the world more base," admonishes the *raisonneur* of Fonvizin's *The Minor.*

The satire of eighteenth-century comedy, when it was not excoriating the ignorance of dark Russia, took as its object this counterfeit nobility. For many, "enlightenment" and "Westernization" were confined to elegant dress, imported baubles, polite manners, the capacity to sprinkle one's conversation with French phrases. It was an exceptional comedy that missed a chance to take a dig at the Frenchified dandy or his twin, the frivolous coquette. "Why was I born Russian!" a typical fop exclaims, "O nature, have you no shame that, in making me a man, you made me from a Russian father!"[6] Spoofing soon turned into serious social criticism, as comedies drove home the fact that the self-indulgent luxury of the few entailed the suffering of many. But eighteenth-century satire, often courageous and far ranging, exposing official corruption and reaching even into the court of Catherine to attack its tinsel and sycophancy, remained essentially moral and pedagogical—if men and women and even tsars had more good sense, all would be well with the world. The great mass of Russians, including most of the nobility, though aware of changing cultural styles, held to the old patriarchal ways. The incongruity of modern fashionable ideas and manners in a backward and largely illiterate country was a natural subject for comedy right through the age of Gogol.

Russia encountered French classicism at the moment it was losing its coherence and vitality. While Marivaux was enclosing comedy in a hothouse of refinement, Diderot and others were satisfying middle-class tastes for an art less severe than the classical models, more personal and intimate. A comedy that would make us weep instead of laugh supplanted the satirical theater of Molière and the popular farces. Russians of the eighteenth century, eagerly receptive to trends from the West, translated and produced the new "tearful comedies" and "bourgeois tragedies" almost as soon as they appeared. Rousseau had a tremendous impact, though he was most often squeezed into a conservative mold. In Russia, the celebration of the countryside easily led to idealization of its fundamental institution—the manorial estate based on serfdom. The new sensibility affected Russian drama in important ways. Discovery of a natural self undermined classical rationalization of character into abstract types; the cult of natural simplicity eroded classical decorum. Writers began to seek out ordinary life and speech and things Russian. Nevertheless the major current of Russian comedy remained strongly satiric. While the French were moving to a drama that would overcome the distance of the classical stage through characters with whom the audience could "identify," the leading

Russian writers of comedy, from Sumarokov through Fonvizin, Knyazhnin, Kapnist, and Krylov, held to the older patterns of ridicule. It is symptomatic that at a time when the authority of Molière was on the wane in France, where he was attacked as "too aristocratic," his popularity in Russia was enormous and continuous. Almost every dramatist of the eighteenth century tried his hand at adaptations from his plays, and his influence was still very much alive in the early nineteenth. Russia, without a bourgeoisie to speak of, was still to develop a middle range of drama—this was to be the achievement of Ostrovsky in the 1850s—and "the choice for a dramatist of [Gogol's] age was almost inevitably between comedy and tragedy."[7]

Fonvizin's *The Minor* (1782), besides being the best eighteenth-century Russian comedy, is exemplary of the tangle of elements that went into the genre and which Gogol was finally to unravel. It is a play with two faces: on the one side, a crisp satire of the boorishness and brutality of the worst segment of the Russian provincial gentry; on the other, a tiresome lecture on the virtues of enlightenment and aristocratic honor. The *raisonneur* Starodum ("Old Thoughts") is brought on stage solely to instruct us; the idealistic young lovers, to offer an opposing model to the barbaric Prostakovs ("Simpletons"). Both types had become staples of Russian comedy. But if Fonvizin's play mirrors the didactic imperatives of his age, it is also indicative of its growing realism. The frighteningly coarse and bullying Mme. Prostakov is the first great creation of the Russian comic imagination; she would be fully at home among Gogol's grotesques. Hovering at the edge of caricature, she is not reducible to a single comic flaw or "humor." With Fonvizin Russian comedy begins to move from a comic vice to a comically vicious character.

The play's conclusion calls for a complexity of response that is also new for Russian comedy. Mme. Prostakov stays unregenerate, and the action, like that of Gogol's plays, resolves in the collapse of a world instead of the usual pedagogical rehabilitation. As dramatists confronted the reality of Russian life, that reality showed itself as more refractory than had been imagined, less yielding to instruction. Fonvizin, however, still clutched at eighteenth-century optimism: the stage at the end presents an image of an alternative society of the virtuous (the play's other face), who have been vindicated by the favorite deus ex machina of classical comedy—the enlightened monarchy. In Griboyedov's brilliant *Woe from Wit* (written 1822-24) the hero Chatsky, like the *raisonneurs* of Fonvizin, lectures his society on civic virtue and honor but finds no social ground on which to stand and speaks to the wind. The characters of Gogol also moralize, but it is sheer bluff—the moralist become ludicrous. The progression is telling.

The classical impulse continued through the first quarter of the nineteenth century and reached its culmination in Pushkin and the remarkable poets of his age. In the reign of Alexander I (1801-25) Russian aristocratic culture achieved an urbanity and sophistication that has made the preceding century seem provincial in comparison. Comedy lost its high moral tone, as wit, elegance, and polish became the order of the day. Whereas eighteenth-century drama tended to be oratorical, addressing a ruling elite from a public tribunal, the new style developed by playwrights like the prolific Prince Shakhovskoy was oriented to the cultivated conversation of the aristocratic salon.

The 1820s witnessed a craze for vaudeville—light and fluffy plays, often accompanied by song and dance, and ancestors of the operetta and musical comedy. Gogol held them in contempt: "just go to the theater; every day you'll see a play where one fellow is hiding under a chair while another is pulling him out by the leg."[8] But serious literature has a way of growing out of even frivolous forms (or degrading into them). Whatever else the vaudeville was, it was performable. Here were plays to be acted, not set speeches strung along a plot line. Griboyedov's *Woe from Wit*, an extremely complex play, has a briskness of pace and a flashing wit that connect it to the lighter forms of the period as well as to Molière. Gogol learned from the vaudeville writers also. Free of all speechifying, his comedies move with lightning speed and exhibit the play of farce and parody that made the vaudevilles so popular. Many of the first actors and spectators of *The Government Inspector*, failing to see its novelty or seriousness, took it as merely another example of the genre.

In the 1830s Russian classical culture disintegrated. Romanticism, introduced in the twenties, dominated the scene. Following upon the heels of the abortive Decembrist revolt of 1825, the rule of Nicholas I (1825-55) was a grimly repressive period. The state became increasingly despotic and bureaucratic, the atmosphere cramped and stifling. But beneath the hard crust of conformity, the rustlings of change might be heard. The social composition of audiences was more varied, and writers gradually focussed their attention on the middle level of society—government clerks, petty merchants, and in time the peasants and urban proletariat. In the theaters, lurid melodramas, in addition to the ever popular vaudevilles, were the rage. No doubt there was an element of escapism in this avid search for cheap laughs and thrills. Indicative of the lowered tastes of more socially mixed audiences, it also expressed their longing for something easier to relate to than the remote aristocratic models. The period was one of growing, often fervent, nationalism. The overblown patriotic potboilers of one Nestor Kukolnik enjoyed a popularity that is today difficult to comprehend.

More significantly, the age marked the beginning of a fateful parting of the ways of the government and the intellectuals. Catherine and her critics, no matter how sharp their disagreements, had proceeded from the shared assumptions of the Enlightenment. In Nicholas's time the bureaucratic leviathan appeared as frightful and alien, and thinking Russians sought a vision of their nation larger than the state of the moment. This broader nationalism, which would form a common ground for otherwise antagonistic Slavophiles and Westerners of the 1840s, brought in its wake an intensified call for a truly national art: "For heaven's sake, give us Russian characters, give us ourselves," Gogol wrote while preparing *The Government Inspector* for production. The wide social spectrum of that play, the recognizable "Russianness" of its characters, its richly colloquial language the likes of which had never before been heard on the Russian stage caused it to be hailed as a realization of the dream of a national theater.

Gogol, more than anyone else, was responsible for the breakup of classical culture in Russia. He did not do it by himself—no artist ever does—but his work had the authority to turn others away from the older models to new forms and subjects. In his task of destruction, however, he was highly dialectical, taking from the past what he could use but manipulating it in such a way as to turn it on its head. His characters are relations, however distant, of traditional comic figures of the Russian and European stage. In *The Government Inspector* Anna Andreyevna is a lineal descendent of the affected coquette of eighteenth-century Russian comedy; Khlestakov, of the Frenchified dandy; the mayor, of the gruff and bumbling paterfamilias who runs through the history of comedy and is still to be seen on our television screens. The wily servant Osip has forbears in hundreds of plays; Marya Antonovna, like Agafya in *Marriage,* recalls the ingénues of classical comedy; and so on. Many of them have been complicated so that their provenance is barely recognizable, or mixed. If Khlestakov is the petit-maître of Russian comedy, he is also the traditional comic braggart, the confidence man, and something else that is not to be easily pinned down. The great mass of characters we encounter in Russian plays before Gogol give us the sense of having been seen before, and where we have seen them is in other plays. Gogol's, though they draw much of their vitality from proven archetypes of comedy, are ultimately larger than literary types.

The plots of the plays are also drawn from the conventions of comedy. *The Government Inspector* and *The Gamblers* turn on the age-old device of mistaken identity; *Marriage,* on the equally conventional pattern of an obstacle in the path of love. Again Gogol modifies an inherited model. The familiar schemes are psychologized: Khlestakov has his impersonation thrust upon him by the fears of the town's officials; the obstacle of *Marriage* is Podkolyosin's terror of marriage.

At a time when the unities were under attack, Gogol came close to adhering to them. In *The Gamblers* the unities of time and place are observed perfectly; in *The Government Inspector* and *Marriage,* approximately. All three plays follow the rule of unity of action—they are without subplots or incidental events. Of course, it was not the rules Gogol cared about, but ways to achieve a fast narrative movement and comic rhythm. His plays possess the only important unity—the unity of form. They are comedies that are altogether comic. The admixture of sentimentalism and didacticism that had been infiltrating comedy for over a century has survived in them only as an object of parody. In holding scrupulously to a comic vision, Gogol is closer to the spirit of Molière than the mass of the Frenchman's eighteenth-century imitators. His world is coarser (he found Molière "too decorous"), his characters cruder, witless rather than witty. Uninterested in the sophisticated repartee of classical high comedy, let alone its appeals to good sense, he nevertheless has affinities with the Molière who springs from the improvisations and slapstick, the pantomime and masks of French and Italian farce. In the manner of Molière, a highly stylized design is imposed on human gestures and speech: see, for example, the mayor's and Khlestakov's simulations of gallantry, their balletic verbal dances of impersonation, the pas de deux of Khlestakov as seducer with the mayor's daughter as imbecilic ingénue. The discrepancy between affectation and vulgarity is wider in Gogol than in his classical predecessors, which only sharpens the parody and heightens the fun. Commedia dell'arte was well known (and imitated) in Russia, and Gogol's plays resonate its theatricality, as well as the comic energies of the puppet theater of his native Ukraine. In bypassing the sentimental moralizing of the eighteenth century (and the literariness of Romantic drama), Gogol looks sideways to the popular forms of his day and backwards to an older, "purer" comedy—of Molière, and also of the man Gogol called the father of comedy, Aristophanes. Aristophanes gave him a model for a comedy that would not be straitjacketed in the narrow limits of "private life," nor, we may add, of class. The scene of *The Government Inspector* was, in Gogol's words, "ideal." Like the Athenian agora, it was "a place of assembly," where the entire polis, if we may so dignify Gogol's scrubby backwater town, flocked to give us a microcosm of Russia and the world. The undomesticated vigor and robust invective of his plays may also have been inspired by the "father of comedy."

If Gogol is something of a throwback, he is also an adventurous innovator. But what is new in his plays is often either an enriching of what had come before or a new twist to an old theme. It has often been remarked that Gogol purged his comedies of the customary love story, and he voiced his scorn for centuries of "theatrical lovers with their cardboard amours!" The conventional lovers are very much there, however, in two of his plays (*The Gamblers* has no women). What was new and unexpected was their failure to get together. Many in the first audiences of *Marriage* and *The Government Inspector* did not realize that the plays were over, fully expecting Podkolyosin and Khlestakov to return to their abandoned sweethearts! In Gogol's hands the young gallants and ingénues of earlier comedy (and with them aristocratic gentilesse) have become ridiculous, their interchanges delightfully parodic.

Indeed, everyone in Gogol is ridiculous. His great innovation for his time was to write a comedy without any ballast of sanity. In doing so he achieved stunning concentration and an organic unity of form. His plays are not split in two—between comic deviants and virtuous representatives of a norm, between "them" and "us." They invoke integral worlds, complete in themselves. After a century of plays whose characters were too frequently vehicles for the author's ideas, Gogol's seemed generated by a sense of life rather than mental abstraction. The plots of previous comedy were often launched by the calculations, or "intrigues," of characters. Gogol's people calculate little, and never deliberate—they improvise. Sometimes they seem oddly motiveless: Kochkaryov bullies, Khlestakov lies, but for no readily apparent end. Even when they have purposes—as do Podkolyosin and the mayor—they arrive at them casually or in response to the exigencies and opportunities of the moment. Mindless creatures of whim and habit, they do what they do simply because it is the way they are. With the partial exception of *The Gamblers,* it is not the characters who plot the action of the plays—for most of *The Government Inspector,* Khlestakov hasn't the faintest notion of what is going on—but the artist standing at lofty remove from the world he has set in motion. In depriving his characters of premeditation, Gogol was able to dispense with the usual expositions of motive as well as the intrigues of drama. "Comedy should cohere spontaneously," he wrote, and his plays seem like analogues of original creation, form coming into being out of the void. In Nabokov's felicitous words:

"[*The Government Inspector*] begins with a blinding flash of lightning and ends in a thunderclap. . . . it is wholly placed in the tense gap between the flash and the crash."[9]

Gogol's uncompromising repudiation of conventional dichotomies of virtue and vice, reasonableness and unreasonableness, resulted in a comic universe without a stable center. His genius for comic illogicality and irrelevance have been justly celebrated, but such devices, in less extreme form, had always been the stock in trade of comedians. More than these, it is the absence of a comfortable standard of normality by which to judge the comic vagaries of his characters that gives his plays their grotesque quality—their sense of displacement from quotidian "reality." The distinctive plot of classical comedy moved inexorably to reconciliation and the integration of society, often symbolized by marriage. Gogol's distinctive plot is one of loss and of the dissolution of things. Comedy, he felt, was like a game of chance in which one reaches for a desired object only to find it eluding his grasp. Hopes are raised—an important government personage will marry your daughter and make you a general; marriage will bring true bliss; a big win at cards will guarantee your future—and it all turns out to be an empty bubble. Spontaneity in place of schematization, whimsy for calculated choice, illusion for what one took to be the firm ground of reality—the formulas were commonplaces of the Romantic revolt. But Gogol was not a writer of formulas. He was a natural comic who looked at the world from an odd angle of vision and found the ways we live—our courtships and marriages, our ambitions and dreams —to be all very funny. The lack of substance and of anchors of certainty in the worlds he portrayed also reflected his profound sense of a crisis in contemporary life—what he called the "terrible splintering" of the nineteenth century.[10]

He looked to his religious faith for bonds to heal the fragmentation of Russian (and modern) life. In his first apologia for *The Government Inspector,* the dramatic piece *Leaving the Theater after a Performance of a New Comedy* (probably written in 1836), a Christian interpretation of the play is already implicit; in *The Denouement of "The Government Inspector"* (written in 1846) the play is read as a Christian allegory. If the world was incoherent, it was because it had turned from patterns of order and justice that lie beyond its chaos. We often remark on the absence of virtuous characters in Gogol's comedies, less often on the fact that they are also without villains. His people make mischief—for themselves as well as others—but they can't help themselves. It's the way they are. "My heroes are not at all villains; were I to add but one good trait to any of them, the reader would be reconciled to all of them. But the banality of all of it taken together frightened readers."[11] Gogol tended, especially in his later years, to view his characters as sinners on the edge of salvation but never quite attaining the "one good trait" that would redeem them. One might also see them as comic caricatures on the edge of becoming human but always falling short.

The history of productions of Gogol's plays in Russia would dismay those who feel there is one right way to perform a play or read a text. There has been a vaudeville Gogol, a realist Gogol, an impressionist, expressionist, and symbolist Gogol, and a futurist Gogol. The temptation to do him as harmless vaudeville began with the first production of *The Government Inspector*. By the 1870s the play was already a museum piece, exhibiting to audiences the manners of a bygone era. In the West these two strains—Gogol as farceur and Gogol as genre painter of the quaint ways of Old Russia —have predominated. Around the turn of the century the Russian symbolists substituted a metaphysical Gogol for the realist Gogol of the nineteenth century. In productions of *The Government Inspector* there was a significant shift of the play's center of gravity, as Khlestakov took the limelight away from the mayor. Gogol himself saw Khlestakov as the "major role" and complained bitterly that, as the play was being performed, it would have been better entitled *The Mayor*.[12] The differing perspectives are indicative of the gulf between the two centuries. The mayor, for all the comic hyperbole that went into the part, came out of more familiar terrain. The gruff, high-handed official could be met with everywhere—in daily life and satirical literature. The mayor is the subject of a clearly recognizable narrative line, whose descent from hope to loss has often evoked the sympathies of audiences. Khlestakov is something else: he flits into town, words tumbling from his lips, improvising the most fantastical tall tales, only to fly off again, leaving chaos as his legacy. Gogol called him a phantasmogorical character; and for the Russian symbolists he became the Devil and the type of modern man: rootless, aimless, cynical, glib, a creature of mass culture, all surface and no substance. These two Gogols—the realistic ethnographer and the fantastical, grotesque poet—have battled each other in criticism, theatrical productions, and literary tradition. On the one hand, Gogol feeds into the realistic theater of Ostrovsky; on the other, he influences the grotesquely satiric, sometimes surrealistic plays of Sukhovo-Kobylin. His fascination with the demoniacal and irrational are continued by Dostoyevsky, later by the symbolists. Prose writers of the pre- and post-Revolution avant-garde seek him out for his exuberance of language as well as his grotesque comedy. Both aspects—realistic and fantastic—were necessary to Gogol. Without a foot in the social realities of his age, he might have fallen into contrivance; without his imaginative leaps, he might have remained a period piece.

Twentieth-century reinterpretations of Gogol have been evident in a number of novel Russian productions, the most famous of which was the staging of *The Government Inspector* by Vsevolod Meyerhold in 1926. Freely drawing from variants and even other works by Gogol, including *Dead Souls,* Meyerhold sought to present an image of the artist's entire created world and, through it, a metaphor of Imperial Russia. Known as the Aristophanic version, it transposed the setting to a larger city suggestive of the capital, and submerged the mayor into a "chorus" of officials. The intent was to dramatize the corporate body of Russian society, while minimizing interest in the narrative of any individual's experience. In one episode the servile officials formed a procession, each mimicking Khlestakov's every move; in the bribe scene, disembodied hands extended from a curved mahogany panel of eleven doors enclosing the rear of the stage. Meyerhold wished, in his words, "to unify the production according to the laws of orchestral composition, in such a way that each actor's part did not sound by itself in isolation."[13]

Khlestakov, gaunt, angular, in dark cloak, dark oddly elongated hat, dark-rimmed rectangular spectacles, swinging a black cane, looked properly diabolical, though Meyerhold eschewed symbolist mysticism, insisting that Gogol conceives of "the world as real but with a shade of something fantastical—not the mystical, but the fantastic." His Khlestakov was "a mystifier and adventurer by way of principle."[14] Very much in tune with Gogol's intentions, Khlestakov altered his attitude from scene to scene, as if putting on a new mask for each person he encountered. Though the production had its share of slapstick, the emphasis was on the darker aspects of the play. In the final scene the mayor went mad and was placed in a straitjacket; the horrified townspeople snaked across the stage and through the audience, like figures in a dance of death, to be replaced on the stage by life-sized mannequins. The use of mannequins, meticulously patterned after the characters, not only solved the technical problem of the dumb scene, but provided a brilliant realization of Gogol's metaphor of a world frozen by terror.

To speed the action the play's classical five acts were broken up into fifteen episodes, all but four of which were played on a small platform propelled toward the audience on rails. Long interested in commedia dell'arte and taken with the silent screen acting of performers like Chaplin and Keaton, Meyerhold made ample use of stylized gestures and pantomime. The production was at times balletic, at times operatic. The settings were extravagantly opulent, as Meyerhold contrasted glossy elegance with crass vulgarity, and also with a claustrophobic oppressiveness probably inspired by his reading of *Dead Souls*. The scenes of Khlestakov and the ladies were played in a light, airy manner; the ponderous bureaucrats were often crowded into close places where they acted their roles in half darkness. The production was guided by a double vision of Imperial Russia which Meyerhold found in Gogol—a Russia of tinsel and gossamer, insubstantial and unreal, and beneath it a hard, ominous meanness of spirit.

We have had three goals in these translations: to be faithful to the original, to produce texts that would seem as if originally written in English, and to make the plays performable. None of these purposes, not even the first, is compatible with a word by word transcription. We have recast Gogol's lines so as to achieve a comic rhythm and diction that actors can speak and contemporary audiences can respond to. What we have not done is to try to improve upon the original, or deliberately mold Gogol into a particular interpretation (though any translation that goes beyond mere copying of dictionary definitions is inevitably a critical act). Unfamiliar references have been dropped; those that might be of interest are explained in the notes. In a few instances where a literal rendering, though unwieldy, was noteworthy, it is also given in the notes. For the convenience of reader and actor, we have accented names in lists of characters or on their first appearance. Gogol, wise about things literary, merits quoting on the art of translation: "About translations. . . . Sometimes it is necessary to distance oneself from the words of the original precisely in order to come closer to it. . . . if we translate them word for word, . . . [they] sometimes obliterate half the power of the original."[15]

A number of friends graciously acted as our audience, and we thank them for their interest and suggestions. We would be remiss if we failed to express our gratitude to Nicholas Rudall, director of the Court Theater at the University of Chicago, and Kenneth Northcott for their advice and discerning criticism. Norman Ingham was an astute reader of the Introduction. Roberta Ehre, whose patience and kindness were of inestimable value, was also a keenly sensitive stand-in for the "general" reader and audience. We are grateful to Katherine Gottschalk and Carol Any for typing the manuscript.

Thanks are also due to the Guggenheim Foundation for a fellowship which allowed me to begin this project.

Marriage
A Completely Unlikely Incident in Two Acts

Characters

AGÁFYA TÍKHONOVNA   A merchant's daughter, the bride
ARÍNA PANTELEYMÓNOVNA   Her aunt
FYÓKLA IVÁNOVNA   A matchmaker
PODKOLYÓSIN, IVÁN KUZMÍCH   A government clerk
KOCHKARYÓV, ILYÁ FOMÍCH   His friend
OMELET, IVÁN PÁVLOVICH   A managing clerk in a government
                                         office
ANÚCHKIN, NIKANÓR IVÁNOVICH   A retired infantry officer
ZHEVÁKIN, BALTAZÁR BALTAZÁROVICH   A naval officer
DUNYÁSHKA   A servant girl
STÁRIKOV, ALEXÉY DMÍTRIYEVICH   A storekeeper
STEPÁN   PODKOLYOSIN's manservant

Act One

Scene One

A bachelor's room. PODKOLYOSIN, *alone, on a sofa, smoking a pipe.*

PODKOLYOSIN. Yes, when you're alone with nothing to do, you realize marriage is the only answer. What's it all about? We go on and on, just living, until we're sick of it. Again I've let a winter slip by. The matchmaker's been coming for three months, everything's arranged. . . . Ugh! I'm feeling disgusted with myself. Stepan! (STEPAN *enters.*)

PODKOLYOSIN. Has the matchmaker arrived?

STEPAN. No, sir.

PODKOLYOSIN. Have you been to the tailor?

STEPAN. Yes, sir.

PODKOLYOSIN. Is he working on my dress coat?

STEPAN. He's working on it.

PODKOLYOSIN. Has he gotten far?

STEPAN. He's already started on the buttonholes.

PODKOLYOSIN. What did you say?

STEPAN. I said, he's already started on the buttonholes.

PODKOLYOSIN. Did he ask, "What does your master need a dress coat for?"

STEPAN. No, he didn't ask.

PODKOLYOSIN. Perhaps he said, "Your master must be getting married?"

STEPAN. No, he didn't.

PODKOLYOSIN. But you saw dress coats? I suppose he's making them for others too?

STEPAN. Yes, he's got lots of them.

PODKOLYOSIN. But the cloth is probably not as good as mine?

STEPAN. No, yours looks nicer.

PODKOLYOSIN. What did you say?

STEPAN. I said, yours looks nicer.

PODKOLYOSIN. Good. But did he ask, "Why has your master ordered a dress coat of such fine cloth?"

STEPAN. No.

PODKOLYOSIN. Didn't he say anything like. . . uh, "is your master getting married?"

STEPAN. No.

PODKOLYOSIN. But of course you told him what my rank is and where I work?

STEPAN. I told him.

PODKOLYOSIN. What did he say to that?

STEPAN. He said, "I'll do my best."

PODKOLYOSIN. Good. You may go now. (STEPAN *goes out.* POD-KOLYOSIN *alone.*) The way I look at it, a black dress coat is somehow more respectable. Color is for secretaries and other small fry—for milksops! Those of a higher rank must observe more of the, as they say, the. . . the word escapes me. It's a fine word, but I've forgotten it. Yes, by God, no matter how you look at it, a court councilor is equal to a colonel. Even if his uniform has no epaulets. Stepan! (STEPAN *enters.*) Did you buy the shoe polish?

STEPAN. Yes.

PODKOLYOSIN. In the store on Voznesénsky Street? The one I told you about?

STEPAN. Yes, sir.

PODKOLYOSIN. Well, is it a good polish?

STEPAN. It's good.

PODKOLYOSIN. Have you tried shining my boots with it?

STEPAN. Yes.

PODKOLYOSIN. Well, do they shine?

STEPAN. They shine all right—real nice.

PODKOLYOSIN. And when he gave you the polish, did he ask, "Why does your master need such an expensive polish?"

STEPAN. No.

PODKOLYOSIN. Maybe he said, "Your master's thinking of getting married, isn't he?"

STEPAN. No, he didn't say anything.

PODKOLYOSIN. Very well, you may go! (STEPAN *goes out.* PODKOLYOSIN *alone.*) Some people may think boots don't matter, but if they're badly made and the polish is too red, you're not respected in the best society. Things aren't as they should be. . . . It's even worse when you get corns. God knows I can stand anything—except corns. Stepan! (STEPAN *enters.*)

STEPAN. What is it, sir?

PODKOLYOSIN. Did you tell the shoemaker I can't stand corns?

STEPAN. I told him.

PODKOLYOSIN. And what did he say?

STEPAN. He said, "Fine." (STEPAN *goes out.*)

PODKOLYOSIN. Getting married is a hell of a business. If it's not one thing, it's another. This has to be just right, that has to be just right—no, damn it, it's not as easy as they say. Stepan! (STEPAN *enters.*) I was about to tell you. . .

STEPAN. The old woman's here.

PODKOLYOSIN. Ah, she's come. Show her in. (STEPAN *goes out.*) What a business. . . not the sort of. . . just a hell of a business! (FYOKLA *enters.*)

PODKOLYOSIN. Hello, hello, Fyokla Ivanovna! Well, what's new? Take a chair and tell me all about it. How's it going? What did you say her name is? Melanie?

FYOKLA. Agafya.

PODKOLYOSIN. Yes, yes. Agafya. Probably some old maid!

FYOKLA. No, not at all. I mean, once you're married, you won't stop raving about her. You'll thank me for it.

PODKOLYOSIN. You're slobbering, Fyokla.

FYOKLA. I'm too old to slobber, my friend. Dogs slobber, not me.

PODKOLYOSIN. And the dowry? What about the dowry? Tell me about it once more.

FYOKLA. Ah, the dowry! A stone house in the city. Two stories.

And what a fine income! A real joy. The grocer alone pays seven
hundred rubles for his store. And the beer hall in the cellar draws
a big crowd. There are two wings—they've got wood siding, but
one's on a stone foundation. Each brings in four hundred rubles.
Then there's a vegetable garden in the Výborg district. A storekeeper rented it three years ago to grow cabbage. Very sober!
Never touches a drop, and he's got three sons. He's married off
two, "and the third," he says, "he's still young; let him stay in
the store. It'll make the work go easier. I'm already old," he
says, "let my son stay in the store. It'll make the work go easier."
PODKOLYOSIN. And the girl? What's she like?
FYOKLA. Sugar candy! All white and pink. Peaches and cream. So
sweet—there's no word for it. She'll take your breath away.
You'll tell your friends and even your enemies, "Oh that Fyokla,
it's all thanks to her."
PODKOLYOSIN. But her father—he wouldn't be an officer, would
he?
FYOKLA. She's the daughter of a respectable merchant. A girl who
wouldn't shame a general. She won't hear of a merchant. "As
for me," she says, "whatever my husband's like, even if he's not
much to look at, he's got to be a nobleman." Yes, very genteel!
And on Sunday, when she wears a silk dress—my God, how it
rustles. A princess, I tell you!
PODKOLYOSIN. Well, I asked you, you know, because I'm a court
councilor, so for me...you understand...
FYOKLA. Of course, that's how things are. I understand. We had
another court councilor, but she turned him down, didn't take to
him. He had such odd ways. Whenever he opened his mouth,
out came a lie, and a fine looking gentleman too. What can you
do? That's how God made him. He's not happy about it himself.
He just can't help lying. God's will, that's what it is.
PODKOLYOSIN. Well, besides this one, do you have any others?
FYOKLA. What do you want others for? She's the best we've got.
PODKOLYOSIN. Really? The best?
FYOKLA. Travel the world over, you won't find another like her.
PODKOLYOSIN. Well, I'll think about it. Drop by the day after
tomorrow. We'll try again...I'll sit back, and you'll tell your

stories.

FYOKLA. Please, sir! I've been coming to you for three months, and there's nothing to show for it. All you do is sit around in your bathrobe and smoke your pipe.

PODKOLYOSIN. I suppose you think marriage is as easy as yelling, "Stepan, bring my boots!" You put them on and off you go! No, I'll have to look into it carefully.

FYOKLA. If you want to look, then look. That's what the merchandise is there for—to be looked at. Listen, it's still morning. Tell the servant to hand you your coat and we'll drive over.

PODKOLYOSIN. Now? But it's cloudy. We'll get caught in the rain.

FYOKLA. Well, it's your loss. For God's sake, you're already turning gray. Soon you won't be fit for a husband's business at all. Acting high and mighty because he's a court councilor! We'll round up the finest gentlemen. We won't even look at the likes of you!

PODKOLYOSIN. How ridiculous! What in the world made you say I'm getting gray? Where do you see a gray hair? (*He feels his hair.*)

FYOKLA. Of course you've got gray hair. That's what a man comes to. So watch out! This one doesn't suit him, that one doesn't suit him. You know, I've got my eye on a captain—the man's a head taller than you, with a voice like a trumpet. He works in the Admiralty.

PODKOLYOSIN. You're lying. I'll take a look in the mirror. Where did you get the idea I'm turning gray? Stepan, bring a mirror! No, wait, I'll get it myself. Just my luck. Heaven help me, it's worse than the pox. (*He goes off to the next room.* KOCHKARYOV *runs in.*)

KOCHKARYOV. Where's Podkolyosin?... (*Seeing* FYOKLA.) What are you doing here? Oh you old... Why the hell did you get me married?

FYOKLA. And what's so bad about that? You did your duty.

KOCHKARYOV. My duty! Some prize—a wife! As if I couldn't manage without one!

FYOKLA. But you came pestering me. "Marry me off, grandma"— that's all I heard from you.

KOCHKARYOV. You old hag! So what are you doing here? Podkolyosin's not going to get...

FYOKLA. What of it? It's God's will.

KOCHKARYOV. No fooling? Ah, the son-of-a-bitch, not a word
about it to me. What a character! It's on the sly, isn't it?
(PODKOLYOSIN *enters with a mirror in his hands. He is looking
at it attentively.*)

KOCHKARYOV, *stealing up behind, startles him.* Boo!

PODKOLYOSIN, *cries out and drops the mirror.* You're mad! What
did you do that for? What a dumb thing! You frightened me out
of my wits.

KOCHKARYOV. Forget it. I was only joking.

PODKOLYOSIN. You and your jokes! I still can't pull myself
together. You scared the life out of me. And the mirror's
cracked. It's not a cheap item, either. I bought it in the English
shop!

KOCHKARYOV. All right, all right. I'll get you another mirror.

PODKOLYOSIN. Yes, you'll get one. I know your mirrors. They
make you look ten years older, and your face shows up crooked.

KOCHKARYOV. By right I should be angry at you. We're friends,
and yet you keep secrets from me. Thinking of getting married,
huh?

PODKOLYOSIN. Nonsense! I never even gave it a thought.

KOCHKARYOV. But here's proof, right in front of your eyes. (*Points
to* FYOKLA.) We know what sort of a bird she is. So you're
getting married. What of it, it's nothing, nothing at all. A
Christian duty, that's what it is. Even the patriotic thing to do.
Leave it to me. I'll take care of everything. (*To* FYOKLA.) Now
tell me, who, how, what, and so on. Nobility, civil service, or
merchant class? And what's her name?

FYOKLA. Agafya Tikhonovna.

KOCHKARYOV. Agafya Tikhonovna Brandakhlýstova?

FYOKLA. No—Kuperdyágina.

KOCHKARYOV. She lives on the Street of Six Shops, doesn't she?

FYOKLA. No, closer to Peskí, on Soapy Alley.

KOCHKARYOV. Of course, on Soapy Alley, right behind the grocery
—the frame house?

FYOKLA. Not behind the grocery—in back of the beer hall.

KOCHKARYOV. In back of the beer hall, you say. Then I don't know her.

FYOKLA. Turn into the alley, and you'll see a sentry box straight ahead. Go past the sentry box, turn left, and in front of your eyes, I mean right smack in front of your eyes, there'll be a frame house—that's where the dressmaker lives, the one who used to live with the First Secretary of the Senate. Now don't go into the dressmaker's, but just behind her place is another house, a stone house—that's her house, I mean the house in which she lives, Agafya Tikhonovna, the young lady, that is.

KOCHKARYOV. Fine, fine. I'll make all the arrangements. You can go—you're no longer needed.

FYOKLA. What's that? You're going to arrange the marriage yourself?

KOCHKARYOV. Of course I am. And don't you poke your nose in.

FYOKLA. What! You ought to be ashamed! This isn't work for a man. You keep out of this, mister!

KOCHKARYOV. Go on, get out of here. You don't understand these things. Don't butt in. Stick to your own business. Get going!

FYOKLA. The devil! Taking the bread out of people's mouths! Getting himself mixed up in this mess. Had I known, I wouldn't have said a word. (*Leaves upset.*)

KOCHKARYOV. Well, old man, these matters can't be put off. Let's go.

PODKOLYOSIN. But I haven't made up my mind yet. I was just mulling it over.

KOCHKARYOV. Nonsense, nonsense! Don't be shy. I'll marry you off so quick you won't feel a thing. We'll go to the girl right now and finish it off. . .just like that!

PODKOLYOSIN. Now! That's all I need.

KOCHKARYOV. Why not? What's keeping you?. . . See what comes of your not being married! Take a look at your room. There's a dirty boot, over there a basin with yesterday's bath water, tobacco all over the table. And you! Lying around all day like some lazy good-for-nothing.

PODKOLYOSIN. That's true. There's no order to my life.

KOCHKARYOV. But when you're married, you won't recognize yourself, or anything else for that matter. You'll have a sofa, a little puppy, some sort of a canary in a cage, needlework. . . . And imagine, you're sitting on your sofa, when suddenly a pretty girl, very attractive, sits down beside you, and with her soft little hand she . . .

PODKOLYOSIN. Ah, damn! When you think about it, really, what soft hands they have—white as milk!

KOCHKARYOV. And that isn't all! As if it's only hands! My friend, they also have . . . But what's the point of saying it—they have, my friend, simply—ah, who the hell knows what they have.

PODKOLYOSIN. You know, to tell the truth, I love it when a pretty little thing sits down next to me.

KOCHKARYOV. See! You've caught on. Now we only have to iron out the details. Don't worry. The wedding dinner and all that— I'll handle it. Champagne—you can't do with less than a dozen bottles, no matter what you say. Madeira also—a half dozen bottles are absolutely necessary. I bet the bride has a gang of aunts and gossipy girl friends—that kind doesn't like to fool around. We don't want any Rhine wine—the hell with it, right? As for the meal—I know a caterer, the son-of-a-bitch feeds you till you can't get up from the table.

PODKOLYOSIN. What is this? You're rushing into it as if the wedding were about to take place.

KOCHKARYOV. And why not? Why put it off? You agreed, didn't you?

PODKOLYOSIN. Me? Well, no . . . not entirely.

KOCHKARYOV. Well I'll be! But you just said you're willing.

PODKOLYOSIN. I only said it wouldn't be a bad idea.

KOCHKARYOV. Wait! Hold on! We had everything . . . What's wrong? Don't you like the idea of married life?

PODKOLYOSIN. No . . . I like it.

KOCHKARYOV. What is it then? What's stopping you?

PODKOLYOSIN. Nothing's stopping me. Only it's strange.

KOCHKARYOV. Strange?

PODKOLYOSIN. Of course it's strange. All my life I've been a bachelor, and now all at once I'm to be a married man.

KOCHKARYOV. Come on. Aren't you ashamed? Well, I see that I can't beat around the bush with you. I better speak frankly, like a father to a son. Take a good look at yourself. What are you? A log, that's what. You don't count at all. What are you living for? Look in the mirror. Well, what do you see? A ridiculous face— nothing else. Now picture this: loads of kids at your knee, not just two or three, but maybe a half-dozen, and every one of them your spitting image, like peas in a pod. Now you're all alone, you're a court councilor, a filing clerk or some kind of a supervisor—God only knows what you are. But think about it, a crowd of tiny filing clerks swarming over you, clever little rascals. A cute little devil will stretch out his chubby hand and tug at your whiskers, and you, you'll make doggy sounds for him. "Bowwow, bow-wow!" Now tell me, can anything top that?

PODKOLYOSIN. But they're such brats. They'll make a mess, toss my papers about.

KOCHKARYOV. So they're brats, but they'll look like you—that's the whole point.

PODKOLYOSIN. Come to think of it, it might even be fun, damn it. Some butterball, a tiny pup, and he looks like you. . . .

KOCHKARYOV. Why won't it be fun? Of course it'll be fun. Well, let's go.

PODKOLYOSIN. All right, let's go.

KOCHKARYOV. Stepan! Hurry up! Help your master dress.

STEPAN *enters.*

PODKOLYOSIN, *dressing before a mirror.* Perhaps I ought to put on a white vest.

KOCHKARYOV. Nonsense. It makes no difference.

PODKOLYOSIN, *putting on a collar.* The stupid laundress! She did such a sloppy job on the collar. There's no way to make it stand up. Stepan, tell her if she's going to iron like that, I'll hire somebody else. Probably spends her time with her boy friends instead of ironing.

KOCHKARYOV. Come on, pal, hurry up! Stop fussing!

PODKOLYOSIN. Just a moment! (*Puts on a dress coat and sits down.*) Listen Kochkaryov, you know what? You'd better go by yourself!

KOCHKARYOV. Now what? Have you gone out of your mind? Me go! But who's getting married—you or me?

PODKOLYOSIN. Really, somehow I don't feel up to it. We'd better go tomorrow.

KOCHKARYOV. Do you have an ounce of brains in your head? Are you a moron, or what? He was champing at the bit—and now he's not up to it! Tell me, please, after this aren't you a pig, a regular bastard!

PODKOLYOSIN. What are you calling me names for? By what right? What did I do to you?

KOCHKARYOV. An idiot, a perfect idiot—everyone will call you that. You're stupid, plain stupid, even though you're a head clerk. You know what I'm knocking myself out for? For your good, that's what. They'll steal the shirt off your back. All he does is lie around, the damn bachelor! Now tell me, please, what sort of man are you? You're dirt, you're a dunce, an imbecile. I'd use another word . . . only it's impolite. You're an old woman! Worse than an old woman!

PODKOLYOSIN. And you're a fine one. (*In a lowered voice.*) Are you in your right mind? Swearing at me in front of a servant. And in language like that. Couldn't you find another spot?

KOCHKARYOV. How can one not swear at you, huh? Who could help but swear at you? Who has the strength not to swear at you? Like a decent fellow, he decides to get married, to follow the path of reason, and suddenly—simply out of stupidity, as if he'd gone crazy . . . Numbskull!

PODKOLYOSIN. That's enough! I'll go. What are you yelling for?

KOCHKARYOV. He'll go! Of course, what else is there to do but go! (*To* STEPAN.) Bring him his hat and coat.

PODKOLYOSIN, *in the doorway.* What a queer fellow. There's no getting along with him. Swearing without rhyme or reason! Absolutely no comprehension of good manners.

KOCHKARYOV. Well, that's all. I'm not swearing now.

Both go out.

Scene Two

A room in AGAFYA TIKHONOVNA'*s home.* AGAFYA *is dealing cards for fortune telling. Her aunt,* ARINA PANTELEYMONOVNA, *looks over her shoulder.*

AGAFYA. Another journey, Auntie! A king of diamonds is interested; tears, a love letter. On the left, the king of clubs shows warm feelings...

ARINA. And who do you think the king of clubs might be?

AGAFYA. I don't know.

ARINA. But I do.

AGAFYA. Who?

ARINA. Who else but the merchant? The one in the cloth business. Starikov.

AGAFYA. I'm sure it's not him. I'd even bet it's not him.

ARINA. Don't argue, Agafya. He has brown hair. No one else is the king of clubs.

AGAFYA. No, it can't be. The king of clubs means a nobleman. A merchant is a far cry from the king of clubs.

ARINA. Oh Agafya! You wouldn't talk like that if your poor old papa were alive. The way he used to bang his fist on the table. "I'll spit on him," he'd shout, "I'll spit on the man who's ashamed to be a merchant. A colonel isn't good enough for my daughter. And as for my son," he'd say, "I won't enter him in the civil service. Doesn't the merchant serve his tsar as well as anyone else?" And how he'd thump his fist on the table! (*Bangs the table.*) A fist as big as a bucket. And what a temper! As a matter of fact, he was the death of your mother. The poor woman might have lived longer if not for him.

AGAFYA. There you are! What if my husband had a hot temper like that! I wouldn't marry a merchant for the world!

ARINA. But Starikov isn't that sort.

AGAFYA. No! I won't hear of it. He has a beard. When he eats, the food dribbles down his whiskers. No, I won't hear of it.

ARINA. But where will you find a decent nobleman? They don't grow on trees, you know.

AGAFYA. Fyokla Ivanovna will find one. She promised us the very best.

ARINA. But my darling, Fyokla's a liar.

FYOKLA *enters.*

FYOKLA. Oh no, Arina Panteleymonovna. It's sinful to slander for no reason.

AGAFYA. Ah, it's Fyokla Ivanovna! Well? Have you found anybody?

FYOKLA. Oh yes, only first let me catch my breath. How I've been running around! For your sake I've searched every house in town, worn myself out going to offices, ministries, hung around army barracks. Do you know, my dear, I was almost beaten up—yes, by God! The old woman that married the Afyórovs, she comes up to me. "You're a so and so," she says, "taking the bread out of the mouths of honest people. Stick to your own district." "Well, what of it," I told her straight off. "For my young lady I'm ready to do anything." But what gentlemen I've got in store for you! Since God made Adam, there's been no one like them. They'll be here today. I ran ahead to warn you.

AGAFYA. Today? Oh Fyokla, I'm frightened.

FYOKLA. Don't be scared, my darling! That's how these things are done. They'll come, they'll look you over, that's all. And you'll look them over. If you don't like them—well, they'll leave.

ARINA. No doubt it's a fine bunch you've hooked!

AGAFYA. How many are there?

FYOKLA. Six.

AGAFYA, *screams.* Oof!

FYOKLA. But why are you in such a flutter, my dear? It's better to have a choice. If one won't do, another will.

AGAFYA. What are they? Noblemen?

FYOKLA. All of them—a first-rate selection. You've never seen such gentlemen.

AGAFYA. Well, what are they like?

FYOKLA. They're marvelous—good-looking, neat. First, there's Baltazar Baltazarovich—just marvelous. A navy man. He'll suit you to a tee. Says he needs a bride with some meat on her.

Doesn't go for the bony kind. And there's Ivan Pavlovich. A
managing clerk. So dignified, there's no getting near him. Very
handsome—stout. The way he yells at me: "Don't give me any
nonsense, that she's such and such a lady. Give it to me straight
—what's she got in property and how much in ready cash?" "So
much and so much, my good sir." "You're lying! Bitch!" Yes,
my dear, and he stuck in another word, only it wouldn't be
polite to repeat it. Right away I said to myself, "Ah, this one
must be an important gentleman."

AGAFYA. And who else?

FYOKLA. Nikanor Ivanovich Anuchkin. This one's so delicate, and
his lips, my darling—raspberries, perfect raspberries. He's just
marvelous. "As for me," he says, "I need a wife who's good-
looking, well-brought up, and can speak French." Yes, a man of
refined manners, a foreign type. And he has such slender little
legs.

AGAFYA. No, these delicate types are somehow not quite. . .I don't
know. . . . I fail to see anything in them.

FYOKLA. Well, if you want 'em a little fatter, take Ivan Pavlovich.
You couldn't pick anyone better. No use arguing—he's a gentleman if anyone's a gentleman. Why, he'd barely fit through that
door—such a marvelous gentleman!

AGAFYA. How old is he?

FYOKLA. He's still young—about fifty, but not yet fifty.

AGAFYA. And what's his last name?

FYOKLA. His last name? Omelet.

AGAFYA. What kind of a name is that?

FYOKLA. A name.

AGAFYA. Oh my God! Do you call that a name? Listen, Fyokla, can
you imagine marrying him and being called Agafya Tikhonovna
Omelet? Good heavens, what an idea!

FYOKLA. Yes, my dear, there are such god-awful names in Russia.
At the sound of them, you just spit and cross yourself. But
please, if you don't like his name, then take Baltazar Baltazarovich Zhevakin—a marvelous gentleman.

AGAFYA. What kind of hair does he have?

FYOKLA. Nice hair.

AGAFYA. And his nose?

FYOKLA. Eh. . . the nose is fine also. Everything's in its right place. He's just marvelous. But don't be upset. All he's got in his apartment is his pipe—not a stick of furniture.

AGAFYA. Who else?

FYOKLA. Akínf Stepanovich Pantelèyev. He's a clerk and a titular councilor. Stammers a bit, but otherwise he's well-behaved.

ARINA. Why do you keep on like that? Nothing but clerks and more clerks. Does he drink? That's what you'd better tell us.

FYOKLA. So he drinks, I won't deny it, he drinks. What can you do? After all, he's a titular councilor. But he's so quiet, smooth as silk.

AGAFYA. No! I won't have a drunkard for a husband.

FYOKLA. As you wish, my dear! You don't want one, take another. But what of it if he has a drop too much now and then? He's not drunk all week. Some days he turns up sober.

AGAFYA. Well, who else?

FYOKLA. There's one more, only he's such a. . . ah, the devil take him! The others are at least decent.

AGAFYA. But who is he?

FYOKLA. I didn't mean to mention him. If you must know, he's a court councilor and wears a ribbon in his buttonhole. But he's got lead in his pants. You'll never get him out of the house.

AGAFYA. But that's only five, and you said six.

FYOKLA. Isn't that enough for you? See how you've gotten carried away, and only a little while ago you felt scared.

ARINA. What good will come of these noblemen of yours? One merchant is worth the lot of them.

FYOKLA. No, Arina. A nobleman is more respected.

ARINA. What can you do with respect? Now take a merchant, wearing a sable hat, driving along in his sleigh. . .

FYOKLA. And some nobleman in epaulets will run into him and yell: "Who do you think you are, you small-time storekeeper? Get out of my way." Or, "Show me some of your best velvet, storekeeper!" And the merchant will tremble in his boots! "As you please, good sir!" "Take off your hat, you oaf!" That's what the nobleman will say.

ARINA. And the merchant won't give him the cloth. And there's your nobleman all naked. The nobleman doesn't have a thing to wear.

FYOKLA. And the nobleman will slash the merchant with his sword.

ARINA. And the merchant will go complain to the police.

FYOKLA. And the nobleman will go complain to the senator.

ARINA. And the merchant will go to the governor.

FYOKLA. And the nobleman...

ARINA. You're talking nonsense, plain nonsense, you and your nobleman. A governor is higher than a senator! How she's carried on with her nobleman. A nobleman also tips his hat when he has to. . . . *(The doorbell rings.)* That must be someone at the door.

FYOKLA. Ah, that's them!

ARINA. Who?

FYOKLA. Them. One of the suitors.

AGAFYA, *shrieks*. Oof!

> FYOKLA *goes out.*

ARINA. Holy saints, have mercy upon us sinners. The room's a mess. *(Snatches up whatever is on the table and runs about the room.)* The tablecloth. The tablecloth is absolutely black. Dunyashka, Dunyashka! (DUNYASHKA *appears*.) Quick! A clean tablecloth! *(She pulls off the tablecloth and scurries about the room.)*

AGAFYA. Oh Auntie, what am I to do? I'm practically in my nightgown.

ARINA. Oh, my dear, run quickly and get dressed! *(Scurries about the room;* DUNYASHKA *brings a tablecloth; the doorbell rings.)* Hurry, tell them, "Just a moment." (DUNYASHKA *calls from a distance:* "Just a moment!")

AGAFYA. Auntie, the dress isn't ironed.

ARINA. Oh, merciful God, don't ruin us! Put something else on.

FYOKLA, *running in.* Why aren't you coming? Agafya, hurry my dear! *(A ring is heard.)* Oh! He's still waiting.

ARINA. Dunyashka, show him in and ask him to wait.

DUNYASHKA *runs into the hall and opens the door. Voices are heard:* "Anyone at home?"—"Yes, sir, please come in." *In their curiosity they all strain to look through the keyhole.*

AGAFYA, *shrieks.* Oh, how fat!

FYOKLA. He's coming, he's coming. (*All run out headlong.* OMELET *and* DUNYASHKA *enter.*)

DUNYASHKA. Please sir, wait here. (*She goes out.*)

OMELET. All right, if we have to wait, we'll wait. As long as they don't take their time. Only took a minute break from the office. The general will suddenly get it into his head to ask, "Where's the managing clerk?" "He's gone to look over a young lady." How he'd give it to me for that young lady. . . . But let me glance over the inventory. (*Reads.*) "Stone house. Two stories." (*Raises his eyes upwards and scans the room.*) Fine! (*Continues reading.*) "Two wings, one on a stone foundation, the other all wood." . . . Hm, the wooden wing's in bad shape. "Carriage, two-horse sleigh with carvings, large rug, small rug." Probably the sort that are fit for the scrap heap. But the old woman swears they're first-rate. All right, let 'em be first-rate. "Two dozen silver spoons." Sure, what's a home without silver spoons? "Two fox furs." Hm. "Four large quilts, two small quilts." (*Purses his lips significantly.*) "Six silk dresses, six cotton, two nightgowns, two. . ." Eh, worthless frills! "Linen, tablecloths. . ." Well, that's her department. But on the other hand, I'd better check it out. Nowadays they're likely to promise houses and carriages, but when you marry 'em, all you find is quilts and feather beds. (*A ring is heard.* DUNYASHKA *runs through the room in a flurry to open the door. Voices are heard:* "Anyone at home?" "Yes, sir." DUNYASHKA *sees* ANUCHKIN *in.*)

DUNYASHKA. Wait here, please. They'll be right out. (*She goes out.* ANUCHKIN *and* OMELET *exchange bows.*)

OMELET. Good day, sir.

ANUCHKIN. Have I not the honor of addressing the papa of the charming lady of the house?

OMELET. No, no. Not papa at all. I don't even have children.

ANUCHKIN. Oh, I beg your pardon! Forgive me!

OMELET, *aside.* That fellow looks a bit suspicious. I'll wager he's here for the same reason I am. (*Aloud.*) No doubt you have some business with the lady of the house?

ANUCHKIN. No, what sort of. . . no, no business at all. I was out for a walk and just dropped in.

OMELET, *aside.* He's lying. The crook wants to get married! (*A ring is heard.* DUNYASHKA *runs through the room to open the door. Voices in the hall:* "Anyone at home?" "Yes, sir." ZHEVAKIN *enters accompanied by* DUNYASHKA.)

ZHEVAKIN, *to* DUNYASHKA. Please, brush me off a bit, sweetie. A good deal of dust has settled on the streets. Right there, take off that speck of fluff, please. (*He turns around.*) Fine! Thanks, dearie. Take another look. Is that a spider? Nothing in the folds in the back? Thanks, pet! And there—I think there's still something. (*He smooths the sleeves of his dress coat with his hand and looks at* ANUCHKIN *and* OMELET.) English cloth, you know! How it wears! I bought it back in '95 when our squadron was in Sicily. I was still a midshipman. Had a uniform made from it. In 1801, when Paul was tsar, I was promoted to lieutenant—the cloth was still as good as new. In 1814 I went on an expedition around the world—well, it only became a bit frayed around the seams. In 1815 I retired—just had it turned inside out—been wearing it ten years since. Still almost like new. Thanks, sweetheart. . . hm . . . you're a peach! (*Throws her a kiss and, walking up to the mirror, lightly ruffles his hair.*)

ANUCHKIN. If I may ask. . . I believe you said Sicily. Is it a pleasant country?

ZHEVAKIN. Beautiful! We spent thirty-four days there. The view, I tell you, is enchanting. What mountains, what. . . some sort of a pomegranate tree; and wherever you look, young Italian girls, such little rosebuds, you just want to kiss 'em.

ANUCHKIN. And are they well-educated?

ZHEVAKIN. Superbly! In Russia only countesses are as well-educated. You'd be walking along the street—well, a Russian lieutenant, naturally epaulets here (*points to his shoulders*), gold braid. . . And these dark little beauties are everywhere. The houses have tiny balconies, and roofs—here, like this floor,

perfectly flat. As it happens, a little rosebud will be sitting on her
balcony... Well, so as not to make a fool of yourself, you...
(*bows and waves his hand*). And she, she only... (*makes a
movement with his hand*). Naturally, she's all dressed up—
taffeta, lace, lovely earrings... in a word, a tasty little piece.
ANUCHKIN. With your kind permission, I'd like to ask another
question. In what language do they express themselves in Sicily?
ZHEVAKIN. In French, of course.
ANUCHKIN. And do all the young ladies actually speak French?
ZHEVAKIN. All of them, sir. Absolutely. Perhaps you won't even
believe what I'm about to tell you. We stayed thirty-four days,
and in all that time I didn't hear a single word of Russian.
ANUCHKIN. Not a single word?
ZHEVAKIN. Not a word. I'm not speaking only of the nobility and
other signori—that is, of their various officers. But take any
simple peasant, someone who hauls all kinds of junk on his back,
try telling him in Russian: "Give me some bread, my good
man." He won't understand, by God he won't. But say in
French: "Dateci del pane" or "portate vino!" and he'll run off
and actually bring them.
OMELET. This Sicily must be a curious country. You said peasant.
What sort of peasant? What's he like? Is he exactly like the
Russian peasant? Is he broad in the shoulders and does he plough
the land? Or doesn't he?
ZHEVAKIN. I can't say. Didn't notice whether he ploughs or not.
But as for sniffing snuff, I can tell you this: not only do they sniff
it, they even stuff it into their mouths. Transportation is also very
cheap. The country is mostly water and there are gondolas
everywhere. Naturally, with a little Italian girl sitting in them,
such a rosebud, all dressed up—a tiny chemise, a tiny kerchief
... We also had some English officers along... well, people like
us, sailors... and at first, of course, it was very strange. We
couldn't make out a word. But later, when we became friendly,
we understood each other perfectly. You would point like this to
a bottle or a glass; right away they'd know—that means "drink."
Or put your fist to your mouth and go "puff-puff" with your
lips; they'd get it—"smoke." On the whole, I can say the

language is pretty easy. In three days or so the sailors were speaking fluently.

OMELET. Life abroad must be extremely interesting. I'm delighted to make the acquaintance of a man of the world. Allow me to inquire, With whom do I have the honor of speaking?

ZHEVAKIN. Zhevakin, sir. Retired naval lieutenant. And allow me to ask, With whom do I have the pleasure of conversing?

OMELET. Omelet, managing clerk.

ZHEVAKIN, *not catching the last words.* Yes, I also had a bite. Knew I had a good trip ahead of me, and it's a bit cool out. Ate a herring and a slice of bread.

OMELET. No, it seems you didn't understand me correctly. That's my name—Omelet.

ZHEVAKIN, *bowing.* Oh, I beg your pardon. I'm a bit hard of hearing. I thought you said you'd eaten an omelet.

OMELET. What can I do? I considered asking the general to let me change my name to Omeletson, but my relatives talked me out of it. Names that end in *son* make them think of son-of-a-bitch.

ZHEVAKIN. Yes, it's like that sometimes. Our entire third squadron, all the officers and men—they all had very peculiar names—Slopsov, Tipsykov, Lieutenant Spoilov. One midshipman, and a very good midshipman too, his name was simply Hole. "Hey you, Hole," the captain would shout, "Come on over here!" And we would always be kidding him—"Hey, you, you're such a little hole!" That's how we spoke to him. (*A ring is heard in the hall;* FYOKLA *runs through the room to open the door.*)

OMELET. Ah, good morning, ma'm!

ZHEVAKIN. Hi, how are you, sweetie?

ANUCHKIN. Good day, Madam Fyokla.

FYOKLA, *rushing headlong.* Fine, fine. Thank you, gentlemen. (*Opens the door; voices are heard in the hall:* "Are they at home?" "Yes, sir." *Then several almost inaudible words to which* FYOKLA *answers with irritation,* "Just who do you think you are!" KOCHKARYOV *and* PODKOLYOSIN *enter, with* FYOKLA.)

KOCHKARYOV, *to* PODKOLYOSIN. Remember, now. Courage. That's all it takes. (*Looks about and bows with some astonish-*

ment. To himself): Whew, what a mob. What's going on? They can't all be after her? (*Nudges* FYOKLA *and says to her quietly*): Where on earth did you come up with these queer birds—eh?

FYOKLA, *in a lowered voice.* Where do you find birds here? They're all honest people.

KOCHKARYOV, *to her.* "An uninvited guest won't be of the best."

FYOKLA. "People who live in glass houses shouldn't throw stones." "His hat's expensive, but his purse is empty."

KOCHKARYOV. And "Many a full pocket has a hole in it." (*Aloud.*) But what's she doing now? I suppose this door leads to her bedroom? (*Approaches the door.*)

FYOKLA. Aren't you ashamed? She's still getting dressed!

KOCHKARYOV. So what? Why the fuss? I'll just take a little peek— that's all. (*Looks through the keyhole.*)

ZHEVAKIN. And permit me to satisfy my curiosity also.

OMELET. And let me take just one little peek.

KOCHKARYOV, *continuing to look through the keyhole.* Nothing to be seen, gentlemen. It's impossible to make out if that white spot is a woman or a pillow. (*All surround the door, however, and press to catch a glimpse.*) Sh! . . . Someone's coming. (*All leap away from the door.* ARINA PANTELEYMONOVNA *and* AGAFYA TIKHONOVNA *enter. All bow.*)

ARINA. Gentlemen, to what do we owe the pleasure of this visit?

OMELET. Well, m'am, I learned from the newspapers that you wish to enter into a contract regarding the sale of lumber and firewood. Seeing as I'm a managing clerk in a government office, I came to inquire—what kind of lumber, how much, and when can you deliver the goods?

ARINA. We don't deal in lumber here, sir, but we're glad you visited. And what's the name?

OMELET. Ivan Pavlovich Omelet, collegiate assessor.

ARINA. Please be seated. (*Turns to* ZHEVAKIN.) May I ask . . . ?

ZHEVAKIN. Also saw it in the papers. They were advertising something or other. All right, I said to myself, I'll go. The weather looked fine, grass all along the road . . .

ARINA. And what's your name?

ZHEVAKIN. Retired Naval Lieutenant Baltazar Baltazarovich

Zhevakin the Second. We had another Zhevakin, but he retired before me. He was wounded, m'am, below the knee. The bullet passed right through him. Very curious. Didn't touch the knee itself, but caught a tendon—threaded it like a needle. Standing next to him, you were always worried his knee was about to kick you in the behind.

ARINA. Sit down, please. (*Turning to* ANUCHKIN.) Allow me to inquire, to what do we owe...?

ANUCHKIN. To my being a neighbor, madam. Finding myself a rather close neighbor...

ARINA. Don't you live in Tulubóva's house—the merchant's wife, right across from here?

ANUCHKIN. No, I'm still living in Peski. But I intend to move some day, madam, to this part of the city, and be your neighbor.

ARINA. Do sit down. (*Turning to* KOCHKARYOV.) And may I ask...?

KOCHKARYOV. You mean to say you don't recognize me? (*Turning to* AGAFYA.) And you also, miss?

AGAFYA. As far as I know, I've never seen you.

KOCHKARYOV. But try to remember. You must have met me some place.

AGAFYA. Really, I don't recall. Could it have been at the Biryúshkins?

KOCHKARYOV. That's it—at the Biryushkins.

AGAFYA. Oh. You haven't heard? She's had a misfortune.

KOCHKARYOV. Yes, I heard—she got married.

AGAFYA. No, that would be wonderful. She broke her leg.

ARINA. And broke it badly. She was coming home late one evening; the coachman was drunk and threw her from the carriage.

KOCHKARYOV. Oh yes, I remember now. Something happened— either she got married or broke her leg.

ARINA. And may I have your name, sir?

KOCHKARYOV. Ilya Fomich Kochkaryov, of course. We're related, you know. My wife's always saying...uh, allow me, allow me. (*Takes* PODKOLYOSIN *by the hand and leads him up.*) My good friend, Court Councilor Ivan Kuzmich Podkolyosin. He's a head clerk; does all the work himself. He's brought his department into perfect condition—it's just remarkable!

ARINA. What's his name?

KOCHKARYOV. Podkolyosin. Ivan Kuzmich Podkolyosin. They have a director for show, but he does all the work—Ivan Kuzmich Podkolyosin.

ARINA. You don't say! Please be seated, gentlemen. (STARIKOV *enters.*)

STARIKOV, *bowing briskly and rapidly in the merchant fashion and holding his sides slightly.* Good morning, Arina Panteleymonovna. The boys down in the shopping district told me you're selling some wool, m'am!

AGAFYA, *turning away in disdain, in a low voice, but so that he hears.* This is not a store.

STARIKOV. Huh? Have we come at the wrong time? Or have you cooked up a deal without us?

ARINA. Please, please, Alexey Dmitriyevich. We're not selling wool, but we're glad to see you. Kindly be seated. (*All are seated. Silence.*)

OMELET. Queer weather we're having. Looked like rain this morning, but now it seems to have cleared up.

AGAFYA. Yes. Have you ever seen anything like it? Sometimes clear, sometimes quite rainy. Very unpleasant.

ZHEVAKIN. Now in Sicily, miss—we were there with the squadron in the springtime—though if you think about it, it turns out to have been our February. You'd leave your house on a sunny day, and after a while it would seem like rain. Look around, and what do you know? It's actually almost raining.

OMELET. Worst of all is being alone in this kind of weather. For a married man things are different—they're not boring. But for a bachelor they're . . .

ZHEVAKIN. Deadly, just deadly.

ANUCHKIN. Indeed, one may say . . .

KOCHKARYOV. You said it! Plain torture! You wish you were dead. God save us from such a condition.

OMELET. And what would you do, miss, if you had to choose a husband? May I inquire about your taste? Pardon me for being so direct. What branch of the service do you regard as more appropriate for a husband?

ZHEVAKIN. Wouldn't you, miss, prefer a man who has known the tempests of the seas?

KOCHKARYOV. No, not at all. The best husband, in my opinion, is a man who almost single-handedly runs an entire department.

ANUCHKIN. Why be prejudiced? Why show contempt for a man who, though he has, of course, served in the infantry, is nevertheless able to appreciate the manners of the best society?

OMELET. Miss, you decide!

AGAFYA *is silent.*

FYOKLA. Answer, my dear. Say something.

OMELET. What's it going to be, miss?

KOCHKARYOV. What are you thinking, miss?

FYOKLA, *aside to her.* Speak up. Say, "I'm grateful" or "I'm pleased." It's not polite just to sit there.

AGAFYA, *softly.* I'm embarrassed. I'm so embarrassed. I'm leaving, I'm really leaving. Auntie, you stay.

FYOKLA. Oh don't. Don't go. You'll disgrace yourself. There's no knowing what they'll think.

AGAFYA, *softly again.* No, I'm leaving. I must, I must! (*Runs off. FYOKLA and ARINA go out after her.*)

OMELET. How do you like that? They've all cleared out! What's going on?

KOCHKARYOV. Something must have happened.

ZHEVAKIN. Something to do with the lady's attire . . . to straighten her dress . . . pin up her chemise . . .

FYOKLA *enters. All go up to meet her with questions: "What is it? What happened?"*

KOCHKARYOV. Anything wrong?

FYOKLA. What could possibly go wrong? So help me, nothing's wrong.

KOCHKARYOV. Then why did she leave?

FYOKLA. You embarrassed her—that's why she left. It was more than she could stand. She asks you to excuse her, and to come for a cup of tea in the evening. (*Goes out.*)

OMELET, *aside.* Oh, I know their cups of tea. Now that's why I don't care for courting. "Today we can't, please come tomorrow for tea," and "Come again the day after tomorrow," and "We still have to think about it." It's all such rubbish, not the least bit challenging for the mind. To hell with it! I'm a busy man, I don't have time to waste.

KOCHKARYOV, *to* PODKOLYOSIN. The lady's not bad looking, eh?

PODKOLYOSIN. Not bad.

ZHEVAKIN. But the lady is attractive.

KOCHKARYOV, *aside.* Damn it! The fool's fallen for her. He may get in the way yet. (*Aloud.*) Attractive? Not at all.

OMELET. Her nose is too big.

ZHEVAKIN. Hm. No, I didn't notice her nose. She's. . . such a rosebud.

ANUCHKIN. I am also of that opinion. No, she's not quite it, not quite it. I even imagine she is hardly conversant with the manners of the best society. And does she know French?

ZHEVAKIN. But why didn't you, if I may presume to ask, why didn't you try, why didn't you speak French with her? Maybe she does know it.

ANUCHKIN. Do you think I speak French? I didn't have the good fortune to enjoy an education of that sort. My father was a scoundrel, a brute. He never even thought of teaching me French. I was a child then; it would have been easy to teach me. He only had to give me a good whipping—and I would speak French, I most certainly would.

ZHEVAKIN. Well, as things stand now, since you don't speak French, what good would it do if she . . .

ANUCHKIN. Oh no, not at all. A woman is an altogether different matter. She must converse in French—without it, why her. . . and her. . . (*pointing with gestures*), everything wouldn't be quite it.

OMELET, *aside.* Well, let the others worry about that. I'll inspect the house and the wings. If they're satisfactory, I'll clinch the deal tonight. I've got nothing to fear from these fellows—a bunch of nobodies. The ladies don't go for their kind. (*Goes out.*)

ZHEVAKIN. I could use a smoke. Say, don't you go my way? May I ask where you live?

ANUCHKIN. In Peski, Petróvsky Lane.

ZHEVAKIN. I'm on the Island. It's roundabout, but I'll walk along with you. (*They go out.*)

STARIKOV. There's something highfalutin going on here. Oh well, you'll think of us yet, Agafya Tikhonovna. My respects, gentlemen. (*Bows and goes out.*)

PODKOLYOSIN. What are we waiting for? Let's go, too.

KOCHKARYOV. But the girl's sweet, isn't she?

PODKOLYOSIN. You think so! Frankly, she doesn't appeal to me.

KOCHKARYOV. I'll be damned! What's that? But you yourself agreed she's pretty.

PODKOLYOSIN. Hm . . . Somehow she's not quite it. Her nose is too long, and she can't speak French.

KOCHKARYOV. Now what? Why do you need French?

PODKOLYOSIN. Well, a young lady should speak French.

KOCHKARYOV. What for?

PODKOLYOSIN. Why? Because . . . I really don't know why. But without French she won't be quite it.

KOCHKARYOV. There he goes again! Some fool said it, and he lapped it up. She's a beauty, a real beauty. You won't find a girl like her just anyplace.

PODKOLYOSIN. You know, at first she seemed attractive to me too, but later, when they began saying "A long nose, a long nose," well, I took a good look and what did I see—a long nose!

KOCHKARYOV. Eh, you! "A fool tries and tries, but can't see in front of his eyes." They were carrying on that way on purpose, to put you off. And I didn't praise her either—that's how things are done. My friend, this is some girl! Look at her eyes. Dammit, what eyes! They speak, they breathe. And her nose? I can't begin to tell you what a nose this is! So white—pure alabaster! And not just any alabaster either. Take a good look at it.

PODKOLYOSIN, *smiling*. Yes, now that I've thought about it, perhaps she is pretty.

KOCHKARYOV. Of course she's pretty. Listen, now that they've left, let's go in, propose, and wrap it all up.

PODKOLYOSIN. Oh, I can't do that.

KOCHKARYOV. Why not?

PODKOLYOSIN. It's presumptuous! There are so many of us. Let her take her pick.

KOCHKARYOV. What do you want to worry about them for? Afraid of competition, eh? If you like, I'll get rid of 'em in a flash.

PODKOLYOSIN. And how will you do that?

KOCHKARYOV. That's my affair. Only give me your word you won't try to weasel out of it later.

PODKOLYOSIN. Why not give my word? All right. I don't object. I want to get married.

KOCHKARYOV. Let's shake on it!

PODKOLYOSIN, *giving his hand.* Here!

KOCHKARYOV. Now that's what I was waiting for. (*Both go out.*)

Act Two

The room in AGAFYA TIKHONOVNA's *house.*

AGAFYA, *alone.* Indeed, making a choice is so complicated! If there were only one or two, but there are four. I'll just have to pick what strikes me. Mr. Anuchkin isn't bad-looking, although he's a bit skinny. Mr. Podkolyosin isn't bad-looking either. And Mr. Omelet, though he's fat, also cuts a fine figure. How am I going to manage here? Baltazar Baltazarovich is also a man with qualities. It's so difficult to choose—there are just no words for it! Now if I could combine Anuchkin's lips with Podkolyosin's nose, and take some of the easy ways of Baltazar Baltazarovich, and perhaps add Omelet's solid build, then I could decide in a moment. Oh, it's all so perplexing! My head is throbbing. I guess it would be best to draw lots. Trust in God's will—whoever turns up, he's my husband. I'll write them all down on scraps of paper, roll them up, and what will be, will be. (*Goes up to a small desk, takes scissors and paper from it, cuts out lots and rolls them up, continuing to speak.*) A girl's situation is so trying, especially when she's in love. Men don't feel any sympathy; they refuse to understand. . . . There, everything's ready! I'll put them into my purse, shut my eyes, and what will be, will be. (*She puts the lots into her purse and shakes them up with her hand.*) How terrifying! . . . Oh God, make Mr. Anuchkin turn up. No, why him? Better Mr. Podkolyosin. But why Mr. Podkolyosin? Are the others worse? . . . No, no . . . whoever turns up, so be it. (*Fumbles in the purse, and instead of one, takes out all.*) Oof! All of them! They've all turned up! My heart is pounding so! No. One! One! I must pick one. (*Puts the lots into the purse and shakes them up. At that moment* KOCHKARYOV *enters stealthily and stands behind her.*) Oh, if only I could draw Baltazar... What am I saying! I meant to say Anuchkin.... No, no... Leave it to fate.

KOCHKARYOV. Take Podkolyosin. He's the best of the bunch.

AGAFYA. Oh! (*Shrieks and covers her face with both hands, afraid to look behind her.*)

KOCHKARYOV. What frightened you? Don't be shy, it's me. Seriously, take Podkolyosin.

AGAFYA. Oh, I'm so ashamed. You overheard.

KOCHKARYOV. Never mind, never mind! After all, I'm one of the family, a relative. No reason to be embarrassed in front of me. Come on, show me your pretty little face.

AGAFYA, *half uncovering her face.* Really, I'm so ashamed.

KOCHKARYOV. Go ahead, take Podkolyosin.

AGAFYA. Oh! (*Shrieks and covers her face again.*)

KOCHKARYOV. The fellow's a marvel; he's brought his office into perfect shape... really, a marvel!

AGAFYA, *uncovering her face a bit.* And what about the others? Mr. Anuchkin—he's a nice man too.

KOCHKARYOV. Please, he's dirt next to Podkolyosin.

AGAFYA. Why is that?

KOCHKARYOV. It's clear why. Podkolyosin is a man... well, a man who... a man who... you won't find anyone like him.

AGAFYA. And what about Mr. Omelet?

KOCHKARYOV. Omelet's garbage. They're all garbage.

AGAFYA. Can it be that all of them...?

KOCHKARYOV. Judge for yourself, just compare—no matter what, it's Podkolyosin! And these others, these Anuchkins, these Omelets, who the hell knows what they are.

AGAFYA. But they're very... well-behaved.

KOCHKARYOV. Well-behaved? Thugs, hooligans of the worst sort! Do you want to be beaten the day after your wedding?

AGAFYA. Oh my God! That's terrible. There couldn't be anything worse.

KOCHKARYOV. You said it! You couldn't even imagine anything worse.

AGAFYA. So you advise me to take Mr. Podkolyosin?

KOCHKARYOV. Podkolyosin, of course, Podkolyosin. (*Aside.*) It seems to be working. Podkolyosin's waiting in the pastry shop. I'll have to run over and get him.

AGAFYA. So you think—Mr. Podkolyosin?

KOCHKARYOV. Absolutely—Podkolyosin!

AGAFYA. And the others. Should I refuse them?

KOCHKARYOV. Certainly. Turn 'em down flat.

AGAFYA. But how can I do that? It would be embarrassing.

KOCHKARYOV. Why embarrassing? Tell them you're too young to get married.

AGAFYA. But they won't believe it. They'll want to know why.

KOCHKARYOV. In that case, end it once and for all. Say, "Scram, you idiots!"

AGAFYA. How could I use such language?

KOCHKARYOV. Just try. I assure you, after that they'll make themselves scarce.

AGAFYA. But it would be uncouth.

KOCHKARYOV. You won't see them again. So it's all the same, isn't it?

AGAFYA. Well, somehow it's not very nice. . . . They'll be angry.

KOCHKARYOV. So what if they're angry? If anything could come of it, that would be another matter. But at worst, one of them will spit in your eye—that's all.

AGAFYA. There, you see!

KOCHKARYOV. What of it? God knows, some people have been spat at several times! I even know one fellow—very good-looking, rosy cheeks and all—well, he was pestering and sucking up to his boss for a raise till the boss finally couldn't stand it—spat right in his face, by God! "Here you are," he says, "here's your raise; now get off my back, you devil!" But just the same, he gave him a raise. So what if they spit? You have a handkerchief in your pocket. Take it and wipe it off. (*A ring in the hall.*) There's the bell. That must be them. I wouldn't care to run into that gang now. Is there another way out?

AGAFYA. Yes, of course, down the back stairs. But, really, I'm trembling all over.

KOCHKARYOV. Don't worry. Just keep your wits about you. So long. (*Aside.*) I'll get Podkolyosin as fast as I can. (*Goes out. OMELET enters.*)

OMELET. I have intentionally come a bit early, miss, to have a word with you alone, and at leisure. Well, miss, as for my rank, I suppose you're aware, I am a collegiate assessor, beloved by my superiors, obeyed by my subordinates. I lack only a companion on the road of life.

AGAFYA. Yes, sir.

OMELET. Now I have found a companion on the road of life. This companion—is you. Tell it to me straight: yes or no. (*Stares at her shoulders. Aside.*) Ah, she's not like those skinny German ladies you run into—there's something to her.

AGAFYA. I'm still quite young, sir. . . . I'm not ready to marry.

OMELET. What's that? . . . Then what's the matchmaker doing here? But perhaps you have something else in mind. Would you explain . . . (*A ring is heard.*) Damn it! They never let a fellow attend to business.

ZHEVAKIN *enters.*

ZHEVAKIN. Pardon me, miss, perhaps I'm a bit early. (*Turns and sees OMELET.*) Ah, someone's already . . . Mr. Omelet, my respects.

OMELET, *aside.* Drop dead with your respects! (*Aloud.*) So what's it going to be, miss? Just say the word: yes or no? (*A ring is heard. OMELET spits in anger.*) The bell again!

ANUCHKIN *enters.*

ANUCHKIN. Perhaps, miss, I'm earlier than is appropriate, as commanded by the rules of propriety. . . . (*Seeing the others, utters an exclamation and bows.*) My respects, gentlemen.

OMELET, *aside.* Shove your respects! Who the hell brought you just now? I wish you'd break those skinny legs of yours! (*Aloud.*) So what's it going to be, miss. Decide! I'm a busy man; I don't have time to waste. Yes or no?

AGAFYA, *in confusion.* I've had enough, sir, enough . . . (*Aside.*) I don't know what I'm saying.

OMELET. What's that? "Enough"? What do you mean,
"enough"?

AGAFYA. Nothing, sir, nothing . . . I didn't intend . . . (*Pulling
herself together.*) Scram! . . . (*Aside, flinging up her hands.*) Oh
my God! What am I saying?

OMELET. What's that? "Scram"? What do you mean—"scram"?
Permit me to ask, What do you mean by that? (*Putting his hands
on his hips, he steps up to her menacingly.*)

AGAFYA, *glancing into his face, shrieks.* Oh, he's going to hit me,
he's going to hit me! (*Runs out.* OMELET *stands open-mouthed.*
ARINA PANTELEYMONOVNA *runs in at the cry and, glancing into
his face, shrieks also,* Oh, he's going to hit us!" *and runs out.*)

OMELET. What the devil is going on here? Now, isn't this
something!

The doorbell rings and voices are heard.

KOCHKARYOV'S VOICE. Go on in, go on in. Why are you stopping?

PODKOLYOSIN'S VOICE. You go ahead. I'll get myself together in a
minute. My shoelace is untied.

KOCHKARYOV'S VOICE. You'll sneak off again.

PODKOLYOSIN'S VOICE. No, I won't sneak off! I promise, I won't!
(KOCHKARYOV *enters.*)

KOCHKARYOV. Now he has to tie his shoelace!

OMELET, *addressing him.* Tell me, please, is the young lady crazy,
or what?

KOCHKARYOV. Why? What happened?

OMELET. Strange goings on. She ran out of the room, started
screaming, "He's going to hit me, he's going to hit me!" I'll be
damned if I know what it's all about.

KOCHKARYOV. Well, yes. She has these fits. She's a bit touched.

OMELET. Say, you're her relative, aren't you?

KOCHKARYOV. Certainly, a relative.

OMELET. May I ask how you're related?

KOCHKARYOV. I really don't know. In some way my mother's aunt
is something or other to her father, or her father is something or
other to my aunt. My wife knows all about it. She keeps track of
these things.

OMELET. And has she had these fits for a long time?

KOCHKARYOV. Since childhood.

OMELET. Well, it would be preferable if she had more brains, but a fool is fine too. As long as the items in the dowry are in proper order.

KOCHKARYOV. But she doesn't have a thing.

OMELET. How's that possible? What about the stone house?

KOCHKARYOV. Stone? That's all talk. If you only knew how they built it. The walls were slapped together with the cheapest bricks. And there's nothing but sawdust holding it up.

OMELET. No!

KOCHKARYOV. Yes. Don't you know how houses are built nowadays? Anything goes, as long as they can get a mortgage.

OMELET. But the house isn't mortgaged?

KOCHKARYOV. Who says so? Not only is it mortgaged, the interest hasn't been paid for two years. And there's a brother in the Senate who's got his eye on the property—a shyster; you've never seen anything like him. The swindler would steal his mother's last skirt.

OMELET. Then how was it that the matchmaker. . . Ah the liar, the fraud. . . (*Aside.*) But maybe *he's* lying. I'll worm the truth out of that old woman! And if he's right. . . well. . . I'll make her sing out of the other side of her mouth.

ANUCHKIN. Please, permit me to trouble you with a question, sir. I confess, not knowing French, I find it extraordinarily difficult to judge whether a woman speaks French or not. As to the lady of house, does she speak French, or doesn't she?

KOCHKARYOV. Not a blessed word.

ANUCHKIN. Indeed?

KOCHKARYOV. Absolutely! I know it for a fact. She was at the same boarding school as my wife—well-known for her laziness, always in the dunce's cap. The French teacher beat her with a stick.

ANUCHKIN. Imagine! From the moment I laid eyes on her I had a feeling she didn't know French.

OMELET. Oh, to hell with French! But how that damn matchmaker . . . Oh the cheat, the witch! If you only knew the pictures she painted, the words she used! An artist, a perfect artist! ''A house," she says, "wings, stone foundations, silver spoons, a sleigh; just sit down and drive off' "—like a page out of some novel. Oh you old hag! Wait till I get my hands on you . . .

FYOKLA *enters. On seeing her, all address her with the following words.*

OMELET. Ah! There she is! Come over here, you snake! Just come here!

ANUCHKIN. So this is how you deceived me, Madam Fyokla.

KOCHKARYOV. Step up and face judgment, you wicked woman!

FYOKLA. I can't make out a word. You're making me deaf.

OMELET. The house is made of brick, you old slut. And how you laid it on—with attics and who the hell knows what else.

FYOKLA. What do I know! It wasn't me that built it. Maybe it had to be built with brick, so they built it that way.

OMELET. And mortgaged into the bargain! I hope you choke, you damned witch! (*Stamping his feet.*)

FYOKLA. Look at him! And swearing too. Anyone else would be thanking me for all the trouble I took.

ANUCHKIN. But Madam Fyokla, you assured me she knows French.

FYOKLA. She knows it, my dear. She knows everything, German too, and all the other languages. Whatever manners you like, she has them.

ANUCHKIN. Oh no! It seems she can only speak Russian.

FYOKLA. What's the harm in that? Russian's easier to understand, so she talks Russian. And if she could talk like some heathen, so much the worse for you—you wouldn't understand. I don't have to explain what Russian is. . . . All the saints spoke Russian.

OMELET. Just come here, damn you! Just step over to me!

FYOKLA, *backing away to the door.* Oh no! I know your kind. You're a bully. You'll hit a person for no reason.

OMELET. Well, watch out! You won't get away with this. I'll pack you off to the police. I'll teach you to hoodwink honest people. You'll see. And tell the young lady she's a bitch! You hear—be sure to tell her—a bitch! (*Goes out.*)

FYOKLA. See what he's like! Lost his head! Because he's fat, he thinks no one's a match for him. And I'll say you're a son-of-a-bitch, that's what!

ANUCHKIN. My dear woman, I confess, I never imagined you were going to deceive me in this way. Had I known how the young lady was educated, I . . . I should have never set foot in here. Yes indeed, madam. (*Goes out.*)

FYOKLA. They've gone out of their minds or had a drop too much. What a bunch of nit-pickers I've come up with! Damn fool education has made 'em crazy!

> KOCHKARYOV *laughs uproariously, looking at* FYOKLA *and pointing his finger at her.*

FYOKLA, *annoyed.* What are you laughing your head off about? (KOCHKARYOV *continues to laugh.*) Eh, what's gotten into him!

KOCHKARYOV. Some matchmaker! Some matchmaker! Mistress of marriages! Knows her business! (*Continues laughing.*)

FYOKLA. Eh, how he's running off at the mouth! You know, your mother must have been cracked when she had you. (*Goes out annoyed.*)

KOCHKARYOV, *continuing to laugh.* Oh I can't, really, I can't. I can't take it, I'll burst laughing! (*Continues laughing.* ZHEVAKIN, *staring at him, begins to laugh also.* KOCHKARYOV *sinks to a chair, exhausted.*) Whew, I'm bushed. If I laugh any more, I'll burst a gut.

ZHEVAKIN. I like the gaiety of your disposition. Now, in Captain Bóldyrev's squadron we had a midshipman, Petukhóv by name —Antón Ivanovich—also of a cheerful disposition. You would show him a finger, like this—that's all—and, by God, he'd start to laugh, and he'd be laughing all day. Well, looking at him you'd get into a funny mood youself, and in no time you'd actually be laughing too.

KOCHKARYOV, *catching his breath.* Oh, Lord, have mercy! Now what could she have had in mind, the old fool? She make a match! She make a match! Now when I marry 'em, I marry 'em!

ZHEVAKIN. No? So you can really arrange a marriage?

KOCHKARYOV. Sure. Anyone to anyone, whatever you like.

ZHEVAKIN. If that's true, arrange a match for me with the young lady here.

KOCHKARYOV. You? But what do you want to get married for?

ZHEVAKIN. What do you mean, "What for"? I must say, that's an odd question! Everybody knows what for.

KOCHKARYOV. But you must have heard, she has no dowry.

ZHEVAKIN. If not, then there's no point complaining. Of course, it's a shame, but she's such a charming girl, so well mannered. Married to her, I could get along without a dowry. A little room (*indicates the size with his hands*), here a small foyer, a tiny screen, or a partition of some sort. . .

KOCHKARYOV. What about her appeals to you?

ZHEVAKIN. Well, to be honest, I like her because she's plump. I'm a great connoisseur in the area of feminine plumpness.

KOCHKARYOV, *with a sidelong glance at him, aside.* He's not much of a dandy himself. Looks like a pouch after you've shaken the tobacco out of it. (*Aloud.*) No, you shouldn't get married.

ZHEVAKIN. What's that?

KOCHKARYOV. Yes, that's so. Between you and me, what sort of a shape do you have? Chicken legs.

ZHEVAKIN. Chicken?

KOCHKARYOV. Sure. That's some figure you've got there!

ZHEVAKIN. Really. . .like a. . .but. . .chicken legs?

KOCHKARYOV. Exactly. Chicken legs.

ZHEVAKIN. It seems to me, however, that this touches upon personal matters.

KOCHKARYOV. I'm speaking frankly because you're a sensible man. I wouldn't say it to anyone else. I'll marry you off, if you wish, only to some other girl.

ZHEVAKIN. No, I beg you. Be so kind as to get me this one.

KOCHKARYOV. All right, but on one condition—don't butt in. Don't even let the young lady set eyes on you. I'll handle it myself.

ZHEVAKIN. But how can you manage without me? I shall at least have to make an appearance.

KOCHKARYOV. That won't be necessary. Go home and wait. By evening it'll all be taken care of.

ZHEVAKIN, *rubbing his hands.* Now that would be splendid! But won't you need my diploma, my service record? Perhaps the young lady would be interested. I'll run and bring them immediately.

KOCHKARYOV. You don't need a thing. Just go home. I'll let you know before the day is over. (*Sees him out.*) Like hell you'll hear from me! But what's going on? How come Podkolyosin's not here? Hm, peculiar. Can he still be tying his shoelace? Maybe I'd better go look for him?

AGAFYA *enters.*

AGAFYA, *looking about.* Have they gone? No one here?

KOCHKARYOV. They've gone.

AGAFYA. If you only knew the way I was trembling! Nothing quite like it has ever happened to me. What a dreadful man that Omelet is! How he would abuse his wife! I keep imagining he'll return.

KOCHKARYOV. Oh, he won't come back. Not a chance. I'll stake my life neither of those two pokes his nose in here again.

AGAFYA. And the third?

KOCHKARYOV. What third?

ZHEVAKIN, *poking his head through the door, aside.* I'm dying to hear her declare her love for me with that pretty little mouth . . . Oh what a rosebud!

AGAFYA. Baltazar Baltazarovich?

ZHEVAKIN. Here it comes! Here it comes! (*Rubbing his hands.*)

KOCHKARYOV. Phew! What the heck! I couldn't imagine who you were talking about. Why, he's a nobody, a complete idiot.

ZHEVAKIN. Now what's this? I must say, I don't understand.

AGAFYA. But he seemed a very nice gentleman.

KOCHKARYOV. A drunk!

ZHEVAKIN. I swear, I don't get it.

AGAFYA. Can he really be a drunkard?

KOCHKARYOV. Trust me. An out-and-out degenerate.

ZHEVAKIN, *aloud.* I beg your pardon, sir. This isn't exactly what I had in mind. Something in my favor, a word of praise—that would have been another matter. But to go on in such a fashion, in such language—no thank you; for that, you can get somebody else.

KOCHKARYOV, *aside.* What on earth made him turn up? (*To*
AGAFYA *in a lowered voice.*) Look at him! He can't stand on his
feet. He's staggering all over the place. Kick him out, and let
that be the end of him! (*Aside.*) And Podkolyosin's still not
here. The bastard! I'll get even with him. (*Goes out.*)

ZHEVAKIN, *aside.* He promised to flatter me, and instead he hurls
insults! What a strange fellow! (*Aloud.*) Miss, don't you
believe . . .

AGAFYA. Excuse me. I'm not feeling well. . . . I have a headache,
sir. (*Tries to go.*)

ZHEVAKIN. But, perhaps there's something about me that dis-
pleases you? (*Pointing to his head.*) Is it my little bald spot?
Don't you pay it any mind. It's nothing—from a fever. The hair
will grow back soon.

AGAFYA. It's all the same to me whatever you have up there, sir.

ZHEVAKIN. When I put on a black coat, miss . . . my complexion
becomes a bit lighter.

AGAFYA. I'm happy for you! Goodbye! (*Goes out.*)

ZHEVAKIN, *alone, calls after her.* Miss, please, tell me the reason.
Why? Why? Do I lack something essential? . . . She's gone! Very
odd! It must be the seventeenth time this has happened to me—
and almost always the same way. At first everything seems to be
going smoothly, but when it comes to a head—bam! They turn
me down. (*Walks around the room pondering.*) Yes . . . she must
be number seventeen! But what can she want? What would she,
for example, uh . . . on what grounds . . . ? (*Thinking a little.*)
Puzzling, very puzzling! It would make sense if something were
wrong with me. (*Looks himself over.*) Seems nobody could say
that. Thank goodness, everything's in its right place. Nature
hasn't been unkind to me. . . . Incredible! Maybe I'd better go
home and search through my trunk. I had a poem there. No
woman could resist it. . . . My God, incredible! At first, it seemed
to be going so nicely. Looks like I'll have to try another approach.
A pity, really a pity. (*Goes out.* KOCHKARYOV *and* PODKOL-
YOSIN *enter, and both look behind them.*)

KOCHKARYOV. He didn't notice us! Did you see the long face he
had on?

PODKOLYOSIN. You think he's been turned down?

KOCHKARYOV. Turned down cold.

PODKOLYOSIN, *with a self-satisfied smile.* It must be very embarrassing.

KOCHKARYOV. Very!

PODKOLYOSIN. I still can't believe it. Did she actually say she prefers me to all the others?

KOCHKARYOV. Prefers! She's wild about you. What love! The pet names she has for you! The passion! The girl's positively sizzling.

PODKOLYOSIN, *laughs with self-satisfaction.* You know, really . . . a woman, when she wants to, can say such things: babyface, my little cockroach, piggy. . . .

KOCHKARYOV. You haven't heard anything yet! Wait till you're married—then you'll hear pet names! My friend, you'll just melt away.

PODKOLYOSIN, *laughs.* You don't say!

KOCHKARYOV. As I'm an honest man! But look here, we have to get to work fast. Have it out with her, open your heart, and ask her hand this minute.

PODKOLYOSIN. This very minute? What are you saying?

KOCHKARYOV. It has to be this minute. . . . And here she is. (AGAFYA *enters.*) I have brought you, miss, the mortal whom you behold. Never was man so enamoured, God help us, and I wouldn't wish my worst enemy . . .

PODKOLYOSIN, *nudging him under the arm, aside.* Really, old man, you may be laying it on a bit thick.

KOCHKARYOV, *to him.* Don't worry. It's all right. (*To her, aside.*) Be a bit bolder—he's very shy. Try to act free and easy. Wiggle your eyebrows, or lower your eyelids and suddenly give it to him, destroy him, the bandit. Or show him a little shoulder, and let the bastard look! It's a pity you didn't put on a dress with short sleeves, but this one will do. (*Aloud.*) Well, I leave you in pleasant company! Meanwhile I'll drop by the dining room and kitchen—have to see to things. The caterer from whom I ordered supper will be here soon. And maybe the wines have come. . . . So long! (*To* PODKOLYOSIN.) Courage! Courage! (*Goes out.*)

AGAFYA. Please be seated, sir. (*They sit and remain silent.*)

PODKOLYOSIN. Do you like rowing, miss?

AGAFYA. Rowing, sir?

PODKOLYOSIN. Rowing is very pleasant in the summer.

AGAFYA. Sometimes we go on hikes with friends, sir.

PODKOLYOSIN. There's no knowing what kind of summer we'll have.

AGAFYA. I'd like it to be nice. (*Both fall silent.*)

PODKOLYOSIN. What's your favorite flower, miss?

AGAFYA. One that has a strong fragrance, sir—carnations.

PODKOLYOSIN. Flowers go well on ladies.

AGAFYA. Yes, it's a pleasant pastime. (*Silence.*) What church did you go to last Sunday?

PODKOLYOSIN. Ascension. The week before, I went to the Kazansky cathedral. They pray the same way no matter what the church, but the ornaments are prettier in the cathedral. (*They fall silent.* PODKOLYOSIN *drums with his fingers on the table.*) The festival will be here soon.

AGAFYA. Yes, in a month, I think.

PODKOLYOSIN. Not even a month.

AGAFYA. It should be fun.

PODKOLYOSIN. Today's the eighth. (*Counts on his fingers.*) The ninth, tenth, eleventh. . . in twenty-two days.

AGAFYA. Imagine, so soon!

PODKOLYOSIN. I'm not even counting today. (*Silence.*) How brave the Russian people are!

AGAFYA. I beg your pardon?

PODKOLYOSIN. The workers. They stand on the very heights. . . . I was passing a house—a plasterer was plastering, and he wasn't in the least afraid.

AGAFYA. Yes, sir. Where was that?

PODKOLYOSIN. On the street I take to the office. You're aware, of course, that every morning I go to the office. (*Silence.* PODKOLYOSIN *again starts to drum with his fingers; at last he takes his hat and bows.*)

AGAFYA. Are you already. . . ?

PODKOLYOSIN. Yes, miss. Forgive me. Perhaps I've bored you.

AGAFYA. How is that possible, sir! On the contrary, I must thank you for passing the time so pleasantly.

PODKOLYOSIN, *smiling*. But I imagine, really... I must have bored you.

AGAFYA. Oh no, not at all.

PODKOLYOSIN. Well, if not, than allow me, some other time, in the evening...

AGAFYA. I would be delighted, sir.

They exchange bows. PODKOLYOSIN *goes out.*

AGAFYA, *alone*. What an excellent man! Only now have I come to know him well. One can't help loving him—he's so modest and sensible. Yes, his friend spoke the truth. Only it's a pity that he left so soon. I should have liked to listen to him some more. How fascinating to converse with him! And it's especially delightful that he's not one to waste words. I wanted to say a thing or two also, but, I admit, I felt shy. My heart began to beat so... What a splendid man! I must go and tell Auntie! (*Goes out.* KOCHKARYOV *and* PODKOLYOSIN *enter.*)

KOCHKARYOV. What do you want to go home for? Ridiculous!

PODKOLYOSIN. But why should I remain here? I've already said all that's necessary.

KOCHKARYOV. Then you've opened your heart to her?

PODKOLYOSIN. Well, not exactly... maybe I haven't yet opened my heart.

KOCHKARYOV. Oh hell! Why didn't you open it?

PODKOLYOSIN. Do you want me all of a sudden, without any preliminaries, to blurt out, "Miss, let me marry you!"

KOCHKARYOV. In that case, what were you chattering about for a solid half-hour?

PODKOLYOSIN. We discussed all sorts of things. I'm quite satisfied. Every moment was extremely interesting.

KOCHKARYOV. But look here, time is running short. In an hour we go to the church for the wedding.

PODKOLYOSIN. What! Are you out of your mind? The wedding today!

KOCHKARYOV. Why not?

PODKOLYOSIN. Today!

KOCHKARYOV. But you gave your word. As soon as we got rid of the others, you were supposed to get married.

PODKOLYOSIN. Well, I'm not going back on my word. But not right now. I need a month at least—as a breathing spell.

KOCHKARYOV. A month!

PODKOLYOSIN. Yes, certainly.

KOCHKARYOV. Are you crazy?

PODKOLYOSIN. Less than a month is out of the question.

KOCHKARYOV. But I've ordered the supper from the caterer, you dimwit!. . . Listen to me, Ivan Kuzmich, dear friend, don't be stubborn, get married now.

PODKOLYOSIN. Now? For God's sake, what are you saying?

KOCHKARYOV. Ivan Kuzmich, I beg you. If not for yourself, then for me.

PODKOLYOSIN. Really, I can't.

KOCHKARYOV. You can, dear friend, you can do it. Please, don't play games, dear boy!

PODKOLYOSIN. Really, no. It's so awkward.

KOCHKARYOV. Why awkward? Who told you it's awkward? Make up your own mind. You're an intelligent man. I'm not saying this to flatter you, and not because you're a head clerk. I'm saying it out of love. . . . Enough of this, my dear boy. Make your decision. Look at it with the eyes of a reasonable man.

PODKOLYOSIN. Well, if it were possible, then I'd. . .

KOCHKARYOV. Ivan Kuzmich! Pet! Angel! If you like, I'll get down on my knees.

PODKOLYOSIN. What on earth for?

KOCHKARYOV, *going down on his knees.* Here I am, on my knees! See, I'm begging you. I shall never forget this favor. Don't be stubborn. Sweetheart!

PODKOLYOSIN. No, I can't, old boy, really, I can't.

KOCHKARYOV, *getting up, very angry.* Pig!

PODKOLYOSIN. Go ahead, curse all you want.

KOCHKARYOV. Idiot! I've never known anyone like you!

PODKOLYOSIN. Swear away!

KOCHKARYOV. For whom did I try so hard? For whom did I rack my brains? For you, you numbskull. What's it to me? I'm through with you. I wash my hands of the whole business.

PODKOLYOSIN. Well, who asked you to trouble yourself? By all means, drop it.

KOCHKARYOV. But you'll be lost without me. Without me you can't do anything. If I don't marry you off, you'll remain a fool the rest of your life.

PODKOLYOSIN. What's it to you?

KOCHKARYOV. It's for you that I'm exerting myself, you block-head!

PODKOLYOSIN. I don't want your exertions.

KOCHKARYOV. In that case, go to hell!

PODKOLYOSIN. Very well, I'll go.

KOCHKARYOV. And have a good trip!

PODKOLYOSIN. Very well, I'll go.

KOCHKARYOV. Go! go! And I hope you break your legs on the way! I hope a drunken cabbie rams his carriage shaft into your throat! You're a rag—not a clerk! I swear it's all over between us. Don't let me ever set eyes on you again!

PODKOLYOSIN. I won't. (*Goes out.*)

KOCHKARYOV. Go to your old friend—go to the devil! (*Opening the door, yells after him.*) Idiot!

KOCHKARYOV, *alone, walks back and forth in great agitation.* Has the world ever seen the likes of him? What an imbecile! But I'm a fine one too. Now tell me, please, I call on all of you as witnesses—aren't I a fool, a dolt? What am I knocking myself out for, yelling till my throat is dry? What is he to me? A relative or what? And what am I to him—an aunt, a mother-in-law, a nursemaid? What possessed me to bother about him? Why? Why do I worry myself sick? The devil take him! Who the hell knows why! Ask anybody why he does anything! What a son-of-a-bitch! What a nasty repulsive face! You dumb beast, I'd like to take you and smack you in the nose, the ears, the mouth, the teeth—every place! (*In anger makes several punches in the air.*) Now what really kills me is that he's gone off—he just doesn't give a damn. For him it's all water off a duck's back—that's what's so unbearable! He'll go to his apartment and lie there smoking his stinking pipe. What a nasty creature! The world's

full of repulsive mugs, but none to match his! You couldn't
dream up anything worse—by God, you couldn't. Well, it's no
use, I'll go bring the pig back! I won't let him slip away. I'll go
get the bastard! (*Runs out.* AGAFYA *enters.*)

AGAFYA, *alone.* My heart is pounding so—I don't know why.
Wherever I turn I see Mr. Podkolyosin. How true it is that you
can't escape your fate. A little while ago I wanted so much to
think of something else—I tried winding wool, embroidering a
purse—but no matter what I do, Mr. Podkolyosin keeps coming
into my thoughts. (*Falls silent.*) So at last I'm to be married!
They'll come and take me to the church . . . then they'll leave me
alone with a man—oof! I'm trembling all over. Goodbye to my
life as a single girl. (*Weeps.*) So many years spent in peace. . . .
I've gone on and on, just living—and now I'm to be a married
woman! The troubles that are in store for me! I'll have children,
little boys—they're always fighting; and girls too—they grow up,
and you have to find husbands for them. All well and good if
they marry decent men, but what if they choose drunkards, or
gamblers ready to risk everything on a card! (*Gradually begins
weeping again.*) I missed out having fun as a girl. It's not even
twenty-seven years that I've been single. . . . (*Changing her
voice.*) But what's keeping Mr. Podkolyosin?

PODKOLYOSIN, *pushed on stage through the door by* KOCHKAR-
YOV'S *two arms; stammering.* I have come to you, miss, to
discuss a small matter. . . . Only I hope you won't find it
peculiar?

AGAFYA, *lowering her eyes.* What is it?

PODKOLYOSIN. No, miss. Tell me first, you won't find it peculiar?

AGAFYA, *still lowering her eyes.* I don't understand, sir.

PODKOLYOSIN. Confess! Most likely you'll think what I'm going to
say is peculiar?

AGAFYA. Oh dear, how could it be? Anything you say is agreeable.

PODKOLYOSIN. You haven't heard this yet. (AGAFYA *lowers her
eyes even more. At this moment* KOCHKARYOV *enters stealthily
and stands behind his back.*) The point is . . . uh, I better tell you
some other time.

AGAFYA. But what is it?

PODKOLYOSIN. It's...I...I was about to declare...but somehow I keep having doubts.

KOCHKARYOV, *to himself, folding his arms.* Good God, what a man! He's an old woman, not a man, a mockery of a man, a satire upon man.

AGAFYA. Why is that?

PODKOLYOSIN. I don't know...I'm just filled with doubt.

KOCHKARYOV, *aloud.* How stupid, how stupid! Look miss, he asks your hand in marriage, would like to say that without you he can't live or exist, and only wants to know, do you consent to make him happy?

PODKOLYOSIN, *almost panic-stricken, nudges him, speaking aside.* For Christ's sake, what are you doing!

KOCHKARYOV. So what'll it be, miss? Do you consent to provide this mortal with happiness?

AGAFYA. I don't dare dream I can make someone happy. But I consent.

KOCHKARYOV. Of course, of course, it's about time! Give me your hands!

PODKOLYOSIN. Just a moment. (*He tries to whisper something in his ear;* KOCHKARYOV *shows him his fist and frowns; he gives his hand.*)

KOCHKARYOV, *joining their hands.* May God bless you. I give my consent and approval to your union. Marriage is a...it's not like getting into a cab and riding off someplace. It's a responsibility of an entirely different sort, a responsibility that... But I haven't the time now. I'll tell you later what sort of a responsibility it is. Come Podkolyosin, kiss the bride. You can do it now. You must do it now. (AGAFYA *lowers her eyes.*) Don't be shy, miss, it's all right. That's the way it ought to be—let him kiss you.

PODKOLYOSIN. No, allow me, miss, allow me. (*Kisses her and takes her hand.*) What a lovely little hand! How come you have such a lovely little hand, miss?... I insist, the wedding must take place right now! At once!

AGAFYA. At once? But perhaps that's too soon.

PODKOLYOSIN. I won't hear a word. I would prefer it even sooner, that the marriage take place this minute.

KOCHKARYOV. Bravo! Excellent! Noble fellow! I must say, I always expected great things from you! And you, miss, you'd better hurry and get dressed. As a matter of fact I've already sent for the carriage and invited the guests. They've all gone directly to the church. I know you have a wedding gown on hand.

AGAFYA. Oh yes. I've had it ready for some time. I'll run and put it on. (*Goes out.*)

PODKOLYOSIN. Well, pal, thanks! Now I fully appreciate your efforts. My own father wouldn't have done what you've done. You acted out of friendship. Thanks again. Your kindness will stay with me all my life. (*Moved.*) Next spring without fail I'll visit your father's grave.

KOCHKARYOV. Think nothing of it, my pleasure. Come here, let me embrace you. (*Kisses him on one cheek, then the other.*) God grant you good health (*they kiss*), happiness, and prosperity, and I wish you a batch of kids. . . .

PODKOLYOSIN. Thanks, old man. I've finally discovered what life is all about. You've opened my eyes to a whole new world—seething, pulsating, bubbling, somehow or other. . . my head's just swimming. Till now all this was hidden from me. My days were spent in ignorance, without a serious thought or idea. I lived, well, as everyone else lives.

KOCHKARYOV. I'm awfully glad. Let me go and check the way they've set the table. Be right back. (*Aside.*) But I'd better hide his hat—just in case. (*Takes the hat and carries it out with him.*)

PODKOLYOSIN, *alone*. Really, what was I till now? Did I understand the meaning of life? No, not at all. And what was my bachelor's existence like? What was I good for? What did I do? I lived, I worked, I went to the office, I ate, I slept—in short, I was the most ordinary and empty of men. Only now do I see how foolish it is not to marry. And to think of all those who go on living in blindness. If I were a king, I'd order everyone to get married, absolutely everyone. Not a single bachelor would be permitted in my kingdom. . . . And come to think of it, in a few minutes, I'll be a married man. I'll taste of the bliss that's perhaps found only in fairly tales, an inexpressible bliss, a bliss

words can't describe. (*After a brief pause.*) But no matter what
they say, the thought of it is frightening. To tie yourself down for
all your days, for your whole life, come what may. And afterwards, there's no begging off, no second thoughts, nothing,
nothing—you're finished, cooked. And it's already too late to
back out of it—in a minute I'll be at the altar. Impossible to get
away—the carriage is waiting, the guests are at the church. But is
it really impossible? Absolutely! Out of the question. People are
standing in the doorway. They'll want to know what I'm up to.
No, it's impossible. Say, the window's open. What about the
window? No, I couldn't—so unbecoming, and besides, it's too
high. (*Goes up to the window.*) Hm, not so high, only the
ground floor, and a low one at that. . . . No, how can I, I don't
even have my hat. How can I without a hat? It's so awkward. But
really, can't I, even without a hat? What about giving it a try,
huh? Do we try it, or not? (*He stands on the window sill, and
saying, "Oh Lord, help me!" jumps to the street; groans and
moans from off stage.*) Ouch! It was high! Cab! Cab!
CABMAN'S VOICE. Where to, sir?
PODKOLYOSIN'S VOICE. Kanávka, near the Semyónovsky Bridge.
CABMAN'S VOICE. Ten kopecks, not a kopeck less.
PODKOLYOSIN'S VOICE. It's a deal! Get going!

The rattle of a departing carriage is heard. AGAFYA *enters
timidly in a wedding dress, her head lowered.*

AGAFYA, *alone.* I don't know what's wrong with me! I feel embar-
rassed again. I'm trembling all over. Oh, if only he weren't in
the room, if only he stepped out for a moment! (*Timidly looks
about.*) But where is he? No one's here. Where did he go?
(*Opens the door to the hall and speaks through it.*) Fyokla,
where's Mr. Podkolyosin?
FYOKLA'S VOICE. He's there.
AGAFYA. What do you mean "there"?
FYOKLA, *entering.* Why, he was sitting right here.
AGAFYA. But you see, he's not here.
FYOKLA. Well, he didn't come out either. I was in the hallway.
AGAFYA. But where is he then?

FYOKLA. I don't know. Maybe he went down the back stairs, or maybe he's in Arina Panteleymonovna's room?

AGAFYA. Auntie! Oh Auntie!

ARINA PANTELEYMONOVNA *enters.*

ARINA, *all dressed up.* What is it?

AGAFYA. Is Mr. Podkolyosin in your room?

ARINA. No, he should be here. He hasn't been to see me.

FYOKLA. Well, he didn't come into the hallway.

AGAFYA. But you can see, he's not here either.

KOCHKARYOV *enters.*

KOCHKARYOV. What's up?

AGAFYA. Mr. Podkolyosin's not here.

KOCHKARYOV. What's that? Not here? He left?

AGAFYA. No, he hasn't left either.

KOCHKARYOV. What? Not here and hasn't left?

FYOKLA. I can't figure out what could've become of him. I was in the hallway all the time, didn't budge from my seat.

ARINA. Well, there's no way he could have gotten down the back stairs.

KOCHKARYOV. Dammit! He also couldn't have gotten lost without leaving the room. Maybe he's hiding? . . . Podkolyosin! Podkolyosin! Where are you? Stop fooling; enough now. Come out right away! What kind of a joke is this? It's time you were in church! (*Looks behind the cupboard, even casts a sidelong glance under the chairs.*) Incredible! No, he couldn't have left. There's no way he could have! He's here. His hat's in the next room—I purposely put it there.

ARINA. Maybe we should ask the maid? She's been outside all this time. She may know something. . . . Dunyashka! Dunyashka! (DUNYASHKA *enters.*) Where's Mr. Podkolyosin? Have you seen him?

DUNYASHKA. The gentleman jumped out of the window, madam.

AGAFYA *shrieks, throwing her arms up.*

ALL THREE. Out the window?

DUNYASHKA. Yes, madam. And after he jumped, he took a cab and drove away.

ARINA. Are you telling the truth?

KOCHKARYOV. You're lying! It can't be!

DUNYASHKA. So help me—he jumped out! The grocer saw him too. He took a cab for ten kopecks and drove away.

ARINA, *stepping up to* KOCHKARYOV. What's this, sir, poking fun at us, are you? Did you think to laugh at us? Did we deserve this from you—to be shamed so? I've lived for almost sixty years and I've never been so disgraced! Even if you're an honest man, sir, I'll spit in your face for this. Even if you're an honest man, after this you're a crook. To shame a girl before the whole world! I'm a simple woman, but I wouldn't do such a thing. And you— you're a nobleman! You're a nobleman for dirty tricks, for making mischief—that's what your being a nobleman is good for! (*Goes out in a rage and takes* AGAFYA *away.* KOCHKARYOV *stands as if thunderstruck.*)

FYOKLA. So! There he stands. Knows all the tricks of the trade. Can arrange a marriage without a matchmaker! Now, I may have a mixed bag of bachelors, riffraff, all sorts, but the kind that jump out of windows I don't have—no thank you!

KOCHKARYOV. Ridiculous! It can't be. I'll run and get him. I'll bring him back! (*Goes out.*)

FYOKLA. Yes, you go, bring him back! Don't know much about the marriage business, do you? Now if a bridegroom runs out the door—that's one thing; but when he jumps out the window— you can kiss him good-bye!

Curtain.

The Government Inspector
A Comedy in Five Acts

No use blaming the mirror
if your face is crooked.
Proverb

Characters

ANTÓN ANTÓNOVICH SKVOZNÍK-DMUKHANÓVSKY   The mayor
ANNA ANDRÉYEVNA   His wife
MÁRYA ANTÓNOVNA   His daughter
LUKÁ LUKÍCH KHLÓPOV   Superintendent of schools
HIS WIFE
AMMÓS FYÓDOROVICH LYÁPKIN-TYÁPKIN   The judge
ARTÉMY FILÍPPOVICH ZEMLYANÍKA   Director of charities
IVÁN KUZMÍCH SHPÉKIN   Postmaster
PYOTR IVÁNOVICH DÓBCHINSKY ⎫
PYOTR IVÁNOVICH BÓBCHINSKY ⎭   Landowners residing in town
IVÁN ALEXÁNDROVICH KHLESTAKÓV   An official from Petersburg
ÓSIP   His servant
KHRISTIÁN IVÁNOVICH HÜBNER   The district doctor
FYÓDOR ANDRÉYEVICH LYULYUKÓV ⎫   Retired officials, respected
IVÁN LÁZAREVICH RASTAKÓVSKY   ⎬   citizens
STEPÁN IVÁNOVICH KORÓBKIN   ⎭
KOROBKIN'S WIFE
STEPÁN ILÍCH UKHOVYÓRTOV   Police captain
SVISTUNÓV ⎫
PÚGOVITSYN ⎬ Policemen
DERZHIMÓRDA ⎭
ABDÚLIN   A storekeeper
FEVRÓNYA PETRÓVNA POSHLYÓPKINA   A locksmith's wife
A CORPORAL'S WIDOW
MÍSHKA   The mayor's servant
A WAITER
Guests, merchants, townspeople, petitioners

Characters and Costumes
Remarks for the Actors

MAYOR. Advanced in years. A life spent in the government service. Shrewd in his own way. A grafter, but conducts himself with considerable gravity. Serious, even a bit sententious. Speaks neither too loudly nor too softly, neither too little nor too much. Every word carries weight. Coarse and hard features of a man who has worked himself up from the lower ranks. Shifts abruptly from fear to joy, servility to arrogance, as do persons of a crude nature. Customarily wears his official uniform with braids and high boots with spurs. His hair is cut short and is greying.

ANNA ANDREYEVNA, *his wife.* A provincial coquette, on the verge of middle age. Her character has been shaped in part by novels and albums, in part by running a house and supervising the maids. Very inquisitive. Given the chance, she'll display her vanity. Sometimes dominates her husband, but only because he is at a loss about how to react. Her power over him extends only to trifles, however, and manifests itself in scolding and sneering. Four changes of dresses in the course of the play.

KHLESTAKOV. A young man, about twenty-three. Extremely thin. Somewhat stupid and, as they say, "not all there." The type known in government offices as a "scatterbrain." Speaks and acts mindlessly. Incapable of keeping his attention fixed on any subject. Speaks in a staccato; the words fly from his lips and are totally unexpected. The more ingenuous and artless the performance, the more it will succeed. He is dressed fashionably.

OSIP, *his servant.* Like any other servant getting on in years. Speaks in a serious manner. Keeps his eyes lowered. A moralizer fond of lecturing his master under his breath. His voice is almost flat, but in conversation with his master it acquires a stern, sharp, even a coarse tone. He is cleverer than his master and quicker to catch on, but doesn't care to talk much. Cunning, he keeps his own counsel. Dressed in a shabby gray or dark blue frock coat.

BOBCHINSKY *and* DOBCHINSKY. Both are short, squat, and very inquisitive. Virtually indistinguishable. Both have little potbellies and speak very rapidly, gesticulating wildly. Dobchinsky is slightly taller and more serious; Bobchinsky is more easy going and livelier.

LYAPKIN-TYAPKIN, *the judge*. Has read five or six books and as a result is something of a freethinker. Given to reading meanings into everything, which is why he lends weight to every word. The actor ought to maintain a portentous air throughout. Speaks in a deep voice. Drawls out each word; wheezes and huffs like an antique clock that hisses before it strikes the hour.

ZEMLYANIKA, *director of charities*. Corpulent, sluggish, and clumsy, but for all that, sly and scheming. Officious and servile.

POSTMASTER. Artless to the point of simplemindedness.

The other roles require no special explanation. Their prototypes are all around us.

The actors must pay particular attention to the last scene. The final words ought to strike everyone like a bolt of lightning. The entire group should change its position instantaneously. The women should let out a cry of astonishment as if in one voice. Disregard of these remarks may ruin the whole effect.

Act One

A room in the MAYOR'S *home.* MAYOR, DIRECTOR OF CHARITIES, SUPERINTENDENT OF SCHOOLS, JUDGE, POLICE CAPTAIN, DOCTOR, *two* POLICEMEN.

MAYOR. Gentlemen! I've summoned you here because of some very distressing news. A government inspector is on his way.

JUDGE. A government inspector?

DIRECTOR OF CHARITIES. An inspector?

MAYOR. From Petersburg, incognito! And with secret instructions to boot!

JUDGE. Well I'll be!

DIRECTOR OF CHARITIES. As if we didn't have enough troubles!

SUPERINTENDENT OF SCHOOLS. Good God! And with secret instructions!

MAYOR. I felt it coming. All night I dreamed of two mysterious rats. I've never seen anything like them—black monstrous things! They stalked in, sniffed—and then vanished. But let me read you Chmýkhov's letter. You know him, Artemy Filippovich. Listen to what he says: "Dear friend, fellow townsman, and benefactor *(mumbles, rapidly skimming the letter)*. . .to inform you." Ah! Here we are. "I hasten to inform you—an official has arrived with instructions to inspect the entire province, and especially our district" *(raises his finger meaningfully)*. "He's been passing himself off as an ordinary traveler, but don't let that deceive you. My information comes from the most reliable of sources. I realize you've been guilty of some indiscretions, as has everyone. You're a clever man, not the sort to let a good thing slip through your fingers." (*Pauses.*) Well, all right, we're among friends. "I advise you to take every precaution. He may turn up at any moment, if he's not there already, living among you incognito. Yesterday I. . .." Hm, the rest is family business: "Sister Anna is here with her husband. Ivan Kirflovich has gotten very fat and keeps on playing the fiddle. . . ." Well, there you are. That's the situation.

JUDGE. Yes, a situation that. . . extraordinary, simply extraordinary. Something's behind it.

SUPERINTENDENT OF SCHOOLS. But why, Anton Antonovich? Why us?

MAYOR. Why! It's clear why. Fate! (*Sighs.*) So far, they've been snooping around other towns. Now it's our turn.

JUDGE. In my opinion there's a subtle motive at work here—most likely of a political nature. Here's what it's all about: Russia. . . hm, Russia wants to declare war, and the Ministry has sent an official to uncover any evidence of treason.

MAYOR. Ech! What put that idea into your head! And you call yourself an intelligent man. Treason in a country town! Are we on the border or what? You could gallop for three years without reaching another country.

JUDGE. No, I must say, you didn't. . . you. . . the authorities keep their ears to the ground. Though they're miles away, nothing escapes them.

MAYOR. Well gentlemen, you've been warned. Look sharp! I've made certain arrangements; I advise you to do the same. Especially you, Artemy Filippovich. This inspector is bound to head straight for the charity hospital—that's your jurisdiction. See to it that the place is presentable. Stick some clean gowns on the patients. I don't want them looking like a gang of chimney sweeps. They can dress like slobs at home but not in the hospital.

DIRECTOR OF CHARITIES. No problem. We can put clean gowns on them, if you like.

MAYOR. And write something over every bed in Latin—or in some other language. That's your department, Dr. Hübner. Each illness, who got what when, day of week, date. And your patients shouldn't be smoking that foul tobacco of theirs. Whenever you

walk in, you sneeze your head off. Besides, we'd be better off if
there were fewer patients—otherwise they'll put it down to poor
management or the doctor's incompetence.

DIRECTOR OF CHARITIES. Oh! As regards medical treatment, Dr.
Hübner and I have our own policy: let nature take its course. We
don't use any of your expensive medicines. Man's a simple
creature—if he has to die, he'll die; if he's going to get well,
he'll get well. Besides, it's difficult for Dr. Hübner to consult
with the patients. He doesn't know a word of Russian.

> DR. HÜBNER *utters a sound, somewhat like the letter* i *and a
> little like* e.

MAYOR. And you, Ammos Fyodorovich, I'd advise you to pay some
attention to the courthouse. Your guards have been breeding
geese in the room where the petitioners wait. The damn geese are
under everybody's feet. Of course poultry farming is an honorable profession, and why shouldn't a guard get into it? Only in a
place like that. . . well, it doesn't look right. I've been meaning
to mention it to you, but somehow I keep forgetting.

JUDGE. I'll have them remove every last goose to my kitchen at
once. Would you like to come for dinner?

MAYOR. Another thing. Everybody's laundry is hung out to dry in
the courtroom. That won't do. And your hunting crop's on the
wall over the cabinet for court documents. I know you enjoy
hunting, but you'd better take it down for the time being. Once
the government inspector passes through, you can hang it up
again. Then there's your clerk—a knowledgeable man, no
doubt. But what a stink he gives off. It's as if he just stepped out
of a distillery. That won't do either. I wanted to speak to you
about him, but I had other business on my mind. If it's really
his natural odor, as he claims, there are remedies. Advise him to
try onions, or garlic. Or Dr. Hübner can prescribe some of his
medicines.

> DR. HÜBNER *utters the same sound.*

JUDGE. No, there's no getting rid of it. He says his nurse hit him
with a bottle when he was a baby and ever since he's smelled of

vodka.

MAYOR. Well, I only thought I'd mention it. As for our private arrangements and what Chmykhov calls our little indiscretions—what can I say? It's even strange to talk about. None of us is without sin. God made us that way, even if the freethinkers deny it.

JUDGE. What do you consider sins, Anton Antonovich? There are sins, and sins. I'm not ashamed to say it—I take bribes. But what kind of bribes? Puppies! That's altogether different.

MAYOR. Puppies or whatever, a bribe is a bribe.

JUDGE. I can't go along with that, Anton Antonovich. Now if someone accepts a five-hundred-ruble fur, a silk shawl for his wife...

MAYOR. So what if you take puppies as bribes? The point is you don't believe in God, you never go to church. At least I'm firm in my faith. I never miss a Sunday. But you! Oh I know you. When you start spouting your crazy theories of the Creation, it's enough to make a man's hair stand on end.

JUDGE. But I arrived at it all by myself, with my own brains.

MAYOR. In some cases too many brains are worse than none at all. But I just wanted to get the courthouse out of the way. No one's likely to go poking his nose into that dump. The place has a charmed life—God Himself must be looking after it. And you Luka Lukich, as superintendent of schools you just have to do something about those teachers of yours. I realize they're learned people, educated in various colleges, but they have some very queer ways about them. Naturally, the sort of thing that goes along with the teaching profession. One of them—what's his name?—the one with the fat face—he can't get up in front of a class without twitching. Let me show you (*grimaces*). Then he starts smoothing out his beard with his fingers. Of course it doesn't matter if he makes a face like that at one of his pupils. It may even be necessary for their education—I'm not one to judge. But suppose he does it to a visitor? That could mean trouble. The government inspector might take it personally. Where the hell would that leave us?

SUPERINTENDENT OF SCHOOLS. What can I do? I've already spoken to him several times. The other day the marshall of the nobility stepped into his classroom, and he pulled such a face—I've never seen anything like it. He means well, but I get blamed. "Why are you filling the heads of our young people with subversive ideas?" everyone asks.

MAYOR. I'm compelled to make a similar remark about the history teacher. His head's crammed with information—no doubt about it, the man's picked up knowledge by the ton. Only he gets so worked up he forgets himself. I listened to him once; well, he was all right on the Assyrians and the Babylonians, but as soon as he came to Alexander the Great he lost his head. I thought the school was on fire. He bolted from his desk, grabbed a chair, and smashed it against the floor. Of course, this Alexander the Great was a hero, but why break chairs? The treasury loses on it.

SUPERINTENDENT OF SCHOOLS. Yes, he's hot-headed. I've reprimanded him more than once. "Say what you like," he answers, "but for the cause of knowledge I'm prepared to lay down my life."

MAYOR. It's true, God moves in mysterious ways. An educated man turns out to be a drunk or he makes faces that would scare the saints.

SUPERINTENDENT OF SCHOOLS. I wouldn't wish the teaching profession on my worst enemy. You're always frightened. Everyone interferes, everyone wants to show he's as smart as you.

MAYOR. That's all well and good. But it's this damned incognito. Any minute he'll stick his head through the door. I can hear him saying: "Aha, here you are, my angels! Who's the judge?" "Lyapkin-Tyapkin, sir." "Hand over Lyapkin-Tyapkin! And who's the director of charities?" "Zemlyanika, sir." "Hand over Zemlyanika!" That's what we're in for.

The POSTMASTER *enters.*

POSTMASTER. What's going on, gentlemen? Who's the visitor?

MAYOR. You mean you haven't heard?

POSTMASTER. I did hear something from Bobchinsky. He was just at the post office.

MAYOR. Well, what do you think?

POSTMASTER. What do I think? I think it means war with the Turks.

JUDGE. I told you! That's my view of it too.

MAYOR. You're both talking through your hats!

POSTMASTER. Certainly. War with the Turks. The damn French have been stirring things up again.

MAYOR. War with the Turks! It's us, not the Turks, who are going to catch it. We all know what's coming. I have a letter.

POSTMASTER. In that case, there won't be war with the Turks.

MAYOR. Well, what about you, Ivan Kuzmich?

POSTMASTER. What about me? What about you, Anton Antonovich?

MAYOR. Me? I'm not scared...well, maybe a little. The merchants and the townspeople make me uneasy. They say I've been tough on them. But if I took a bribe now and then, it was without hard feelings. I even (*takes him by the arm and leads him aside*)...I even suspect someone may have complained about me. Otherwise, why are they sending an inspector? Listen, Ivan Kuzmich, couldn't you, for the common good, hold up every letter that passes through the post office and, you know, open it slightly. Skim through it to see whether it contains a secret report. If it's only a personal letter, you can easily seal it up again. Or you can deliver it as is—open.

POSTMASTER. I know, I know. You don't have to instruct me in these things. I've been doing it for years. Not because I'm cautious. Because I'm curious. I'm dying to find out what's new in the world. I assure you, it makes for very interesting reading. Some letters you read with sheer joy. How beautifully people write! And so educational! It's better than the *Moscow News!*

MAYOR. Well, tell me. You haven't come across anything about an official from Petersburg, have you?

POSTMASTER. From Petersburg—no. But plenty about officials from Kostromá and Sarátov. What a pity you don't read letters. I've found some marvelous passages! Just the other day an army officer described a ball to a friend in a most amusing... Really, it was quite charming. "Life, dear friend, flows," he says, "through Elysian fields—plenty of young ladies, the band plays, flags flap." Such feeling! I simply had to keep it. Would you like me to read it?

MAYOR. I've no time for that now. Do me a favor, Ivan Kuzmich. If you come across a complaint, don't have any qualms, hold on to it.

POSTMASTER. It'll be a pleasure.

JUDGE. Be careful. Some day you'll have to face the music.

POSTMASTER. Oh no! You can't mean that!

MAYOR. Don't worry. It's not as if we're about to make it public. All in the family, I say.

JUDGE. Well, trouble's brewing! And to think, Anton Antonovich, I came over to present you with a little bitch—the sister of the hound I told you about. You must have heard—Cheptóvich and Varkhovínsky are suing each other, so I'm in clover. I can hunt rabbits on both their lands.

MAYOR. Good God! I can't bother about your rabbits now. That damned incognito is on my mind. Any minute the door is going to open and. . .

BOBCHINSKY *and* DOBCHINSKY *tumble in, breathlessly.*

BOBCHINSKY. It's extraordinary!

DOBCHINSKY. Surprising!

ALL. What? What?

DOBCHINSKY. Totally unexpected. We went to the inn. . .

BOBCHINSKY, *interrupting.* I went to the inn with Pyotr Ivanovich. . .

DOBCHINSKY, *interrupting.* Please, Pyotr Ivanovich, let me tell it.

BOBCHINSKY. Oh, no. Please, let me, let me. You don't have the proper style.

DOBCHINSKY. And you'll make a mess of it. You'll forget the best parts.

BOBCHINSKY. I won't, I won't, I promise I won't. Don't butt in; let me tell it. Now don't butt in! Please, gentlemen, tell Pyotr Ivanovich not to butt in.

MAYOR. For God's sake, get on with it! My heart's in my mouth. Be seated, gentlemen! Pyotr Ivanovich, here's a chair for you! (*All sit about the two* PYOTR IVANOVICHES.) Well, go on, what's it all about?

BOBCHINSKY. Allow me. I'll tell it all in the right order. As soon
as I had the pleasure of leaving you...you had just seen fit to
become upset by that letter...well, I dashed over to... Please,
don't interrupt, Pyotr Ivanovich. I remember all of it, yes sir,
all of it. So there I was, you'll be pleased to note, dashing over to
Korobkin's. I didn't find Korobkin at home, so I headed for
Rastakovsky. Rastakovsky wasn't at home either, so I dropped in
on Ivan Kuzmich...to inform him of the news. And on my way
from there, I ran into Pyotr Ivanovich...

DOBCHINSKY, *interrupting*. ...near the stand where they sell pies.

BOBCHINSKY. ...near the stand where they sell pies. So I met
Pyotr Ivanovich, and I asked: "Have you heard the news? Anton
Antonovich has got it from a reliable source." But Pyotr Ivano-
vich had already heard it from Avdótya, who had been sent to
Pochechúyev for...

DOBCHINSKY, *interrupting*. ...a keg of French brandy.

BOBCHINSKY, *pushing* DOBCHINSKY *aside*. ...a keg of French
brandy. Well, I set out for Pochechuyev's with Pyotr Ivanovich.
... Now, Pyotr Ivanovich, this is simply...don't interrupt,
please don't interrupt! So we set out for Pochechuyev's, and on
the way Pyotr Ivanovich said, "Let's," he said, "stop at the inn.
I haven't eaten since breakfast. My stomach's rumbling." That's
Pyotr Ivanovich's stomach. "They've just delivered some fresh
salmon," he said. "We can have a bite to eat." No sooner do we
step into the inn than we see...

DOBCHINSKY, *interrupting*. ...a young man, not bad looking, in
civilian clothes.

BOBCHINSKY. ...not bad looking, in civilian clothes. He's pacing
up and down the room, and he has such a thoughtful expression
on his face...and his appearance, the way he carries himself...
you could see at once (*points to his head*) he's deep, very deep. I
had a hunch, so I said to Pyotr Ivanovich, "Pyotr Ivanovich,
there's more here than meets the eye." Pyotr Ivanovich had
already snapped his fingers to call over the innkeeper...inn-
keeper Vlas, that is. His wife gave birth three weeks ago. Such a
clever little rascal, some day he's going to run a tavern, just like
his daddy. So we called over Vlas, and Pyotr Ivanovich asks him

quietly, "Who," he asks, "is that young man?" "That," Vlas
answers, "That. . ." Oh don't interrupt, Pyotr Ivanovich, please
don't interrupt. You won't tell it right. God knows you won't.
You lisp. One of your teeth whistles. "That young man," Vlas
says, "is an official from Petersburg." Yes sir! "His name," Vlas
says, "is Ivan Alexandrovich Khlestakov, and he's travelling to
Saratov. He acts very peculiar," he says. "It's his second week
here and he never leaves the inn. He takes all his meals on credit
and won't pay a kopeck." Well, it suddenly dawned on me—
"Aha!" I said to Pyotr Ivanovich.

DOBCHINSKY. No, Pyotr Ivanovich, it was me who said, "Aha!"

BOBCHINSKY. You said it first, then I said it. We both said: "Aha!
Why does he stay on if he's really headed for Saratov?" Yes, sir!
That's him. That's the official.

MAYOR. What official?

BOBCHINSKY. *The* official. The one you received a warning about.
The government inspector.

MAYOR, *in terror.* My God! What are you saying? It can't be him.

DOBCHINSKY. It's him. He doesn't pay his bills and he doesn't go
on his way. Who else could it be?

BOBCHINSKY. It's him. It's him. It must be him. He's so observant, he examined everything. Noticed we were eating salmon—
on account of Pyotr Ivanovich's stomach, that is. He even peered
into our plates. He's very sharp. I was scared stiff.

MAYOR. God save us! What room is he in?

DOBCHINSKY. Number five, under the staircase.

BOBCHINSKY. Where those officers got into a brawl last year.

MAYOR. Has he been here long?

DOBCHINSKY. Two weeks.

MAYOR. Two weeks! (*Aside.*) The Holy Saints preserve me! In these
two weeks the corporal's widow was flogged! The convicts
haven't been fed! The streets are a pig sty. Oh, the shame of it!
The humiliation! (*Clutches his head.*)

DIRECTOR OF CHARITIES. What do you think, Anton Antonovich?
Should we pay him an official visit?

JUDGE. No, no. First to go are the town council and the clergy.
The merchants too. I read it in a book on protocol.

MAYOR. No! Let me handle it my way. I've been in some tight
spots in my time, but things worked out. I was even thanked
afterwards. Maybe God will pull us through this time too.
(*Addressing* BOBCHINSKY.) You say he's young?

BOBCHINSKY. Yes. Not much over twenty-three or twenty-four.

MAYOR. All the better. A young man's easier to feel out—he's an
open book. It can be murder when they send some old devil. . . .
Gentlemen, put your departments in order. I'll stroll over by
myself, or maybe with Pyotr Ivanovich, and, you know, casually
drop in to inquire how the travelers are getting along. Svistunov!

SVISTUNOV. Yes, sir?

MAYOR. Quick, get the police captain. No, wait, I'll need you. Tell
someone out there to hurry and bring the police captain. And
come right back.

OFFICER SVISTUNOV *rushes out.*

DIRECTOR OF CHARITIES. Let's go, Ammos Fyodorovich. Things
look bad.

JUDGE. What are you frightened about? Shove your patients into
clean gowns and you're in the clear.

DIRECTOR OF CHARITIES. Clean gowns—my foot! The regulations
say keep the patients on oatmeal, and my corridors stink of
cabbage. You don't dare walk through without holding your
nose.

JUDGE. I'm not worried. Who on earth would want to visit a district
court? And if he does look at our files, he'll soon curse the day he
was born. Fifteen years on the bench and I still can't make sense
of their depositions. Solomon himself couldn't judge who's lying
and who's telling the truth. (*The* JUDGE, DIRECTOR OF CHARI-
TIES, SUPERINTENDENT OF SCHOOLS, *and* POSTMASTER *go out,
colliding in the doorway with* OFFICER SVISTUNOV, *who is
returning.*)

MAYOR. Is my carriage ready?

SVISTUNOV. Yes, sir.

MAYOR. Go out to the street. . .no, wait! Go get. . .but where are
the others? Just you? I ordered Prókhorov to be here too. Where
the hell's Prokhorov?

SVISTUNOV. He's at the station house, but he's not fit for duty.

MAYOR. What's that?

SVISTUNOV. They carried him in this morning, dead drunk. We soused him with two buckets of water, but he hasn't sobered up yet.

MAYOR, *clutching his head.* My God! My God!... Quick, go to the street, no, wait, first run to my room—do you hear!—and bring me my sword and my new hat. Let's go, Pyotr Ivanovich.

BOBCHINSKY. Me too, me too, please; me too, Anton Antonovich.

MAYOR. No, Pyotr Ivanovich, out of the question. It would be awkward, and besides, we couldn't all fit into the carriage.

BOBCHINSKY. It doesn't matter. I can run alongside...like this: Hop, hop! Hop, hop! I just want to peek through the keyhole and see how he behaves.

MAYOR, *taking his sword, to* OFFICER SVISTUNOV. Run, quick; take some men and have each of them grab a... Oh hell, the sword's scratched. Damn that Abdulin—he knows the mayor's sword is in bad shape, but does he think to send a new one? Oh, they're a sly bunch—those storekeepers! I bet the bastards are already getting up their petitions.... Have each of them grab a street—what the!—grab a broom and sweep up the street that leads to the inn. And sweep it up clean. Do you hear! And watch your step! You! Yes, you! I'm on to you. You act chummy with everyone, and then go around swiping silver spoons. Just watch out! I've got eyes! What did you pull on Chernyáyev? Eh? He slipped you two yards of cloth for a uniform, and you made off with the roll. I'm warning you! Take your bribes according to your rank! Get going! (OFFICER SVISTUNOV *goes out; the* POLICE CAPTAIN *enters.*) Ah, Stepan Ilich. For Christ's sake, where've you been hiding? What do you think you're doing?

POLICE CAPTAIN. I was outside, right behind the gate.

MAYOR. Look here, Stepan Ilich! The official from the capital has arrived. What arrangements have you made?

POLICE CAPTAIN. We're following your orders. I sent Sergeant Pugovitsyn and his men to clean up the sidewalk.

MAYOR. Where's Derzhimorda?

POLICE CAPTAIN. Derzhimorda's gone off on the fire truck.

MAYOR. And Prokhorov's drunk?

POLICE CAPTAIN. Yes.

MAYOR. How could you allow it?

POLICE CAPTAIN. God only knows. We had a brawl outside of town
yesterday. He went to restore order and came back plastered.

MAYOR. Listen, here's what I want you to do. Sergeant Pugovitsyn
is very tall—station him on the bridge, it'll make a nice impression. And get rid of that rotten fence by the shoemaker's. Set
up a boundary mark, so it looks like we have a project planned.
The more we tear down, the better for us. It shows the mayor is
doing something. Oh my God! I forgot, there's enough garbage
dumped around that fence to load up forty carts. What a cess-
pool this town is! Put up anything, from a monument to a fence,
and they litter it with their trash. Where the hell do they get it all
from! (*Sighs.*) And if the inspector asks our civil servants whether
they're satisfied, have them say, "We're completely satisfied,
Your Excellency." If anyone's unhappy, well, I'll give him
something to be unhappy about!... Oh, oh, oh, I've sinned,
I've sinned a lot (*picks up a hatbox instead of his hat*). Dear God,
let me off the hook this time, and I'll light such a candle for You
...it'll be enormous. I'll make every son-of-a-bitch of a merchant come across with a ton of wax. Oh my God, my God!
Let's go, Pyotr Ivanovich! (*Instead of the hat he puts on the
cardboard box.*)

POLICE CAPTAIN. Anton Antonovich, that's a box, not a hat.

MAYOR, *throwing it aside.* So it's a box. The devil take it. And if
he asks how come the chapel for the charity hospital hasn't been
built—you know, the one for which funds were appropriated five
years ago—Remember! We started on it but it burned down. I
even submitted a report. Otherwise some damn fool will let on
that it wasn't even begun. And tell Derzhimorda not to be too
free and easy with his fists. I realize he's strong for law and order,
but he's been giving everyone a shiner, the innocent along with
the guilty. Let's go, Pyotr Ivanovich. (*Goes out and returns.*)
And don't let the soldiers out in the street half naked. That scum
will put on a uniform with nothing on down below. (*All go out.*)

ANNA ANDREYEVNA *and* MARYA ANTONOVNA *run on stage.*

ANNA. Where are they? Where are they? Good heavens, where . . .
(*Opening the door.*) Anton! Anton! Antosha! (*Speaks rapidly.*)
It's all your fault. The way you fuss. "I'll just fix my pin,
straighten my kerchief." (*Runs to the window and cries out.*)
Anton, where are you going? Has he arrived? Is he really the
inspector? Does he have a mustache? . . . What sort of a
mustache?

MAYOR'S VOICE. Later, dear, later.

ANNA. Later? That's a fine piece of news! Later! I don't want your
later. Just tell me, What's his rank? Is he a colonel? What?
(*Contemptuously.*) He's gone! (*To* MARYA.) I won't let you
forget this! The way you carried on. "Mama, Mama, wait for
me, I'll only tie my kerchief, I won't be a minute." So here's
your minute! We haven't found out a thing. You and your silly
flirting. You heard the postmaster was here, and you just had to
primp in front of the mirror, first one pose, then another. You
think he's interested in you, but he turns up his nose the
moment you look away.

MARYA. Oh Mama! It doesn't matter. We'll know in a few hours.

ANNA. A few hours! Thank you very much. That's brilliant. Why
not a month while you're at it. (*Leans out the window.*) Avdotya!
Avdotya! What have you heard? Has someone arrived? You
haven't heard? Oh, the fool! He shooed you away? But you
might have asked. You couldn't? What a featherbrain; nothing
but men on her mind. What? They rushed off? You should have
run after them. Go now. Hurry! Do you hear? Run—ask where
they've gone. Find out the details. Who is he? Is he handsome?
Do you hear? Peek through the keyhole. I must know everything.
Are his eyes dark? Is he tall? And come right home. Do you hear?
Hurry, hurry, for God's sake, hurry! (*Shouts until the curtain
drops. The curtain closes upon them standing at the window.*)

Act Two

A small room in the inn. A bed, table, suitcase, empty bottle, boots, clothes brush, and so forth. OSIP, *alone, is lying on his master's bed.*

OSIP. Damn, I'm hungry! My stomach's rumbling. Sounds like an army band beating out a drum roll. . . . We'll never get home, and that's the truth! What the hell am I supposed to do? It's over a month since we left Petersburg. He blew all his money along the way, the sport! Now he's sitting on his tail and won't budge. There'd be enough—more than enough—to pay for horses. But no, you had to show what a big spender you are. (*Mimics* KHLESTAKOV.) "Osip, book me a room, the best they've got, and order a first-rate dinner. I can't stomach bad cooking; I've got to have the best." As if he amounted to something! He's only a lousy clerk—the botton of the heap. He takes up with some stranger, out come the cards—and before you know it, he's down to his last kopeck. Ugh! I'm fed up with this life! Things are easier back in the village—not so much going on, but less to worry about. Find yourself a woman and lie around all day stuffing yourself on home cooking. . . .

But when you come right down to it, there's no place like Petersburg. If you got the cash, life's nice 'n refined—teeayters, dancing dogs for your pleasure, the works! Everybody talks so genteel, almost like aristocrats. At the market the storekeepers call you "sir"! On the ferry you get to rub elbows with a government official. Feel like company? Just drop into any store: some soldier'll chew your ear about army life, or tell you what the stars in the sky mean. An officer's lady will come traipsing in, maybe a chambermaid . . . and what a chambermaid! Wow! (*Bursts out laughing, shaking his head.*) Damn it, what polish, what manners! You never hear a word that ain't polite. Everybody calls you "mister." Tired of walking? Then take a cab and sit back like a lord. If you don't want to pay, it's up to you. All the houses have alleys—you can duck through so fast the devil himself couldn't catch you. It ain't all peaches and cream though. Some days you eat grand, and some days you're croaking from hunger. Like now. And it's all his fault. You'd think he'd hang on to the money his old man sends him. Fat chance! Give him a ruble and off he goes. All I hear is, "Osip, get me teeayter tickets." And in a week—what do you know, he's sending me to hock his new coat in the flea market. He'll pawn everything, down to his last shirt. Honest to God, it's true. And what cloth—classy English stuff! The coat alone set him back a hundred and fifty rubles, and he sells it for twenty. No use talking about the pants—they go for nothing. And it's all because he won't do an honest day's work. Catch him going to the office! He'll be strutting along the avenoo or out playing cards. Oh, if your old man got wind of it! Government clerk or no, he'd drop your pants and give you a good hiding. You'd be rubbing yourself for the next four days. If you're going to work, then work. The landlord says he won't feed us till we pay up. So, what happens if we don't pay? (*Sighs.*) God! What I wouldn't give for a bowl of cabbage soup. I'm so hungry I could eat a bale of hay. Somebody's knocking. I bet it's him. (*He jumps off the bed.*)

KHLESTAKOV. Here, take these (*hands* OSIP *his hat and cane*). Aha, lying on my bed again?

OSIP. What do I want your bed for? You think I've never seen a bed before?

KHLESTAKOV. Liar! You were sprawling all over it. It's rumpled.

OSIP. You think I don't know what a bed is? I've got legs. I can stand. What do I need your bed for?

KHLESTAKOV, *pacing up and down the room.* See if there's any tobacco left in my pouch.

OSIP. Where are you going to find tobacco? You smoked it up four days ago.

KHLESTAKOV, *pacing, pursing his lips in various ways. Finally speaks in a loud and decisive voice.* Look here, Osip!

OSIP. Yes, sir.

KHLESTAKOV, *in a loud but not so decisive voice.* Go down. . .

OSIP. Where?

KHLESTAKOV, *in a voice not at all decisive or loud, almost an entreaty.* Down to the dining room. Tell them. . . tell them to send up some lunch.

OSIP. Oh no. I'm not going. No, sir.

KHLESTAKOV. How dare you! Idiot!

OSIP. It's no use. The landlord says we've had our last meal.

KHLESTAKOV. How dare he refuse! Ridiculous!

OSIP. He says he's going to the mayor. "Your master hasn't paid for two weeks. You're chiselers," he says, "and your master's a crook. We," he says, "we've seen such dead beats and riffraff before."

KHLESTAKOV. And you're only too glad to repeat it to me, you pig!

OSIP. "At this rate," he says, "all my customers will make themselves at home, run up a bill, and I can't even kick 'em out. I'm not one to fool around," he says. "I'm off to make a complaint. It'll be the clink for you two."

KHLESTAKOV. That's enough, you moron. Go on, go on, tell him about my lunch. What a clod you are!

OSIP. Better I call the landlord and you tell him.

KHLESTAKOV. What do I want with the landlord? Go on, tell him.

OSIP. But sir, I . . .

KHLESTAKOV. All right, damn it! Call the landlord! (OSIP *goes out.*)

KHLESTAKOV, *alone.* It's terrible, being so hungry. I thought a walk would make my hunger pass. No, dammit, it won't go away. Now if it wasn't for that fling in Pénza, I'd have enough money to get home. That infantry officer really put one over on me. Amazing the way the son-of-a-bitch plays cards. He sat in for no more than a quarter of an hour and cleaned me out. Still, I'm dying to have another crack at him. Just haven't had the chance yet. What a grubby town! The grocers won't give anything on credit. How stingy can you get! (*Whistles, first from "Robert le diable," then "Red Sarafan," and finally nothing in particular.*) What's keeping them?

OSIP *returns with a* WAITER.

WAITER. The landlord sent me to see what you want, sir.

KHLESTAKOV. Hello, hello, my good man! How are you? Well, I hope?

WAITER. Yes, sir—thank God.

KHLESTAKOV. And how are things in the inn? Everything going smoothly?

WAITER. Yes, thank God, everything's fine.

KHLESTAKOV. Many guests?

WAITER. Enough.

KHLESTAKOV. Look here, my good man, they haven't brought me my lunch yet. Please, hurry it up a bit. You see, I have some important business to attend to this afternoon.

WAITER. The landlord says he's not serving you any more. He means to complain to the mayor today.

KHLESTAKOV. What's he got to complain about? Think about it, my friend, how am I supposed to manage? I have to eat! If things go on like this, I'll waste away. I'm famished.

WAITER. Right, sir. The landlord says, "I'm not serving him any more meals till he's paid up." That's what he said.

KHLESTAKOV. Then reason with him, persuade him.

WAITER. But what do I tell him?

KHLESTAKOV. Explain that it's serious—I have to eat. The money will take care of itself. Just because a peasant like him can go a day without eating, he thinks others can do the same. That's absurd!

WAITER. All right, I'll tell him. (OSIP *and* WAITER *go out.*)

KHLESTAKOV, *alone.* It'll be rough though, if he won't give me anything to eat. I never dreamed I could feel so hungry. Maybe I can raise some cash on my clothes? Sell my pants? No, I'd rather starve. I've just got to show up at home in my Petersburg suit. A pity nobody would rent me a carriage. It would have been marvelous, dammit, coming home in style. I'd fly like the devil right up to some neighbor's front door, lamps lighted, Osip behind me in livery. I can just imagine the stir, everybody shouting: "What's going on? Who is it?" And I can see my footman, all in gold braid (*drawing himself up and impersonating a footman*). "Ivan Alexandrovich Khlestakov of Petersburg, will you receive him?" Of course those yokels haven't the slightest idea what "receive him" means. When one of our landowners pays a visit, the clumsy bear just rumbles straight into the living room. As for me, I'd waltz over to their prettiest daughter. "Miss, how delighted I am..." (*rubbing his hands, bowing and scraping*). Pfoo! (*Spits.*) Damn, I'm hungry! I'm even feeling nauseous.

 OSIP *enters.*

KHLESTAKOV. Well?
OSIP. They're bringing it.
KHLESTAKOV, *claps his hands and bounces on his chair.* Food! Food! Food!

 WAITER *enters, with a tray.*

WAITER. The landlord says it's the last time.
KHLESTAKOV. Landlord! Landlord! I spit on your landlord! What've you got there?
WAITER. Soup and a roast.
KHLESTAKOV. What? Only two courses?
WAITER. That's it, sir.
KHLESTAKOV. Nonsense! I won't accept it. You tell him this is preposterous! It's not nearly enough.
WAITER. He says it's too much.
KHLESTAKOV. And how come there's no gravy.
WAITER. There isn't any, sir.
KHLESTAKOV. Why not! I saw them preparing heaps of it when I passed the kitchen. Just this morning two little runts were gorging themselves on salmon in the dining room.
WAITER. Well, maybe there is, and maybe again there ain't.
KHLESTAKOV. What do you mean "ain't"?
WAITER. There just ain't.

KHLESTAKOV. And salmon? Fish? Cutlets?

WAITER. That's for them as are more respectable, sir.

KHLESTAKOV. You're an idiot!

WAITER. Yes, sir.

KHLESTAKOV. A filthy swine! How is it they can eat and I can't? Why can't I eat like them, dammit? Aren't they guests just like me?

WAITER. But everybody knows they're not the same kind.

KHLESTAKOV. What kind are they then?

WAITER. The regular kind! Everybody knows the difference. They pay cash.

KHLESTAKOV. I'm not going to argue with you, you imbecile. (*Helps himself to some soup and eats.*) You call this soup? It's dishwater, not soup. It has no taste, though it smells bad enough. I don't want it. Bring me something else.

WAITER. I'll take it away, sir. The landlord says if you don't want it, you don't have to eat it.

KHLESTAKOV, *protecting the food with his hands.* Keep your paws off it, you numbskull. You're used to treating others like this, but I'm a different sort, my friend! I don't advise you to try anything with me. (*Eats.*) My God, what soup! Has anyone ever eaten such slop? There are chicken feathers swimming around in it. (*Cuts up the chicken in the soup.*) Ugh! Where did you get that chicken? Give me the roast! Osip, there's a drop of soup left, you can have it. (*Slices the roast.*) What's this supposed to be? It's not a roast.

WAITER. What is it then?

KHLESTAKOV. Who the hell knows what it is, only it's not a roast. You roasted the cleaver instead of the beef. (*Eats.*) Bandits, cheats! The garbage they feed you! One bite and your jaws ache. (*Picks his teeth with his fingers.*) Sons-of-bitches! It's like tree bark; I can't get it out. My teeth'll turn black. Rotten bastards! (*Wipes his mouth with his napkin.*) Any more?

WAITER. No, sir.

KHLESTAKOV. You could have at least served me gravy or a pastry. You're just a pack of thieves out to fleece the traveler.

The WAITER *and* OSIP *clear the table and carry the dishes out.*

KHLESTAKOV, *alone.* I feel I haven't eaten, only whetted my
appetite. Now if I had some change, I could send out for a roll.
OSIP, *entering.* The mayor's downstairs. He's asking about you.
KHLESTAKOV, *taking fright.* What? Oh no! That pig of a landlord
has managed to complain already. Suppose he really drags me off
to jail? Well, what of it? If they treat me like a gentleman,
maybe I'll... No, I won't go. Officers hang around the inn, they
might see. Just to show them a thing or two, I put on airs and
winked at that storekeeper's pretty daughter. No, I won't go!
Who does he think he is? How dare he? What does he take me
for? A storekeeper? A laborer? (*Screwing up his courage and
standing erect.*) Yes, I'll tell him straight to his face, "How dare
you, how...?"

The door knob turns. KHLESTAKOV *turns pale and shrinks.
The* MAYOR *and* DOBCHINSKY *enter. The* MAYOR *freezes,
and he and* KHLESTAKOV *stare at each other for several
moments, both frightened, their eyes popping.*

MAYOR, *recovering a bit and coming to attention.* Greetings, sir.
KHLESTAKOV, *bowing.* How do you do?
MAYOR. I hope I'm not intruding.
KHLESTAKOV. Not at all.
MAYOR. It is my duty, as chief official of the town, to see to it
that travelers and people of quality suffer no inconveniences
which...
KHLESTAKOV, *at first stammering a bit, but speaking loudly toward
the end of the speech.* I couldn't help it. It's not my fault. I'll...
honest, I'll pay. They'll send money from home. (BOBCHINSKY
peeks in from behind the door.) Blame the landlord, not me.
The roast beef was as tough as shoe leather. And the soup—God
knows what he slopped into it. I should have tossed it out the
window. He's been starving me for days. There's something
funny about the tea. It smells like fish, not tea. Why pick on...
This is outrageous!
MAYOR, *frightened.* I'm very sorry. It's really not my fault. We

always keep quality meat in our market. Reliable dealers supply it, sober, decent people. I have no idea where he got his from. But if anything's wrong, I'll. . . . May I suggest you accompany me to other lodgings.

KHLESTAKOV. No, nothing doing! I know what "other lodgings" mean. They mean jail. How dare you? By what right? I, I. . .I hold a government post in the capital. *(Proudly.)* I, I, I. . .

MAYOR, *aside.* Oh my God, he's losing his temper. He's on to us. Those damn storekeepers have tipped him off.

KHLESTAKOV, *blustering.* Even if you bring the entire police force, I won't budge! I'll speak to the minister! *(Banging his fist on the table.)* Just who do you think you are? Just who?

MAYOR, *drawing himself up and trembling.* Your Excellency, spare me, I have a wife, children. Don't ruin me.

KHLESTAKOV. No, I won't budge. What's it to me? Just because you have a wife and children, I'm supposed to go to jail. That's rich! (BOBCHINSKY *peeks in at the door and hides himself in fright.*) No, thanks, I'm staying here.

MAYOR, *trembling.* It was my inexperience. I assure you, merely inexperience. And an insufficient income. Please, Your Excellency, judge for yourself. An official's salary doesn't even keep me in tea and sugar. If I took any bribes, they were mere trifles— a little something for the dinner table or cloth for a suit. As for the story about my flogging the corporal's widow, it's slander. Take my word for it—sheer slander. My enemies thought it up. They can't wait to do away with me.

KHLESTAKOV. So what? They're no concern of mine. *(Thinks for a moment.)* But why are you telling me about enemies, or some corporal's widow? A corporal's widow is one thing. . .no, you'd better not lay a hand on me. You're not big enough for that. What nerve! I'll pay, I'll pay cash, only I don't have it on me now. That's why I'm stuck here. I'm flat broke.

MAYOR, *aside.* Ah, he's a sly one. So that's his game! He lays down a smokescreen, so you can't tell what he's after. From what angle do you approach him? Well, let's give him a try. Take a stab and see what comes of it. *(Aloud.)* If you're actually in need of funds, sir, I'm at your service. At a moment's notice. It's my duty to assist travelers.

KHLESTAKOV. Excellent! Give me a loan. I'll settle with the landlord. About two-hundred rubles should do it.

MAYOR, *offering the bills.* Exactly two-hundred rubles. Don't bother counting.

KHLESTAKOV, *taking the money.* Much obliged. I'll send it to you the minute I get home. All this happened so. . .I see you're a gentleman. Now things are looking up.

MAYOR, *aside.* Phew! Thank God! He took the money. It'll be smooth sailing from now on. Just to make sure, I slipped him four hundred instead of two.

KHLESTAKOV. Osip! (OSIP *enters.*) Call the waiter. (*To the* MAYOR *and* DOBCHINSKY.) But why are you standing? Please be seated. (*To* DOBCHINSKY.) Take a seat, please.

MAYOR. Don't trouble yourself, sir. We can stand.

KHLESTAKOV. Oh, please, do sit down. It's become quite clear to me that you people are generous as well as hospitable. I admit, I thought you'd come in order to. . . (*To* DOBCHINSKY.) Will you sit down!

MAYOR *and* DOBCHINSKY *sit.* BOBCHINSKY *peeks in at the door and eavesdrops.*

MAYOR, *aside.* I must be bolder. He wants to remain incognito. Fine. We can bluff too, act as if we don't have a hint who he is. (*Aloud.*) Pyotr Ivanovich Dobchinsky and I—Dobchinsky here is one of our local landowners—well, since we were in the neighborhood on official business, we made a point of stopping in to determine whether the guests are being treated properly. Some mayors may not concern themselves with the welfare of others, but I, I. . .insist that a good reception be extended to all persons. Not only because my position demands it, but also out of Christian love for humanity. And now, as if in reward, fortune has afforded me such a pleasant acquaintance.

KHLESTAKOV. I'm also glad. If not for you, I might have been stranded here for ages. I was racking my brains how to pay the bill.

MAYOR, *aside.* Sure, tell it to the birds! Didn't know how he'd pay, did he? (*Aloud.*) May I be so bold as to ask to what parts you are bound?

KHLESTAKOV. Saratov. I'm on my way home.

MAYOR, *aside, an ironic expression on his face.* Saratov, eh? And without a blush! Oh, you've got to be on your toes with him. (*Aloud.*) A most worthy enterprise, sir. They say there's great inconvenience from delays in getting horses; but on the other hand, traveling does divert the mind. I imagine you're making the trip chiefly for your own amusement?

KHLESTAKOV. No, my father sent for me. The old man's sore because I still haven't gotten anywhere in Petersburg. He thinks the minute you arrive they stick a medal on your lapel. Well, I'd like to see him scrambling in the office for a while.

MAYOR, *aside.* Listen to him pile it on! He's even dragged in his father! (*Aloud.*) Will you be staying long, sir?

KHLESTAKOV. I really can't say. My old man's as stubborn as a fence post. Really stupid. I'll tell him straight to his face: "I just can't live outside of the capital." Why on earth should I waste my life among filthy peasants? Nowadays people have different needs. My soul thirsts for culture.

MAYOR, *aside.* How nicely he strings it all together! Lies and lies, and never trips up. And he's not much to look at either, a little pip-squeak. I could squash him under my thumbnail. Well, just wait. I'll make you come clean yet! (*Aloud.*) Very true, sir. What can one accomplish in the provinces? Take this town; you spend sleepless nights doing your best for the fatherland, you don't spare yourself, and as for rewards—who knows when they'll come. (*Glances around the room.*) This room seems a bit damp?

KHLESTAKOV. It's a wretched room. The bedbugs! I've never seen anything like them. They bite like dogs.

MAYOR. That's shocking! A distinguished guest like yourself, and what you have to put up with! Worthless bedbugs who ought to be wiped off the face of the earth. The room's a bit dark too, isn't it?

KHLESTAKOV. Pitch-black! The management has taken to refusing me candles. Now and then I feel like doing something—reading, or scribbling a word or two. But I can't—it's always dark.

77

MAYOR. Might I venture to suggest. . . Oh no, I'm not worthy of the honor.

KHLESTAKOV. Why, what is it?

MAYOR. No, I can't. I'm not worthy.

KHLESTAKOV. Come on, what's this all about?

MAYOR. If I'm not being presumptuous. . . I have an excellent room at home, sunny, quiet. But no, I fear the honor is too great. Don't be offended. I assure you, I offered it in all sincerity.

KHLESTAKOV. On the contrary, I'm delighted. I'll be much more comfortable in a private home than in this flophouse.

MAYOR. How pleased I'll be! And my wife will be overjoyed! That's the way I am—hospitable since childhood, especially if my guest is a man of culture. Don't think I'm saying this to flatter you. No, I'm free from that vice. I say it from the bottom of my heart.

KHLESTAKOV. Much obliged. I'm like that too, don't care for two-faced people. Your generosity is gratifying. You know, I ask for nothing in life but devotion and respect, and respect and devotion.

The WAITER *enters, accompanied by* OSIP; BOBCHINSKY *peeks in at the door.*

WAITER. You called, sir?

KHLESTAKOV. Yes, give me the bill.

WAITER. I've been giving you a bill every day.

KHLESTAKOV. I can't keep track of your stupid bills. Well, how much?

WAITER. On the first day you ordered the dinner, on the second salmon, and then you started taking everything on credit.

KHLESTAKOV. He's going to itemize! How much altogether, you numbskull?

MAYOR. Don't trouble yourself, Your Excellency. He can wait. (*To the* WAITER.) Go on, get out of here. We'll send it.

KHLESTAKOV. Certainly. That's correct. (*Puts his money away. The* WAITER *goes out.* BOBCHINSKY *peeks in at the door.*)

MAYOR. Would Your Excellency care to inspect some of our local institutions now? The charity hospital, for example.

KHLESTAKOV. Why? What have you got there?

MAYOR. Oh, just to see how we're running things. . . the way the town is administered.

KHLESTAKOV. Delighted! At your service. (BOBCHINSKY *pokes his head through the door.*)

MAYOR. Also, if you feel so inclined, we might proceed to the district school and observe our methods of instruction.

KHLESTAKOV. Of course, by all means!

MAYOR. Then you might wish to visit the town jail—to see how the prisoners are cared for.

KHLESTAKOV. The jail? I'd really prefer the hospital.

MAYOR. As you please, sir. Shall we go in your carriage or mine?

KHLESTAKOV. We'd better take yours.

MAYOR, *to Dobchinsky.* Well, Pyotr Ivanovich, there won't be room for you now.

DOBCHINSKY. Don't mind me, I'll manage.

MAYOR, *aside to* DOBCHINSKY. Listen, run as fast as your legs'll carry you. Take two notes—one to Zemlyanika at the charity hospital, the other to my wife. (*To* KHLESTAKOV.) Will you excuse me, sir, if I jot down a line to my wife so she can prepare to receive our distinguished guest?

KHLESTAKOV. Why bother?. . . Well, all right, there's the ink, only I don't know about paper. . . Can you write on this bill?

MAYOR. The bill will do fine. (*Writes, talking to himself.*) Now we'll see how things go after a good lunch and a couple of bottles. We have a local Madeira in the house, nothing to brag about, but it'll knock an elephant off its feet. If I could only find out who he is and how much I've got to fear from him. (*After writing the notes, he hands them to* DOBCHINSKY, *who walks to the door. At that moment the door falls off its hinges and* BOBCHINSKY, *who has been eavesdropping, flies on to the stage with it. All exclaim.* BOBCHINSKY *picks himself up.*)

KHLESTAKOV. Are you all right? You haven't hurt yourself?

BOBCHINSKY. It's nothing, sir, nothing to speak of. No cause to be disturbed, sir, only a tiny bump on the tip of my nose. I'll run over to Dr. Hübner—his plaster will heal it in no time.

MAYOR, *making a sign of reproach to* BOBCHINSKY. It's really nothing, Your Excellency. With your permission, we'll go now. I'll have your servant bring your luggage. (*To* OSIP.) Be a good fellow and bring your master's things over to my place, to the mayor's; anyone can show you the way. After you, Your Excellency. (*Shows* KHLESTAKOV *out and follows him, but turning back, scolds* BOBCHINSKY.) That's you all over! Couldn't find another place to take a flop! Sprawling out like the devil knows what! (*Goes out,* BOBCHINSKY *after him.*)

   Curtain.

Act Three

The MAYOR'S *home, the same room as in Act I.* ANNA ANDRE-YEVNA *and* MARYA ANTONOVNA *are standing at the window without having changed their positions.*

ANNA. See here, we've been waiting for an hour and you haven't stopped your silly preening. You were completely dressed; but no, you had to go on fussing. (*Looking out the window.*) I shouldn't pay her any mind. Oh, it's so annoying! Not a soul about—as if to spite me. How dead the town seems!

MARYA. Really, Mama, in a few minutes we'll know what it's all about. Avdotya should be here soon. (*Looks out the window and shouts.*) Oh, Mama, Mama, someone's coming. There, at the end of the street.

ANNA. Where? You're always imagining things. Ah yes, someone is coming. Who is it?... Very short...in a dress coat... Who could it be? Now, this is annoying!

MARYA. It's Dobchinsky, Mama.

ANNA. Dobchinsky? Where do you get these peculiar notions? It's not Dobchinsky at all. (*Waves her handkerchief.*) You! Come here! Quickly!

MARYA. Really, Mama, it is Dobchinsky.

ANNA. That's just like you. Anything to start an argument. I've told you—it's not Dobchinsky.

MARYA. Well, Mama? Well? You see!

ANNA. Of course it's Dobchinsky. I can see for myself. Why are you arguing? (*Cries out the window.*) Hurry! Hurry! How you dawdle! Well, where are they? What? Speak from there—it

81

doesn't matter. What's that? Very stern, you say? What? And my husband?... (*Stepping back from the window, annoyed.*) The fool, he won't talk till he's inside! (DOBCHINSKY *enters.*) Well? Aren't you ashamed of yourself? I was counting on you; I thought you were a gentleman—but you had to go flying after the rest of them. I was left without a shred of news! Really! You ought to be ashamed! I stood godmother to your Vánichka and Lízanka, and see how you treat me.

DOBCHINSKY. As God is my witness, madam, I ran so quickly to pay my respects I'm out of breath. My respects, Marya Antonovna.

MARYA. Good day, Pyotr Ivanovich.

ANNA. Well? Speak! What happened?

DOBCHINSKY. Here's a message from your husband.

ANNA. But what is he? A general?

DOBCHINSKY. No, not exactly, but every bit as good as a general. Such a cultured gentleman! And so dignified.

ANNA. Ah! Then he must be the one in Chmykhov's letter.

DOBCHINSKY. It's him all right. I was the first to spot him, along with Pyotr Ivanovich.

ANNA. Tell me, how did everything go?

DOBCHINSKY. Thank God, everything went well. At first he gave your husband a cool reception. Yes, ma'm. He lost his temper and said the inn was atrocious. He refused to visit you or go to jail either. But when he realized it wasn't Anton Antonovich's fault, his attitude changed. Then, thank God, everything went smoothly. They've gone to inspect the charity hospital.... And, you know, your husband was sure there'd been a secret denunciation. I was a little edgy myself.

ANNA. But what have you to be afraid of? You don't work for the government.

DOBCHINSKY. Yes, but you know how it is. When an important official speaks, you shake in your boots.

ANNA. But this is all so trivial. I'd rather you tell me what he looks like. Is he old or young?

DOBCHINSKY. Young. Quite young. About twenty-three. But he talks like an old man. "If you please," he says, "I'll go—I'll go

there and there too." (*Waves his arms.*) And he said it so nicely!
"I," he says, "am fond of both reading and writing, but I
can't," he says, "because the room's dark."

ANNA. But what does he look like? Does he have blond hair?
Brown?

DOBCHINSKY. No, more of a light brown. And the way his eyes
dart about—like two little animals. It makes you very uneasy.

ANNA. What's in my husband's note? (*Reads the note.*) "Dearest,
I hasten to inform you that my situation was extremely unfor-
tunate, but trusting in God's mercy for two pickles extra and a
side order of caviar—one ruble, twenty-five..." I can't make
this out. What have pickles and caviar to do with it?

DOBCHINSKY. Your husband was in a hurry and wrote on a scrap of
paper. I think it's a bill.

ANNA. Oh, yes. Certainly. (*Continues reading.*) "...trusting in
God's mercy, I believe we'll pull through safely in the end. Get a
room ready for our distinguished visitor as quickly as you can.
The room with the yellow wall paper should do fine. Don't fuss
over dinner, as we'll be having a bite at the charity hospital. But
order plenty of wine. Tell Abdulin to send the very best—or else
I'll turn his cellar upside down. Kissing your little hand, I remain
your Anton Skvoznik-Dmukhanovsky." Oh good heavens! I
must hurry! Mishka! Mishka!

DOBCHINSKY, *rushes to the door and yells.* Mishka! Mishka!
(MISHKA *enters.*)

ANNA. Listen, Mishka. Dash over to Abdulin's...wait, I'll give
you a note. (*Sits at a table and writes while speaking.*) Hand this
to Sídor and tell him to run to Abdulin's for wine. And you,
hurry and straighten out the guest room. Put in a bed, a washbasin, a lamp, anything! (MISHKA *runs off.*)

DOBCHINSKY. Excuse me, Anna Andreyevna, I'll run along and see
how he's conducting the inspection.

ANNA. Run along, run along, I won't keep you. (DOBCHINSKY
goes out.) Well Máshenka, what shall we wear? He's one of your
Petersburg gentlemen—we mustn't give him a chance to laugh
at us. Your blue dress, the one with the tiny flounces, is very
becoming.

MARYA. Oh, Mama, not the blue! I don't care for it at all. The Lyapkin-Tyapkin girl wears blue, and so does Zemlyanika's daughter. No, I'll put on my flowered print.

ANNA. The print! Really, you'll say anything to spite me. The blue will be far more appropriate, since I'll be in yellow. I simply adore yellow.

MARYA. Oh, Mama, yellow doesn't suit you!

ANNA. What do you mean, it doesn't suit me?

MARYA. It doesn't, I'm quite certain it doesn't. You have to have dark eyes to wear yellow.

ANNA. You're so clever! I suppose I don't have dark eyes? They're as dark as dark can be. How silly you are! They must be dark—I always turn up the queen of clubs when I tell my fortune.

MARYA. Oh, Mama, you know you're the queen of hearts.

ANNA. Ridiculous! Quite ridiculous! I've never been the queen of hearts. (*Goes out quickly with* MARYA *and speaks from off stage.*) The things that pop into your head! The queen of hearts! Good heavens! (*As they leave, a door opens and* MISHKA *sweeps out rubbish.* OSIP *enters from another door carrying a suitcase on his head.*)

OSIP. Where do I dump this?

MISHKA. This way, grandpa, right here.

OSIP. Hold on. Let me catch my breath. Whew! It's a dog's life. On an empty belly any load weighs a ton.

MISHKA. Well, grandpa, what do you say, will the general show up soon?

OSIP. General? What general?

MISHKA. Your master. Who else?

OSIP. My master? What kind of a general is that?

MISHKA. You mean he's not a general?

OSIP. He's a general all right—only the other way round.

MISHKA. Is that more or less than a real general?

OSIP. More.

MISHKA. You don't say! So that's why they've been whipping up a storm around here.

OSIP. Look here, sonny, I can see you're a sharp young fellow. How about whipping up something for me to eat?

MISHKA. Nothing's ready yet for the likes of you, grandpa. You won't eat our plain grub. When your master sits down at the table, you'll get the same.

OSIP. And what do you have of the plain?

MISHKA. Cabbage soup, kasha, meat pies.

OSIP. Cabbage soup! Meat pies! Let me at 'em! I'm not choosy, I'll eat anything. Come on, let's lug the suitcase in. Is that the way out?

MISHKA. Right.

> *They carry the suitcase into the side room.* POLICEMEN *fling open both halves of the door.* KHLESTAKOV *enters; after him the* MAYOR, *followed by the* DIRECTOR OF CHARITIES, SUPERINTENDENT OF SCHOOLS, DOBCHINSKY, *and* BOBCHINSKY, *who has a plaster on his nose. The* MAYOR *points out a piece of paper on the floor to the* POLICEMEN; *they run to pick it up, colliding in their rush.*

KHLESTAKOV. Excellent institutions! I like the way you show visitors the sights of the town. In other towns, they didn't show me a thing.

MAYOR. If I may say so, in other towns the mayors and officials are primarily concerned with their own advantage. Here we think only about meriting the attentions of our superiors by our vigilance and virtue.

KHLESTAKOV. The lunch was delicious. I really ate too much. Do you eat like that every day?

MAYOR. Something special for our most welcome guest.

KHLESTAKOV. I'm wild about good food. That's what life is all about—to pluck the blossoms of pleasure. What do you call that fish?

DIRECTOR OF CHARITIES, *rushing up*. Filet of sole, sir.

KHLESTAKOV. Very tasty. Where was it that we had lunch? Seemed like a hospital.

DIRECTOR OF CHARITIES. That's right, sir. The charity hospital.

KHLESTAKOV. Yes, I recall now. I saw the beds. Have all the patients recovered? There didn't seem to be very many.

DIRECTOR OF CHARITIES. No more than ten. All the others have recovered. It's the way things are arranged, the system we have here. You may not believe it, but since I've taken over, they've been recovering like flies. A patient no sooner sets foot in the hospital than he's cured. And it's not so much our medicines as honest and efficient administration.

MAYOR. If I dare say so, such are the obligations that rack the brains of a mayor! So many matters rest on his shoulders: sanitation, repairs, civic improvements. . . . Even a genius would find himself in trouble. But, thank heavens, everything's running smoothly. Other mayors may be feathering their nests, but I assure you, even in bed, I'm consumed by a single thought! "Almighty God," I pray, "teach me to satisfy my superiors and show them my zeal.". . . Not that I'm after rewards—that's up to them—but at least I'll have a clear conscience. The streets are swept, the convicts are treated well, we have very few drunkards —what more could I ask? No, honors don't interest me. Of course, they're tempting, but compared to virtue, all is vanity.

DIRECTOR OF CHARITIES, *aside*. The grafter! How he lays it on! God gave him one hell of a talent!

KHLESTAKOV. That's very true. I admit I like to philosophize myself—sometimes I do it in prose, and sometimes I fall into verse.

BOBCHINSKY, *to* DOBCHINSKY. Nicely put, Pyotr Ivanovich, very nicely put. You can see he's widely read.

KHLESTAKOV. Say, what do you have in the way of entertainment around here? Are there any clubs where a fellow can try his hand at a game of cards?

MAYOR, *aside*. Oho, my boy, I can see what you're driving at! (*Aloud.*) God forbid! We won't hear of allowing such establishments here. In all my life I've never held a card in my hand, and if I did, I wouldn't know what to do with it. The sight of a king of diamonds is enough to turn my stomach. Once, merely to amuse the children, I built a house of cards, and the blasted things gave me nightmares. How can people waste their precious time like that?

SUPERINTENDENT OF SCHOOLS, *aside*. And the son-of-a-bitch took me for a hundred rubles last night.

MAYOR. I prefer to spend my time serving my country.

KHLESTAKOV. Well. . . but that's going a bit far. It all depends on how you look at it. . . . Now if you pass when you ought to raise . . . then, of course . . . No, no matter what you say, it's very enjoyable to play a hand now and then. (ANNA ANDREYEVNA *and* MARYA ANTONOVNA *enter.*)

MAYOR. Allow me to present my family, Your Excellency. My wife, my daughter.

KHLESTAKOV, *bowing.* How delighted I am, madam, to have the pleasure of your acquaintance.

ANNA. It's even more of a pleasure for us to meet you.

KHLESTAKOV, *posturing.* Oh no, madam, not at all. It's far more pleasant for me.

ANNA. How can you say that, sir! You're only trying to flatter us. Please be seated.

KHLESTAKOV. Standing near you, madam, is joy itself. But if you insist, I'll sit. . . . How delighted I am at last to be sitting beside you.

ANNA. Oh my! I dare not dream your compliments are intended for me. . . . I imagine, after the capital, traveling through the provinces must have been quite disagreeable.

KHLESTAKOV. Exceedingly so. Accustomed as I am, *comprenez-vous,* to moving in the best society, and suddenly to find myself on the road—filthy inns, the dark gloom of ignorance . . . I must say, if not for the good fortune . . . (*glancing at* ANNA ANDRE-YEVNA *and posturing*) that has rewarded me for all my trials and tribulations . . .

ANNA. Indeed, how disagreeable it must have been.

KHLESTAKOV. At this moment, madam, everything is most agreeable.

ANNA. You can't mean that, sir! You do me too much honor. I'm not worthy.

KHLESTAKOV. Why aren't you worthy? Madam, you *are* worthy.

ANNA. I live in the country.

KHLESTAKOV. Yes, but the country also has its hillocks, its rivulets. . . . Of course, there's no comparing it with the capital. Ah, Petersburg! That's the life. You may think I'm only a copy clerk.

Not at all. I'm on a friendly footing with my department head. He'll pat me on the back and say, "Come on over for dinner, my good man." I only drop in at the office for a minute or so, merely to issue instructions—"Do this like this, that like that" —and before you know it, the clerks are scratching away like a pack of rats. "Scr, Scr, Scr." They even wanted to promote me, but I said to myself, "What for?" The doorman runs after me with a brush. "Allow me, sir," he says, "may I polish your shoes." (*To the* MAYOR.) But why are you standing, gentlemen? Please, sit down.

All in Unison

MAYOR. Men of our rank can stand, sir. We know our place.

DIRECTOR OF CHARITIES. We can stand.

SUPERINTENDENT OF SCHOOLS. Don't bother about us, sir.

KHLESTAKOV. Forget about rank. Do sit down. (MAYOR *and others sit.*) I'm not one to stand on ceremony. In fact, I always do my best to slip by unnoticed. But it's impossible to escape attention. Simply impossible! The minute I step out the door, people shout, "There goes Khlestakov!" Once I was even taken for the commander-in-chief. The soldiers leaped out of the guardhouse and presented arms. The officer, who's a great friend of mine, said to me later, "You know, old man, we actually took you for the commander-in-chief."

ANNA. No!

KHLESTAKOV. Yes, I'm known everywhere. Acquainted with all the pretty actresses. You see, I also write for the stage...amusing little pieces...all kinds. I'm in with the literary crowd. Very chummy with Pushkin. Often I'll say to him, "Well, Pushkin, my boy, how goes it?" He'll answer, "So-so, my friend, so-so." Yes, he's quite a character.

ANNA. So you write, too? An author's life must be fascinating. No doubt you write for the magazines?

KHLESTAKOV. Oh yes, the magazines also. By the way, I have many works to my name—*The Marriage of Figaro, Norma, Don Giovanni*...I can't even remember all the titles. And it was luck —I didn't intend to write anything, but the directors kept begging me, "Please Ivan Alexandrovich, write something for us." So I said to myself, "Why not?" Right on the spot I dashed them all off. Everybody was flabbergasted. My mind works with extraordinary speed. Everything published under the name of Baron Brambeus—"The Frigate Hope," *The Moscow Monthly Telegraph*—I wrote it all!

ANNA. Imagine! So *you're* Baron Brambeus?

KHLESTAKOV. Certainly. I correct the poems of all the best poets. A publisher pays me forty thousand for that alone.

ANNA. Then *The War of 1612* must be yours.

KHLESTAKOV. Yes, of course.

ANNA. I knew it all along.

MARYA. But Mama, it says on the cover it's by Mr. Zagóskin.

ANNA. There you go again! Arguing even about this!

KHLESTAKOV. Oh, yes. She's right. It's actually by Zagoskin. There's another *War of 1612*. That one's mine.

ANNA. Well, I must have read yours. How beautifully it was written!

KHLESTAKOV. It's true, I live for literature. I keep the best house in Petersburg. Everybody knows it. They call it Khlestakov House. (*Addressing everyone.*) Please, gentlemen, if you're ever in the capital, I urge you to visit me, by all means. I give parties, you know.

ANNA. I can imagine the glitter and elegance of a party in the capital.

KHLESTAKOV. Words can't describe them! I'll have a watermelon on the table that sells for seven-hundred rubles! A tureen of soup straight off the boat from Paris! You lift the lid, and the aroma —ah! There's nothing in the world to compare to it. I'm at a party every day of the week. We have our own card game: the foreign minister, the French ambassador, the German ambassador—and me. We play till we're exhausted. It's incredible! I'm barely able to drag myself up to my room on the fourth floor and say to the cook, "Hey, Mavrúshka, take my coat." What am I blabbering about? I forgot, I live on the first floor. My staircase alone is worth . . . But you'd find my vestibule extremely interesting—counts and princes jostling each other, buzzing like bees—all you hear is bzz, bzz, bzz. Sometimes even a cabinet

minister drops by... (*The* MAYOR *and the others get up from
their chairs, trembling.*) My letters are addressed, "Your
Excellency." Once I even ran a ministry. Very curious—the
director had vanished, nobody knew where. Well, naturally,
there was a lot of talk. "How will we manage?" "Who will
replace him?" The generals were keen on taking over, and some
of them gave it a whirl. But the job was too much for them.
What seemed easy enough turned out to be the damndest thing.
They saw it was no use—they had to call on me. In a flash messengers came pouring down the streets, then more messengers,
and more messengers.... Think of it—thirty-five thousand messengers! "What's the problem," I asked. "Ivan Alexandrovich
Khlestakov! Come! Take charge!" I confess, I was a bit taken
aback. I came out in my robe, meaning to turn them down. But
I thought to myself, the tsar will hear of it, and there's my service
record to worry about.... "All right, gentlemen, I accept. Very
well," I said, "I accept. Only I won't stand for any nonsense.
No, sir! I'm always on my toes! I'm the sort who..." And that's
exactly the way it turned out. When I made my rounds of the
ministry, you'd have thought an earthquake had struck—
everyone quivering, shaking like a leaf. (MAYOR *and others
tremble in terror.* KHLESTAKOV *is carried away.*) Oh! I'm not one
to play games! I put the fear of God into every last one of them!
Even the cabinet is scared stiff of me. And why not, I ask you?
That's how I'm made! No one gets in my way. I tell one and all
—I know who I am. I'm everywhere! Everywhere! I pop in and
out of the palace. Tomorrow they're promoting me to field
marshal! (*Slips and almost falls to the floor. The officials support
him deferentially.*)

MAYOR, *approaches, trembling, making an effort to speak.* Yo...
Yo...Yo...Yo...

KHLESTAKOV, *in an abrupt sharp tone.* What is it?

MAYOR. Yo...Yo...Yo...

KHLESTAKOV, *in the same tone.* I can't make out a word. You're
talking gibberish.

MAYOR. Yo...Yo...Yo Lexency...Excellency might wish to rest
up.... Your room is ready.

KHLESTAKOV. Rest? Nonsense! But maybe I could use a rest. The lunch, gentlemen, was excellent. I'm satisfied, completely satisfied. (*Exits declaiming.*) Filet of sole! Filet of sole! (*Goes off into the side room, followed by the* MAYOR.)

BOBCHINSKY, *to* DOBCHINSKY. Now that's a man for you, Pyotr Ivanovich. That's what I call a man. In all my life I've never been in the presence of such an important person. I nearly died of fright. What's your opinion, Pyotr Ivanovich? Who is he . . . I mean, what's his rank?

DOBCHINSKY. I'd say he must be a general.

BOBCHINSKY. And I'd say a general isn't fit to tie his shoelaces! He must be the generalissimo himself! You heard how he wiped the floor with the cabinet. Let's run and tell Lyapkin-Tyapkin and Korobkin. Goodbye, Anna Andreyevna.

DOBCHINSKY. Goodbye, madam. (*They go out.*)

DIRECTOR OF CHARITIES, *to* SUPERINTENDENT OF SCHOOLS. I've never been so scared. And it makes no sense—we're not even in uniform. What if he sobers up and whips off a report to Petersburg? (*Goes out, sunk in thought, accompanied by the* SUPERINTENDENT OF SCHOOLS. *Both say,* "Goodbye, madam.")

ANNA. What a charming man!

MARYA. Oh! He's a darling!

ANNA. So refined. You can see at once he's from the capital. His manners are exquisite. Oh, it was simply delightful. I'm terribly fond of young men like him. He was much taken with me, too. Did you notice how he stared at me?

MARYA. Oh, Mama, it was me he was staring at.

ANNA. Don't be silly, my dear. It's quite out of the question.

MARYA. No, Mama, he really was.

ANNA. What? Again! Must you always argue! It's impossible! Why on earth should he want to look at you?

MARYA. Honestly, Mama, he *was* looking at me. When he talked about literature, he glanced at me, and also when he told about playing cards with the ambassadors.

ANNA. Well, perhaps once or twice, but only out of politeness. He must have said to himself, "All right, I might as well give her a look."

MAYOR, *entering on tiptoe*. Shhh...sh!

ANNA. What is it?

MAYOR. I'm sorry I got him drunk. Suppose even half of what he says is true? (*Reflects.*) And why shouldn't it be true? When a man's drunk, it all slips out. Sure, he stretched things a bit. But then, without fibbing, nobody would ever say a word. So he hobnobs with the ministers and drops by the palace... Oh, what the hell's going on in my head? I feel as if I'm standing on the edge of an abyss or waiting to be hanged.

ANNA. And he didn't intimidate me in the least. As far as I'm concerned, he's a gentleman of culture and good breeding. His rank doesn't interest me.

MAYOR. Women! That says it all. You and your feathers and flounces! You'll blurt out any rubbish. They'll let you off with a bawling out, and I'll get it in the neck. By the way, you were very familiar with him—as if he were some Dobchinsky.

ANNA. I wouldn't worry if I were you. We women know a thing or two... (*glances at her daughter.*)

MAYOR, *to himself.* Try and talk to them!... What a predicament! I still can't get over the scare he gave me. (*Opens the door and calls out.*) Mishka, call officers Svistunov and Derzhimorda. They're outside, by the gate. (*After a brief pause.*) The world's gone cockeyed. You expect a man who looks the part, and you wind up with a skinny little twerp. How can I figure out his rank? When a man's in uniform, you know who he is, but in a suit he's like a fly with its wings clipped. Back at the inn, he wouldn't open up. With all his double talk and claptrap, I thought I'd never squeeze anything out of him. But he finally gave way, even spilled more than was necessary. You can see he's still young.

OSIP *enters. All rush to him, beckoning him.*

ANNA. Come here, my good fellow!

MAYOR. Shhh!... Well? Is he asleep yet?

OSIP. No, just stretching.

ANNA. What's your name?

OSIP. Osip, ma'm.

MAYOR, *to his wife and daughter.* That'll do! I'll handle it. (*To*

OSIP.) Well, my friend, did they feed you enough?

OSIP. They fed me fine—real fine. Thank you kindly, Your Honor.

ANNA. Osip, dear, I imagine many counts and princes call on your master?

OSIP, *aside.* What do I say? They fed me fine now, and it can only get better. (*Aloud.*) Yes, ma'm, counts and everything.

MARYA. Osip, dear, your master is so handsome!

ANNA. Please, Osip, how does he . . .

MAYOR. Be still! You're in my way with your silly chatter. Well, my friend . . .

ANNA. What's your master's rank?

OSIP. Er . . . the usual.

MAYOR. Good God! You and your stupid questions! I can't get a word in edgewise. Well, Osip, tell me about your master. Is he strict? Does he give people a hard time?

OSIP. Yes, he's one for order. Wants everything just right.

MAYOR. You know, Osip, I very much like your looks. You seem to be a decent fellow. Now what does your master . . .

ANNA. Osip, does your master wear a uniform in the capital or . . .

MAYOR. Enough! Damn, what chatterboxes! We have a crisis on our hands. A matter of life or death. . . . (*To* OSIP.) Osip, my friend, I've grown very fond of you. You know, an extra cup of tea doesn't hurt any when you're on the road—and it's a bit cold out. Here, take a few rubles . . . for tea.

OSIP, *taking the money.* Much obliged, sir. God bless you. You helped a poor man.

MAYOR. Think nothing of it. And now, Osip . . .

ANNA. Osip, what color eyes does your master prefer?

MARYA. Osip, dearest! Your master has such a sweet nose!

MAYOR. Shut up, you two, and let me get a word in! (*To* OSIP.) Osip, can you tell me what sort of things your master is especially interested in . . . I mean, what does he enjoy when traveling?

OSIP. Well, it all depends on what turns up. Mostly he likes a friendly welcome, and to be served good food.

MAYOR. Good food?

OSIP. Yes, Your Honor, good food. I'm only a peasant, but still he sees to it that I'm well fed. Honest! Whenever we make a stop, he'll ask, "Well, Osip, did they treat you proper?" "Rotten, Your Excellency!" "Osip," he'll say, "that one's a poor host. You just remind me when we get back." But (*waving his hand*) who am I to make a fuss?

MAYOR. Very true, very true, you make a lot of sense, my friend. I gave you something for tea; here, this is for biscuits.

OSIP. Very kind of you, Your Honor. I'll be sure to drink to your health.

ANNA. Come here, Osip! I've got something for you, too.

MARYA. Osip, dear! Give your master a kiss for me! (KHLESTAKOV *coughs in the other room.*)

MAYOR. Shhh! (*Stands on his tiptoes. The remainder of the conversation is in a whisper.*) God help you if you make a sound! You've prattled enough. Get out!

ANNA. Come, Mashenka! There's a little thing I noticed about our guest we can only discuss in private. (ANNA *and* MARYA *go out.*)

MAYOR. The drivel they'll spout! It's enough to make you want to plug your ears. (*Turning to* OSIP.) Well, Osip, my friend... (DERZHIMORDA *and* SVISTUNOV *enter.*) Shhh! Stomping in here like a pair of overgrown bears! I thought a ton of bricks dropped someplace. Where the hell have you been?

DERZHIMORDA. Proceeding per orders we was...

MAYOR. Sh! (*Claps his hand over* DERZHIMORDA'S *mouth.*) Stop your quacking! Are you a duck or what? (*Mimics him.*) "Proceeding per orders!" What a bag of wind! (*To* OSIP.) Osip, my friend, you run along and get everything ready for your master. My house is at your disposal. (OSIP *goes out.*) As for you two—stand by the front door and don't budge! And don't admit anyone who doesn't belong here, especially the storekeepers! If you let even one of them in, I'll.... The minute you see anybody with a petition, or even someone who looks like he might be thinking of a petition, grab him by the neck and throw him out! Smash him one! Let him have it! (*Demonstrates a kick.*) You get me? Shhh...shhh...(*Goes out on tiptoe after the policemen.*)

Act Four

The same room in the MAYOR'S *house. The* JUDGE, DIRECTOR OF
CHARITIES, POSTMASTER, SUPERINTENDENT OF SCHOOLS,
DOBCHINSKY *and* BOBCHINSKY *enter cautiously, almost on
tiptoe. All are in their official uniforms. They speak in hushed
voices.*

JUDGE, *arranging them into a semicircle.* For heaven's sake, gentlemen, hurry, in line! More orderly, please. The man is in and out
of the palace and tells off the cabinet, damn him. In formation!
At attention! It must be in military order. Pyotr Ivanovich, hop
over there; and you, Pyotr Ivanovich, stand here.

> *Both* PYOTR IVANOVICHES—BOBCHINSKY *and* DOBCHINSKY
> *—skip over to their places on tiptoe.*

DIRECTOR OF CHARITIES. This is all very well, Ammos Fyodorovich
. . . but we ought to take some action.

JUDGE. What do you have in mind?

DIRECTOR OF CHARITIES. We all know what.

JUDGE. Slip him something?

DIRECTOR OF CHARITIES. Well, yes, let's say we slip him something.

JUDGE. It's risky, damn it. He's liable to raise the roof—you know
these Petersburg types. But maybe we can dress it up as a
contribution for a monument?

POSTMASTER. Or we can say, "Here, sir, we found this money in the
mail and don't know who it belongs to."

DIRECTOR OF CHARITIES. Watch out he doesn't pack you off in the mails. Look here, this isn't how things are handled in a well-ordered state. Why are we all here? We ought to pay our respects one by one and, behind closed doors, with no one looking on, do what has to be done. Now that's how things are handled in a well-ordered state! Ammos Fyodorovich, you go first.

JUDGE. No, you go first. After all, our distinguished visitor dined in your department.

DIRECTOR OF CHARITIES. It would be more appropriate if Luka Lukich were to go first—as the educator of our young people.

SUPERINTENDENT OF SCHOOLS. I couldn't, gentlemen, I couldn't! It's the way I was brought up. If an official even a rank higher speaks to me, I go to pieces. My tongue sticks in my throat. No, gentlemen, you must excuse me. I simply couldn't.

DIRECTOR OF CHARITIES. Well, Ammos Fyodorovich, that leaves you. You're our Cicero.

JUDGE. Really. . .Cicero! The things you say. Just because I sometimes get carried away about my kennels and dogs. . .

ALL. No, Ammos Fyodorovich, not only about dogs; you can talk about all sorts of things.

About the Creation, and the Tower of Babel, and God knows what.

Please, Ammos Fyodorovich, don't let us down.

Save us!

Please, Ammos Fyodorovich.

JUDGE. Leave me be, gentlemen! (*Footsteps and coughing in* KHLESTAKOV'S *room. All rush headlong to the door, jostling and struggling to get out. Several are jammed in the doorway. Exclaim in hushed voices.*)

BOBCHINSKY'S VOICE. Ouch! Pyotr Ivanovich, Pyotr Ivanovich! You stepped on my toe.

DIRECTOR OF CHARITIES' VOICE. Step back, gentlemen. You're squashing me. I can't breathe. (*A few more cries of* "Ow!" "Ouch!" *At last all squeeze out.* KHLESTAKOV *enters looking sleepy.*)

KHLESTAKOV, *alone.* I must have had a good snooze. Where on earth did they get those mattresses and feather beds? I'm dripping sweat. That was some wine they gave me to drink at lunch. My head's still pounding. . . . Seems I can have a good time around here. It warms my heart to meet cordial people. Especially when they sincerely mean to please and aren't trying to get something out of me. The mayor's daughter isn't half bad, and her mother's the type who just might. . . Ah, I really go for this life.

JUDGE, *enters with money clenched in his fist, halts, and speaks to himself.* Please, Lord, please! See me through safely. Oh, my knees are buckling. (*Aloud, snapping to attention and placing his hand on his sword.*) I have the honor of introducing myself, Your Excellency: Judge of the District Court, Collegiate Assessor, Lyapkin-Tyapkin.

KHLESTAKOV. Have a seat. So you're the judge here?

JUDGE. Twenty years ago our nobility graciously elected me for a three year term, and I've held the office ever since.

KHLESTAKOV. Do you find being a judge profitable?

JUDGE. After my third term I was presented with the Order of St. Vladimir, Fourth Class, and a commendation from my superiors. (*Aside.*) If he'd only take the money! My fist is on fire!

KHLESTAKOV. I prefer the Vladimir myself. Now a Third Class St. Anne isn't nearly so impressive.

JUDGE, *extending his clenched fist with the money in stages. Aside.* Oh Lord! Where am I? I'm on hot coals.

KHLESTAKOV. What's that in your hand?

JUDGE, *flustered, drops the money.* Nothing, sir.

KHLESTAKOV. What do you mean ''nothing''? Didn't you drop some money?

JUDGE, *trembling in fright.* No, Your Excellency. It's not money. (*Aside.*) Oh my God! It's jail for me! I can hear the police wagon coming.

KHLESTAKOV, *picking it up.* Of course it's money.

JUDGE, *aside.* That's it! I'm lost!

KHLESTAKOV. You know what? Lend it to me.

JUDGE, *hastily.* Certainly, Your Excellency, certainly. Delighted! (*Aside.*) Courage, now! Courage!. . . Holy Mother of God! Give me strength.

KHLESTAKOV. I ran through all my money on the road, what with one thing and another...you know how it is.... I'll send it to you as soon as I get home.

JUDGE. Don't give it a thought, sir! How can you even suggest... I consider it an honor. .... You may rest assured, I'll zealously employ all my meagre powers to show my devotion to my superiors and merit their approval. (*Stands up, snaps to attention, his hands at his sides.*) I dare not disturb you with my presence any longer. Does Your Excellency have any instructions for me?

KHLESTAKOV. Instructions?

JUDGE. I mean, will you be issuing any directives to our district court?

KHLESTAKOV. What on earth for? I have no use for the court now.

JUDGE, *bowing and going out. Aside.* The town is ours!

KHLESTAKOV, *upon the* JUDGE'S *exit.* That judge is a splendid fellow.

The POSTMASTER *enters, holding himself erect, in uniform, his hand on his sword.*

POSTMASTER. I have the honor of introducing myself, Your Excellency: Postmaster, Court Councilor Shpekin.

KHLESTAKOV. Ah! Please, do come in. It's always a pleasure having congenial company. Have a seat. I suppose you're a permanent resident here?

POSTMASTER. Quite right, sir.

KHLESTAKOV. I've grown very fond of this little town. Of course, it doesn't have many people—but why should it? After all, it's not the capital. Am I right—it's not the capital?

POSTMASTER. Quite right, sir.

KHLESTAKOV. Only in the capital does one find the right *bon ton.* None of your boorish provincials. Don't you think so?

POSTMASTER. Precisely. (*Aside.*) He's not a bit snobbish; he asks my opinion about everything.

KHLESTAKOV. But one can live well in a small town too. Do you agree?

POSTMASTER. Exactly.

KHLESTAKOV. After all, what does a man need? To be treated with respect and to be genuinely liked. That's true, isn't it?

POSTMASTER. Perfectly true, sir.

KHLESTAKOV. I must say, I'm awfully glad you agree with me. You know, some people might consider me odd, but that's how I'm made. (*Looking the* POSTMASTER *over, speaks to himself.*) Wonder if I can touch him for a loan! (*Aloud.*) An extraordinary thing has happened. I completely ran out of money on my trip. Could you lend me three-hundred rubles?

POSTMASTER. Of course. I'd consider it a supreme pleasure. Here, sir, kindly accept it. I'm only too happy to be of service.

KHLESTAKOV. That's very generous of you. You know, when I'm traveling I hate to deny myself anything. And why should I? Do you agree?

POSTMASTER. Completely, sir. (*Stands, snaps to attention, placing his hand on his sword.*) I don't dare disturb you with my presence any longer. . . . But perhaps Your Excellency has some observations regarding the postal system?

KHLESTAKOV. Not a blessed thing. (*The* POSTMASTER *bows and goes out.* KHLESTAKOV *lights up a cigar.*) The postmaster is a fine fellow, too. At least he's eager to please. I appreciate people like that.

> *The* SUPERINTENDENT OF SCHOOLS *is shoved through the door. A muffled voice off stage:* "What are you afraid of?"

SUPERINTENDENT OF SCHOOLS, *coming to attention while trembling, his hand on his sword.* I have the honor of introducing myself, Your Excellency: Superintendent of Schools, Titular Councilor Khlopov.

KHLESTAKOV. Ah, do come in. Sit down, sit down. Would you care for a cigar? (*Offering one.*)

SUPERINTENDENT OF SCHOOLS, *to himself, hesitating.* Oh my God! I never expected anything like this. Should I take it, or shouldn't I take it?

KHLESTAKOV. Take it, take it. It's not a bad cigar. Of course, it's not what you find in Petersburg. Why, in Petersburg, my friend, I smoke cigars that sell for twenty-five rubles a hundred. One puff and you're smacking your lips. Here, light up. (*Hands him a candle. Trembling he attempts to light up.*) Hey, not that end!

SUPERINTENDENT OF SCHOOLS, *drops the cigar in fright, spits, and with a wave of the hand, says to himself.* Damn! My blasted shyness has ruined everything.

KHLESTAKOV. I can see you're not a connoisseur when it comes to cigars. I'm afraid they're my weakness. Women too. I can't resist them. How about you? Which do you go for—brunettes or blondes? (*The* SUPERINTENDENT OF SCHOOLS, *nonplussed, remains silent.*) Come on, you can be frank with me—brunettes or blondes?

SUPERINTENDENT OF SCHOOLS. I don't dare think about such things, sir.

KHLESTAKOV. No, no. Don't try to wriggle out of it. I'm very curious about your tastes.

SUPERINTENDENT OF SCHOOLS. Might I venture the opinion . . . (*Aside.*) My God! What am I saying!

KHLESTAKOV. Aha! You're not talking! I'll wager some pretty little brunette already has you in her clutches. Come clean—she has, hasn't she? (*The* SUPERINTENDENT OF SCHOOLS *remains silent.*) Ah! Ah! Look, you're blushing! Why aren't you saying anything?

SUPERINTENDENT OF SCHOOLS. I'm s-s-scared, Your Hon . . . Your Excel . . . Your High-n-n-ess . . . (*Aside.*) I'm done for! My damn stammer!

KHLESTAKOV. Scared? Well, I can understand. Something about my eyes does inspire awe. At least I never met a woman who could resist them. Am I right?

SUPERINTENDENT OF SCHOOLS. Quite right, Your Excellency.

KHLESTAKOV. By the way, the strangest thing happened to me. I ran out of all my money. Could you lend me three-hundred rubles?

SUPERINTENDENT OF SCHOOLS, *searching his pockets frantically, to himself.* What a pickle I'm in if . . . Whew! I've got it. (*Hands over the bills, still trembling.*)

KHLESTAKOV. I'm very grateful.

SUPERINTENDENT OF SCHOOLS. I don't dare disturb you with my presence any longer.

KHLESTAKOV. Goodbye.

SUPERINTENDENT OF SCHOOLS, *hurries out, almost at a run, saying aside.* Well, thank God for that! Now maybe he won't look into the classrooms.

> DIRECTOR OF CHARITIES *enters, snaps to attention, his hand on his sword.*

DIRECTOR OF CHARITIES. I have the honor of introducing myself, Your Excellency: Director of Charities, Court Councilor Zemlyanika.

KHLESTAKOV. How are you? Come, sit down.

DIRECTOR OF CHARITIES. I had the privilege of personally accompanying Your Excellency to the charity hospital entrusted to my care.

KHLESTAKOV. Oh yes. I remember. You served an excellent lunch.

DIRECTOR OF CHARITIES. Only too happy to be of service to the fatherland.

KHLESTAKOV. You know, food is my weakness—I'm just wild about good cooking. Say, weren't you a little shorter this morning?

DIRECTOR OF CHARITIES. It's quite possible, Your Excellency. *(Falls silent for a moment.)* I can truthfully say that I spare no efforts in zealously performing my duties. *(Moves his chair closer and speaks in hushed voice.)* Now take the postmaster. He doesn't do a lick of work; everything's neglected, parcels are piled up—you might wish to investigate for yourself. The judge too—he was here a while ago—all he does is chase rabbits. He kennels his dogs in the courthouse, and as for his morals. . . may I be frank with you? He's a relative and a friend, but for the good of my country I'm obliged to say it—his morals are simply shameful. We have a landowner in our town—Pyotr Ivanovich Dobchinsky —you've met him. Now the moment this Dobchinsky leaves the house, the judge pops in to while away the time with his wife. I'm prepared to take an oath on it. You only have to look at the children—not one of them resembles Dobchinsky. All of them, even the little girl, are the spitting image of the judge.

KHLESTAKOV. No! I never would have thought it.

DIRECTOR OF CHARITIES. The superintendent of schools too. It's beyond me how the authorities could have entrusted him with such a responsible position. He's a flaming radical. He's cramming the heads of our young people with subversive ideas— things too shocking to repeat. If you like, I'll put it all in writing.

KHLESTAKOV. Why not? It will be quite entertaining. You know, I very much enjoy some light reading when the time drags. . . . What did you say your name was? I keep forgetting.

DIRECTOR OF CHARITIES. Zemlyanika, sir.

KHLESTAKOV. Oh yes, Zemlyanika. Well, Zemlyanika, tell me, do you have any children?

DIRECTOR OF CHARITIES. Certainly, sir. Five. Two are already grown up.

KHLESTAKOV. How about that? Grown up! And what do they. . . uh, what are their. . . ?

DIRECTOR OF CHARITIES. Does Your Excellency wish to ask their names?

KHLESTAKOV. Yes. What are their names?

DIRECTOR OF CHARITIES. Nikolay, Ivan, Elizaveta, Marya, and Petunia.

KHLESTAKOV. That's charming.

DIRECTOR OF CHARITIES. I dare not disturb you with my presence any longer, or take up time devoted to sacred duty. (*Bows.*)

KHLESTAKOV, *seeing him to the door.* Not at all. What you told me was all very amusing. Please, any time. I enjoy this sort of thing. (DIRECTOR OF CHARITIES *goes out.* KHLESTAKOV *calls after him.*) Say! What do they call you? I keep forgetting.

DIRECTOR OF CHARITIES. Zemlyanika, Your Excellency.

KHLESTAKOV. Do me a favor, Zemlyanika. A curious thing has happened to me. I ran through all my money. Would you happen to have four-hundred rubles on you?

DIRECTOR OF CHARITIES. Yes, sir.

KHLESTAKOV. What luck! Thank you very much.

BOBCHINSKY *and* DOBCHINSKY *enter.*

BOBCHINSKY. I have the honor of introducing myself, Your Excellency: Pyotr Ivanovich Bobchinsky, a local resident.

DOBCHINSKY. Pyotr Ivanovich Dobchinsky, Your Excellency, a local landowner.

KHLESTAKOV. Oh yes. We've met. You took a flop, didn't you? Well, how's your nose?

BOBCHINSKY. First rate, sir! Please don't trouble yourself about it. It's healed, quite healed.

KHLESTAKOV. I'm glad. (*Suddenly and abruptly.*) Got any money on you?

BOBCHINSKY. Money?

KHLESTAKOV, *loud and quick.* A thousand rubles.

BOBCHINSKY. I don't have anything like that. Honestly. Perhaps you do, Pyotr Ivanovich.

DOBCHINSKY. Not on me. Forgive me, Your Excellency, but all my money is tied up in the state bank.

KHLESTAKOV. Well, if not a thousand, then make it a hundred.

BOBCHINSKY, *rummaging in his pockets.* Do you have a hundred rubles on you, Pyotr Ivanovich? All I've got is forty.

DOBCHINSKY, *searching his wallet.* Twenty-five—that's all.

BOBCHINSKY. Now, look thoroughly, Pyotr Ivanovich. You have a hole in your pocket. I know you do. Most likely something slipped into the lining.

DOBCHINSKY. No, nothing in the hole.

KHLESTAKOV. Well, it doesn't matter. Just thought I'd ask. All right then, make it sixty-five. It's all the same. (*Takes the money.*)

DOBCHINSKY. May I presume to ask Your Excellency about a very delicate circumstance?

KHLESTAKOV. What is it?

DOBCHINSKY. It's extremely delicate, Your Excellency. You see, I had my oldest son before I was married.

KHLESTAKOV. You don't say!

DOBCHINSKY. Only in a manner of speaking, Your Excellency. He was born exactly as children of married people are born. And afterwards we did the proper thing by assuming the lawful bonds of matrimony. So you see, Your Excellency, I want him to be my legitimate son, and to bear my name—Dobchinsky, Your Excellency.

KHLESTAKOV. Fine. Let him be Dobchinsky! It can be arranged.

DOBCHINSKY. I wouldn't have bothered you, only I'm sorry for the boy. The little fellow shows great promise! He recites poems by heart, and if you put a knife in his hand, he'll carve a very clever horse and wagon. The boy's a magician, sir. Pyotr Ivanovich can vouch for it.

BOBCHINSKY. Yes, he has great talent.

KHLESTAKOV. All right. I'll do my best. I'll put a word in with. . . uh, I hope. . . Rest assured, it'll all be taken care of. (*Turning to* BOBCHINSKY.) Don't you want to ask me something?

BOBCHINSKY. Yes, Your Excellency. I have a very humble request.

KHLESTAKOV. What about?

BOBCHINSKY. I humbly beg you, sir, when you return to the capital, tell all those great gentlemen—the senators and admirals and all the rest—say, ''Your Excellency or Your Highness, in such and such a town there lives a man called Pyotr Ivanovich Bobchinsky.'' Be sure to tell them, ''Pyotr Ivanovich Bobchinsky lives there.''

KHLESTAKOV. Very well.

BOBCHINSKY. And if you should happen to meet with the tsar, then tell the tsar too, ''Your Imperial Majesty, in such and such a town there lives a man called Pyotr Ivanovich Bobchinsky.''

KHLESTAKOV. Fine.

DOBCHINSKY. Excuse us for troubling you with our presence, Your Excellency.

BOBCHINSKY. Excuse us for troubling you with our presence, Your Excellency.

KHLESTAKOV. Not at all. It's been a pleasure. (*Sees them out. Alone.*) The place is crawling with officials. . . . Seems they've taken me for someone from the ministry. I must have laid it on thick this morning. What a pack of fools! I really ought to write Tryapíckhin about them. He'll stick them into one of those pieces he scribbles for the papers. They'll be the laughingstock of Petersburg. Osip! Bring me paper and ink! (OSIP *peeks in the door and says,* ''Right away.'') Now if Tryapichkin gets his teeth into anybody—watch out! He wouldn't spare his own father for a wisecrack. Anything for a ruble. But on the whole these officials

are a good-natured lot. It's a point in their favor that they lent
me money. I'll just check what I've got. Three hundred from the
judge. Three hundred from the postmaster...six hundred,
seven, eight... Ugh! What a greasy bill! Eight, nine... Oho!
Over a thousand... Well, captain! Just let me catch you in a
game now. We'll see who takes who! (OSIP *enters with paper and
ink.*) So, dimwit, see how these people treat me, the fuss they
make over me! (*Begins writing.*)

OSIP. Yes, we've been lucky! Only you know what, Ivan Alexandrovich?

KHLESTAKOV, *writing.* What?

OSIP. Let's clear out. God knows, it's high time.

KHLESTAKOV, *writing.* Ridiculous! What for?

OSIP. Really, Ivan Alexandrovich. Go while the going's good.
We've been living high off the hog—well, enough is enough. To
hell with this town. Before you know it, someone will turn up.
Honest to God, Ivan Alexandrovich, the horses here are terrific.
We'd race along like the...

KHLESTAKOV, *writing.* No. I want to hang around for a while.
Tomorrow.

OSIP. Tomorrow! For God's sake, Ivan Alexandrovich, let's go. I
know they're treating you like a prince, but still, we'd better get
out of here. It's certain they've taken you for someone else.
Besides, your father'll fly off the handle—we're late as it is. . . .
Oh, what a grand ride we'd have! The horses here are out of this
world.

KHLESTAKOV, *writing.* All right. Mail this letter, and you can
arrange for horses on the way. And see to it that they're first-
rate. Tell the drivers, if they speed me through like the tsar's
courier, it's a ruble each. And have them sing songs! (*Continues
writing.*) I can just picture Tryapichkin. He'll die laughing.

OSIP. I'd better pack, and send your letter with one of the servants.

KHLESTAKOV, *writing.* Fine. But bring me a candle.

OSIP, *goes out and speaks from off-stage.* Listen, pal! Deliver a
letter for us to the post office, and tell them there's no charge.
And send over the best troika on hand—the one for official
messengers. As for the fare, my master don't pay. We're on

government business. And see that they hop to it, or my
master'll have their heads. Wait! The letter isn't ready yet.

KHLESTAKOV, *still writing.* Wonder where he's living these days—
Post Street or Pea Street. He's also one to move around. Skips out
whenever the rent comes due. I'll take a chance on Post Street.
(Folds the letter and addresses it. OSIP *brings in a candle.*
KHLESTAKOV *seals the letter.* POLICEMAN DERZHIMORDA'S *voice,
offstage:* "Hey you old goat! Where do you think you're going!
No one's allowed in.")

KHLESTAKOV, *giving* OSIP *the letter.* Here, take it.

VOICES OF STOREKEEPERS. Let us in! You've no right to keep us
out. We're here on business.

DERZHIMORDA'S VOICE. Move along! Move along! He's not seeing
anybody. He's asleep. *(The hubbub outside grows louder.)*

KHLESTAKOV. What's going on, Osip? See what the commotion is
all about?

OSIP, *looking out the window.* Some merchants are trying to get in,
but the policeman won't admit them. They're waving papers. I
guess they want you.

KHLESTAKOV, *going up to the window.* What can I do for you good
people?

VOICES OF STOREKEEPERS. We're here to appeal to Your Gracious
Excellency. Order them to accept our petitions, Your Lordship.

KHLESTAKOV. Let them through! Osip, tell them they can come in.
It's all right. (OSIP *goes out.* KHLESTAKOV *receives the petitions
through the window, opens and reads one of them.)* "To His
Most Noble and Illustrious Excellency and Distinguished Lord of
Finances, from the merchant Abdulin." What the hell's this!
There's no such title.

The STOREKEEPERS *enter, carrying a basket filled with bottles
of wine and sacks of sugar.*

KHLESTAKOV. Well, my friends, what can I do for you?

STOREKEEPERS, *bowing to the ground.* We most humbly beg Your
Grace's mercy.

KHLESTAKOV. But what do you want?

STOREKEEPERS. Save us from ruin, Your Lordship! We're suffering unjustly. We're being abused.

KHLESTAKOV. By whom?

A STOREKEEPER. It's the mayor, it's all his doing. We've never had a mayor like him, Your Honor. The ways he insults us...billeting soldiers in our homes till we're squeezed dry. Grabbing us by our beards and calling us godless bastards. It's true, Your Honor. His abuses are more than we can stand—we might as well hang ourselves. And it isn't as if we're disrespectful; we always do the right thing by him: a silk dress for his wife, a petticoat for his daughter—we're not against that sort of thing. But nothing is enough for him. Whatever he can lay his hands on, he takes. "Hey, my good man," he'll say, "a fine piece of cloth you've got there. Send it over." And what he calls a piece will have close to fifty yards in it!

KHLESTAKOV. Really? But that's highway robbery!

STOREKEEPERS. God help us—it's so! No one can recall a mayor like him. When we see him coming, we hide everything under the counter. And it's not only the caviar and sturgeon. He'll make off with worthless garbage—prunes moldering in a barrel for seven years—my helper wouldn't touch them with a stick, and he grabs them by the handful. His birthday's on St. Anthony's Day—you'd think we'd brought him all that a man could need. "No," he says, "give me more. I celebrate on St. Onúfry's, too."

KHLESTAKOV. The man's a criminal!

STOREKEEPERS. He is, by God, he is! And just try saying no—he'll put up an entire regiment in your house. Or he'll order your store locked up. "I won't flog you," he says, "and I won't torture you, because it's against the law. But before I'm through, you'll be eating dirt."

KHLESTAKOV. Ha! What a crook! Siberia's too good for him!

STOREKEEPERS. Wherever Your Excellency sends him is fine with us. Just make it far. May we offer you a few sacks of sugar and this basket of wine. Be so kind as to accept our modest gifts, Your Grace.

KHLESTAKOV. I wouldn't dream of it. It's against my principles to take bribes. Now if you were to offer me, let's say, a three-hundred-ruble loan, well, that would be altogether different. I do take loans.

STOREKEEPERS. By all means, Your Honor. Whatever you like. (*They take out money.*) But why three hundred! Here, take five hundred. Only protect us from him.

KHLESTAKOV. Fine. I accept. I've got nothing against loans.

STOREKEEPERS, *offer him money on a silver tray.* Please, Your Grace, take the tray too.

KHLESTAKOV. I might as well.

STOREKEEPERS, *bowing.* May we throw in the sugar now.

KHLESTAKOV. Oh, no. I couldn't possibly accept a bribe.

OSIP. Your Highness! What are you doing? Take it! Everything comes in handy on the road. Hey, give us those sacks and the basket! Fork 'em over! We'll find a use for them. What's that? Rope? Throw in the rope, too! Rope is also handy when you're traveling. If the carriage breaks down, you can tie things together.

STOREKEEPERS. We beg you, Your Excellency, take our part. What will become of us if you refuse to help us? We might as well hang ourselves.

KHLESTAKOV. Of course, of course. I'll do my best. (STOREKEEPERS *go out.*)

VOICES OF TWO WOMEN, *off-stage.* How dare you turn me away! I'll complain to His Excellency! Stop your shoving! You're hurting me!

KHLESTAKOV. Who's out there? (*Goes to the window.*) What's the trouble?

VOICES OF TWO WOMEN. Have pity on us, kind sir! Order them to admit us, Your Honor. Hear us out.

KHLESTAKOV. Let them in.

The LOCKSMITH'S WIFE *and* CORPORAL'S WIDOW *enter.*

LOCKSMITH'S WIFE, *bowing at* KHLESTAKOV'S *feet.* Have mercy on me, kind sir.

CORPORAL'S WIDOW. Have mercy . . .

KHLESTAKOV. But who are you?

CORPORAL'S WIDOW. Corporal Ivanov's widow, Your Honor.

LOCKSMITH'S WIFE. Fevronya Petrovna Poshlyopkina. My husband's the town locksmith, and I . . .

KHLESTAKOV. Slow up. One at a time. (*To the* LOCKSMITH'S WIFE.) Now, what can I do for you?

LOCKSMITH'S WIFE. Pity a poor woman. I beg you. It's the mayor. I pray God send all His plagues on him. May he, the swindler, and his children and his uncles and his aunts never have a moment's peace.

KHLESTAKOV. Why? What has he done?

LOCKSMITH'S WIFE. Shaved my husband's head and sent him off to be a soldier, that's what! And it wasn't even our turn. Oh, the snake! Besides, it's against the law—him being a married man.

KHLESTAKOV. How could he do such a thing?

LOCKSMITH'S WIFE. Oh, he did it all right—the bandit! God strike him down in this world and in the next too! May boils grow on his flesh and vermin crawl over his body, and on his aunt too, if he's got an aunt. And his father, if his father's still living, the stinking dog, he can choke and rot in hell. By right he ought to have taken the tailor's son, but the boy's a drunk; and besides, the parents bought him off with a fancy gift. So he came to me. "What do you need a husband for?" he says. "He's of no use to you any longer." Now that's my business. I'm the one that knows if he's of any use, you crook. "Your husband's a thief," he says. "Maybe he hasn't stolen anything yet, but it's all the same; he's bound to steal sooner or later. And anyhow, they'll take him next year," he says. Now what'll become of me without a husband, you bastard! I'm a helpless woman, and you're a son-of-a-bitch. I pray none of your relatives ever again sees the light of day, and if you've got a mother-in-law, may the old hag . . .

KHLESTAKOV. Enough, enough! (*Sees the old woman out.*) Well, what about you?

LOCKSMITH'S WIFE, *going out.* Don't forget me, kind sir. Have mercy!

CORPORAL'S WIDOW. It's the mayor, Your Honor. I've come to

complain about...

KHLESTAKOV. What is it? Make it short.

CORPORAL'S WIDOW. He flogged me.

KHLESTAKOV. What's that?

CORPORAL'S WIDOW. By mistake, Your Honor. Some of us women got into a fight in the marketplace. The police didn't show up in time—so they grabbed me. Whipped me so I couldn't sit down for two days.

KHLESTAKOV. Well, what can be done about it now?

CORPORAL'S WIDOW. Of course, what's done is done. But make him pay me a fine for the mistake. No sense in turning my back on a piece of good luck. And besides, I can use the money.

KHLESTAKOV. Very well. Run along now. I'll see to it. (*Hands extend through the window holding petitions.*) What now? (*Goes up to the window.*) No more. No more. I've had enough for today! (*Stepping back.*) Damn it, but I'm sick of them. Osip! Don't let anyone else in!

OSIP, *yelling through the window.* Get going! Scram! We've no time for you now. Try tomorrow!

The door opens, and an enigmatic figure in a shaggy coat emerges. He is unshaven, with a swollen lip and bandaged cheek. Several others appear behind him in perspective.

OSIP. Move on! Move on! Where do you think you're going? (*Shoves the foremost figure in the belly and pushes him into the hallway. Goes out with him, slamming the door.* MARYA ANTONOVNA *enters.*)

MARYA. Oh!

KHLESTAKOV. Don't be frightened, miss.

MARYA. But I wasn't frightened.

KHLESTAKOV, *posturing.* Let me assure you, I'm very flattered to be taken for a man who... May I ask where you were going?

MARYA. Nowhere in particular.

KHLESTAKOV. And why, may I ask, weren't you going anywhere in particular?

MARYA. I thought Mama might be here...

KHLESTAKOV. But you must tell me, Why weren't you going

anywhere in particular?

MARYA. I'm afraid I disturbed you. You were occupied with important business.

KHLESTAKOV, *posturing.* Your eyes fascinate me as no business possibly could. No, you're incapable of disturbing me. On the contrary, you might offer me much pleasure.

MARYA. You talk as they do in the capital.

KHLESTAKOV. Only to such a lovely creature as yourself. Allow me the happiness of offering you a chair. Oh, how I wish it were a throne!

MARYA. Really, I shouldn't. . .I ought to be going. (*She sits.*)

KHLESTAKOV. That's a beautiful scarf you're wearing.

MARYA. Oh, you men. Anything to laugh at us provincials.

KHLESTAKOV. How I wish I were your scarf, miss, that I might embrace your lily white neck.

MARYA. What can you have in mind, sir? It's only a scarf. . . . Funny weather we're having lately.

KHLESTAKOV. Your lips, miss, entice me as no weather possibly could.

MARYA. The things you say!. . . Would you write a verse or two in my album as a keepsake? I expect you know many.

KHLESTAKOV. For you, miss, I'd do anything. What sort of verses would you like?

MARYA. Well, something pretty and up-to-date.

KHLESTAKOV. Ah, poetry! Nothing to it. I know loads of poems.

MARYA. Oh! Which will you recite for me?

KHLESTAKOV. Why recite them? I know them well enough.

MARYA. But I'm terribly fond of verses.

KHLESTAKOV. Well, all right. Here's one I wrote myself: "O my love is like a red, red rose, that's newly sprung in June; O my love is like the melody. . ." and I've got others too. . . . Only I can't remember them right now. Anyhow, it's all such rubbish. I'd much rather speak to you of my love. One glance from your eyes has. . .(*Drawing his chair closer.*)

MARYA. Love? What do you mean by that, sir. . .? (*Moving her chair away.*) I know nothing about love. . .

KHLESTAKOV, *moving his chair closer.* Don't move your chair away.

It's more intimate sitting side by side.

MARYA, *moving away.* Why side by side? We can be intimate at a distance.

KHLESTAKOV, *moving closer.* Why at a distance? We can be even more intimate side by side.

MARYA, *moving away.* But for what purpose?

KHLESTAKOV, *moving closer.* Though we may appear to be side by side, pretend we're at a distance. How happy it would make me, miss, if I could enfold you in my arms.

MARYA, *glancing out the window.* Look. Something flew by. A magpie, wasn't it?

KHLESTAKOV, *kisses her on the shoulder and looks out the window.* Precisely.

MARYA, *gets up indignantly.* What impudence! Now you've gone too far. . .

KHLESTAKOV, *detaining her.* Forgive me, miss. I did it out of love, true love.

MARYA. I'm not a common provincial, you know. (*Makes an effort to leave.*)

KHLESTAKOV, *still detaining her.* It was love, true love. I didn't mean anything by it. Don't be angry, Marya Antonovna. I'll even get on my knees to beg your forgiveness. (*Falls to his knees.*) Forgive me, please forgive me. See, I'm on my knees.

ANNA ANDREYEVNA *enters.*

ANNA, *seeing* KHLESTAKOV *on his knees.* Oh, good heavens!

KHLESTAKOV, *getting up.* Damn!

ANNA, *to her daughter.* What's the meaning of this, young lady! Is this a way to behave?

MARYA. Mama, I was only. . .

ANNA. Leave the room! Do you hear? Out, out! And don't dare let me set eyes on you. (MARYA ANTONOVNA *goes out in tears.*) I must apologize for her, Your Excellency. You have my word, I was simply astounded. . .

KHLESTAKOV, *aside.* She's a tasty dish herself—not bad, not bad. (*Throws himself on his knees.*) Madam, you see me consumed by love.

ANNA. What are you doing, sir? On your knees? Oh, do get up.
The floor is so dusty.

KHLESTAKOV. No. On my knees. Absolutely! Madam, decide my
destiny—will it be life or death?

ANNA. I beg your pardon, sir, but I don't fully grasp the drift of
your conversation. If I'm not mistaken, you're declaring your
intentions regarding my daughter.

KHLESTAKOV. Not at all. It's you I'm in love with. My life hangs
by a thread. If you reject my undying love, I no longer deserve
to dwell in this vale of tears. My heart ablaze, I ask your hand.

ANNA. But allow me to point out—in a certain sense . . . I'm
married.

KHLESTAKOV. Well, love knows no barriers, and as the poet says,
" 'Tis the laws that condemn." We shall flee to a haven of shady
streams. Your hand, madam, your hand.

MARYA ANTONOVNA *runs in.*

MARYA. Mama, Papa says you're to . . . (*Seeing* KHLESTAKOV *on his
knees.*) Oh, good heavens!

ANNA. Well? Well? What is it? Such a scatterbrain! Rushing in
here as if the house were on fire. Well, what are you gaping at?
What ideas have popped into your head? A child, simply a
child! No one would believe she's eighteen years old. When will
you start behaving like a well-brought-up young lady? When will
you finally learn to conduct yourself properly?

MARYA, *in tears.* Honestly, Mama, I didn't realize . . .

ANNA. Your head's always in a whirl. Why copy those Lyapkin-
Tyapkin girls? Why them? There are better examples for you to
follow—you have your mother!

KHLESTAKOV, *grabbing the daughter's hand.* Madam, don't stand
in the way of our happiness! Give your blessing to our undying
love.

ANNA, *in astonishment.* So it's her?

KHLESTAKOV. Decide! Life or death?

ANNA. There, you silly fool! It was you! It was for trash like yourself
that His Excellency deigned to get down on his knees. Bursting
in here like some lunatic! It would serve you right if I said No.

You don't deserve such happiness.

MARYA. I'll never do it again, Mama. I promise I won't.

The MAYOR *bursts in.*

MAYOR. Have mercy, Your Excellency, don't destroy me.

KHLESTAKOV. What's wrong?

MAYOR. I know the storekeepers have been complaining. On my word of honor, not half of it is true. They're the ones who cheat and shortchange their customers. The corporal's widow lied to you. As if I flogged her! It's a lie, I swear it, a damn lie! She flogged herself.

KHLESTAKOV. The corporal's widow can drop dead. I've got better things to think about.

MAYOR. Don't listen to them! They're all liars—a child would know better than to trust them. The whole town knows they're liars. And swindlers too. Of the worst sort!

ANNA. Are you aware of the honor His Excellency is conferring on us? He's asking for our daughter's hand in marriage.

MAYOR. What? What?... You're out of your mind! Please, Your Excellency, don't lose your temper. She's a bit touched. Her mother was the same way.

KHLESTAKOV. It's true. I'm asking for your daughter's hand. I'm in love.

MAYOR. I can't believe it, Your Excellency.

ANNA. Are you deaf? He just told you.

KHLESTAKOV. It's serious. I'm head over heels in love.

MAYOR. I can't believe my ears. I don't deserve such an honor.

KHLESTAKOV. Yes, it's so. If you don't give your consent, there's no telling what I might do.

MAYOR. I just can't believe it. You must be joking.

ANNA. What an imbecile! Can't you get it through your thick skull!

MAYOR. I still can't believe it.

KHLESTAKOV. Consent! Consent! I'm desperate. Who knows what I might do? I'll shoot myself, and they'll bring *you* to trial.

MAYOR. Trial? Oh my God! But I didn't do anything. I'm innocent. Spare me, spare me! I'll do whatever Your Excellency asks. My head's spinning... What's happening to me? I'm turning into a complete fool.

ANNA. For heaven's sake, give them your blessing! (MARYA *and* KHLESTAKOV *approach the* MAYOR.)

MAYOR. God bless you, and don't forget, I'm innocent. (KHLESTAKOV *and* MARYA ANTONOVNA *kiss. The* MAYOR *stares at them.*) What the devil! It's true! It's true! (*Wipes his eyes.*) They're kissing. Holy Saints, they're kissing! What do you know —a bridegroom! (*Shouts and prances for joy.*) Hey, Anton! Hey, Anton! Three cheers for the mayor! How things have worked out!

OSIP *enters.*

OSIP. The horses are ready, sir.

KHLESTAKOV. Fine... give me a minute.

MAYOR. Your Excellency is leaving?

KHLESTAKOV. Yes, I'm on my way.

MAYOR. But when... I mean, didn't Your Excellency drop a hint about... a wedding?

KHLESTAKOV. Only for a moment... well, a day. To visit my uncle. The old boy's rich. I'll be back tomorrow.

MAYOR. Looking forward to your safe return, we won't presume to detain you.

KHLESTAKOV. Of course, of course. Back in a flash. Goodbye, my love. I can't begin to tell you what's in my heart. Goodbye, my darling! (*Kisses* MARYA ANTONOVNA'S *hand.*)

MAYOR. May I be of any service? I seem to recall you were a bit short on cash.

KHLESTAKOV. Oh no, no need for that. (*After a moment's reflection.*) But if you insist.

MAYOR. What would be sufficient?

KHLESTAKOV. Let's see now. You lent me two hundred—no, it was four—I don't want to take advantage of your mistake. Well, why not the same amount again, to make it an even eight.

MAYOR. At once, Your Excellency! (*Takes the money out of his wallet.*) And I happen to have it in brand new bills, too.

KHLESTAKOV, *takes the bills and examines them.* Very nice. As they say, new bills mean a new life.

MAYOR. That's right, sir.

KHLESTAKOV. Goodbye then, Anton Antonovich! Much obliged
for your hospitality. I've never had so warm a reception. Goodbye Anna Andreyevna. Goodbye, my dearest Marya Antonovna.

All go out. From off-stage:

KHLESTAKOV'S VOICE. Farewell, my angel, my heart. Farewell, my
Marya Antonovna.

MAYOR'S VOICE. What? You're not going by public coach!

KHLESTAKOV'S VOICE. Well, yes. I'm used to it. Smooth rides give
me a headache.

COACHMAN'S VOICE. Whoa! Whoa!

MAYOR'S VOICE. At least let me spread a rug on the seat. Shall I
send for one?

KHLESTAKOV'S VOICE. No, don't bother. It's not necessary. But...
fine. A rug can't do any harm.

MAYOR'S VOICE. Avdotya! Run to the storeroom for a rug—the
best we've got—the Persian with the blue border. And make it
quick!

COACHMAN'S VOICE. Whoa!

MAYOR'S VOICE. When may we expect Your Excellency?

KHLESTAKOV'S VOICE. Tomorrow or the day after.

OSIP'S VOICE. Say, is that our rug? Spread it out! And some hay on
this side.

COACHMAN'S VOICE. Whoa!

OSIP'S VOICE. Right over there! Good! It'll be a grand ride! (*Slaps
his hand on the rug.*) Now you can sit, Your Lordship!

KHLESTAKOV'S VOICE. Goodbye, Anton Antonovich!

MAYOR'S VOICE. Goodbye, Your Excellency!

WOMEN'S VOICES. Goodbye, Ivan Alexandrovich!

KHLESTAKOV'S VOICE. Goodbye, Mama!

COACHMAN'S VOICE. Giddyap, my beauties, giddyap.

Ringing of coach bells. Curtain.

Act Five

The same room. MAYOR, ANNA ANDREYEVNA, *and* MARYA
ANTONOVNA.

MAYOR. What do you say, Anna Andreyevna? Eh? Did you ever
expect anything like this! What a catch, dammit! Confess—it's
beyond your wildest dreams. From the wife of a small-town
mayor to. . . Ah! Damn, a man that powerful in our family!
ANNA. I knew it all along. It's extraordinary for you because you're
so common. You've never met people of quality.
MAYOR. What's that? I'm a person of quality myself. But think
about it, Anna Andreyevna—we've turned into a fine pair. Eh,
Anna Andreyevna? We're flying high now, dammit! Just wait
and see—I'll make it hot for them, sneaking about with their
complaints and petitions!. . . Who's out there? (POLICEMAN
enters.) Ah, it's you, Pugovitsyn. Get the storekeepers in here.
I'll fix those sons-of-bitches! Complain about *me!* Goddamn
Judases. Just wait, sweethearts! Before, I only twitted your
mustaches; now I'll rip out your beards by the roots. . . . I want
the name of everyone who so much as grumbled about me.
Especially the grubby scribblers who wrote up their petitions.
And announce it everywhere—the whole damn town ought to
know. This is how God has chosen to honor their mayor. He's
not marrying his daughter to a nobody; he's marrying her to the
most important man in the world, a man who can do anything,
anything! Shout it from the rooftops, ring the church bells,
dammit! If we're going to celebrate, let's celebrate! (POLICEMAN
goes out.) So, Anna Andreyevna? What's it going to be? Eh?

Where will we live? Here or Petersburg?

ANNA. The capital, of course. How could we possibly stay here?

MAYOR. Then it's the capital. But it wouldn't be bad here either. Well, it's all over with being a mayor. To hell with it, eh, Anna Andreyevna?

ANNA. Certainly. What does a mayor amount to?

MAYOR. Well, Anna Andreyevna? Could we wangle a top rank now? After all, he pals around with the ministers and is in and out of the palace. He can arrange for a promotion, even make me a general. What do you think, Anna Andreyevna? Could I become a general?

ANNA. I should say so! Indeed you can.

MAYOR. Ah! Damn, a general's life must be glorious! They hang a sash across your shoulder. Which sash do you prefer—the red or the blue?

ANNA. What a question! The blue. It's more elegant.

MAYOR. So that's what you've set your heart on! But the red's not bad either. You know why I want to be a general? Adjutants and couriers gallop ahead of you, shouting, "Horses, give the general horses!" All those captains, mayors, and officials are screaming for horses, while you're as cool as a cucumber. You get to dine with the governor. And if some mayor shows up, they tell him: "Wait your turn. You're in the presence of a general!" Ho, ho! (*Bursts into hearty laughter.*) Yes, dammit, that's what I like about being a general!

ANNA. Your tastes are so coarse, my dear. Remember, we shall have to change our way of life completely. You won't be running around with a judge who kennels dogs in his parlor. Or a fool like Zemlyanika. On the contrary, your friends will be the most refined aristocrats. . . . Only I'm apprehensive about your behavior. The shocking things you say! Words never heard in polite society.

MAYOR. So what? Words can't hurt.

ANNA. That's all very well for the mayor of a provincial town. But life in a metropolis is entirely different.

MAYOR. Yes, I've heard they have two kinds of fish there—eels and smelts. They make your mouth water at the first taste.

ANNA. Fish! Is that all you can think about! I am determined to
have the finest home in the capital. I'll have my boudoir
drenched in perfume. It will be impossible to enter without
sniffing. (*She squints and sniffs.*) Ah! Delicious!

The STOREKEEPERS *enter.*

MAYOR. Aha! So here you are, my fine friends!

STOREKEEPERS, *bowing.* We wish you the best of health, Your
Honor!

MAYOR. So, my pets, how's it going, eh? How's business? You
tea-swilling pedlars! Went and complained, eh? You thieving
bastards, double dealing scum, cross-eyed swindlers! Complained? Well, did it get you much? Thought you'd see me
clapped behind bars? Eh?... You know what it'll get you? A
pack of screaming devils and an old witch stuffed into your teeth,
that's what!

ANNA. Dear heavens! What language, Antosha!

MAYOR, *irritated.* I can't worry about language now... That
inspector you complained to—are you aware he's engaged to my
daughter? What do you say to that? Eh? Oooo! I'll fix you!
Hoodwinking people left and right.... You chisel the government out of a hundred thousand by supplying rotten cloth,
donate twenty yards of the stuff to charity, and expect a medal
for it! If they caught on, they'd... Look at them! Strutting
about with their fat bellies. "We're merchants, don't anyone
touch us, we're as good as the nobility." Some noblemen! You
stinking swine! A nobleman has some education. They may whip
him in school, but it's for a purpose. So he can learn something
useful. But you! Before you've even memorized the Lord's
Prayer, you're shortchanging. And when your paunches are filled
out and your pockets are bulging, there's no talking to you. Look
at them! God's gift to the world! As if guzzling sixteen samovars
of tea a day makes them important. Well, I spit on you! And I
spit on your importance!

STOREKEEPERS, *bowing.* We were wrong, Anton Antonovich.

MAYOR. Complain, will you? What about the bridge? Who helped
you with your scheming then! Charging twenty thousand for

lumber and not even using a hundred rubles worth. I helped you, you old goats! Did you forget that? Had I squealed, I could have had the lot of you shipped off to Siberia! What do you say to that? Eh?

ONE OF THE STOREKEEPERS. We were wrong, Anton Antonovich. The devil tempted us. We swear, we'll never do it again. Anything you ask, only forgive us.

MAYOR. Forgive! Now you're groveling at my feet. How come? I'll tell you how come! Because I'm on top. If the scales had tipped the other way, you'd have trampled me into the mud, you bastards.

STOREKEEPERS, *bowing to the ground.* Spare us, Anton Antono-vich.

MAYOR. Now it's "Spare us, spare us!" But what did you say then? Eh? I'd like to take you by the throats and... (*With a wave of the hand.*) Well, God can forgive you! I'm not one to bear a grudge. But watch your step from now on! My daughter isn't marrying just anybody. Make sure your congratulations are appropriate to the occasion. Do you follow me? There'll be no getting off with a bit of sturgeon or a bag of sugar this time. Now get going!

The STOREKEEPERS *go out. The* JUDGE *and* DIRECTOR OF CHARITIES *enter.*

JUDGE, *still in the doorway.* If we can credit the rumors, Anton Antonovich, fortune has certainly smiled upon you.

DIRECTOR OF CHARITIES. Congratulations on your extraordinary good fortune. I was sincerely delighted to hear it. (*Kisses* ANNA ANDREYEVNA'S *and* MARYA ANTONOVNA'S *hands.*) Anna Andreyevna! Marya Antonovna!

RASTAKOVSKY, *entering.* Warmest congratulations, Anton Antonovich. God grant you and the young couple long life. May he bless you with a numerous posterity of grandchildren, great-grandchildren... Anna Andreyevna! Marya Antonovna! (*Kisses their hands.*)

KOROBKIN, *his* WIFE, *and* LYULYUKOV *enter.*

KOROBKIN. It's a privilege to congratulate you, Anton Antonovich.
Anna Andreyevna! Marya Antonovna! (*Kisses their hands.*)
KOROBKIN'S WIFE. My heartfelt congratulations on your happiness, Anna Andreyevna.
LYULYUKOV. Permit me to congratulate you, Anna Andreyevna!
(*Kisses her hand and, turning to the audience, clicks his tongue with an air of bravado.*) Marya Antonovna! It's a great pleasure!
(*Kisses her hand, turning to the audience with the same bravado.*)

A crowd of guests in tails enters and kisses ANNA ANDRE-YEVNA'S *and* MARYA ANTONOVNA'S *hands, repeating:*
"Anna Andreyevna! Marya Antonovna!" BOBCHINSKY *and* DOBCHINSKY *push to the front.*

BOBCHINSKY. I have the honor of congratulating you...
DOBCHINSKY. Anton Antonovich! I have the honor of congratulating you.
BOBCHINSKY. ...on your good fortune!
DOBCHINSKY. Anna Andreyevna!
BOBCHINSKY. Anna Andreyevna! (*They collide, banging their heads together.*)
DOBCHINSKY. Marya Antonovna! (*Kisses her hand.*) It's an honor!
You'll be supremely happy. Imagine! Parading about in gold dresses, dining on delicate soups. What fun you'll have!
BOBCHINSKY, *interrupting.* Marya Antonovna, it's an honor! God grant you prosperity, piles of money, and a bouncing baby boy—a tiny one (*indicates with his hand*), so small he can fit in the palm of your hand. Oh, how the little rascal will cry! "Wah! Wah! Wah!"

Several more guests, among them the SUPERINTENDENT OF SCHOOLS *and his* WIFE, *enter and kiss* ANNA ANDREYEVNA'S *and* MARYA ANTONOVNA'S *hands.*

SUPERINTENDENT OF SCHOOLS. I have the honor...
SUPERINTENDENT'S WIFE, *dashing ahead of him.* Congratulations, Anna Andreyevna! (*They kiss.*) I was so thrilled to hear the news. They told me, "Anna Andreyevna is marrying off her

daughter." "Oh good heavens!" I thought. I was so thrilled, I just had to tell my husband. "Lukánchik," I said, "how wonderful for Anna Andreyevna!" "Well," I thought, "thank God for that!" And I said to Lukanchik, "Lukanchik, I'm so delighted I can't wait to tell Anna Andreyevna." "Oh my," I thought, "Anna Andreyevna was always searching for a good match, and what luck! Things have worked out just as she wanted." I was so thrilled I cried and cried. There I was, sobbing away. Finally Lukanchik said to me, "Why are you crying, Nástenka?" "Lukanchik," I said, "I don't know myself. The tears just keep streaming down my face."

MAYOR. Please be seated, ladies and gentlemen. Mishka, bring some more chairs.

The GUESTS *sit. The* POLICE CAPTAIN *and* POLICEMEN *enter.*

POLICE CAPTAIN. Allow me to congratulate Your Honor, and wish you a long and prosperous life.

MAYOR. Thank you, thank you. You may sit, gentlemen. (*They sit.*)

JUDGE. Please, Anton Antonovich, can you tell us, step by step, how all this came about?

MAYOR. It came about in an extraordinary fashion. His Excellency was kind enough to do the proposing himself.

ANNA. And in the most respectful and refined manner imaginable. He spoke beautifully. "Anna Andreyevna," he said, "I'm prepared to do anything out of respect for your rare qualities." Such an excellent man, extremely well-bred, and of the noblest principles... "Believe me, Anna Andreyevna, life without you isn't worth living. Admiration for your rare virtues compels me..,"

MARYA. Oh Mama! He said that to me.

ANNA. Hush! What do you know? Mind your own business! "Anna Andreyevna, I'm overwhelmed by your...." Oh, he said the most flattering things! I was about to reply, "We don't dare dream of such an honor," when he fell to his knees and spoke like a true gentleman—"Anna Andreyevna! Don't deny me my happiness. My life is in your hands."

MARYA. Really, Mama! He was speaking to me.

ANNA. Yes, of course. There was something about you too. I don't deny that.

MAYOR. He gave us quite a scare. Kept shouting, "I'll shoot myself, I'll shoot myself."

GUESTS. Is that so!
          Really?

JUDGE. Well I'll be damned!

SUPERINTENDENT OF SCHOOLS. It must be fate.

DIRECTOR OF CHARITIES. Not fate, gentlemen. Fate is too fickle. I'd call it a reward for true merit. (*Aside.*) Some pigs have all the luck!

JUDGE. How about it, Anton Antonovich? I'll sell you the puppy we were dickering about.

MAYOR. I can't be bothered about puppies at a moment like this.

JUDGE. Well, if not that one, perhaps another.

SUPERINTENDENT'S WIFE. Oh Anna Andreyevna, you can't imagine how thrilled I am!

KOROBKIN. May I inquire where our illustrious guest is now? I heard he had to leave town.

MAYOR. Oh yes. But just for the day. On very important business.

ANNA. To visit his uncle and ask his blessing.

MAYOR. To ask his uncle's blessing, but tomorrow he's sure to... (*Sneezes. A roaring chorus of* "Bless you!") Thank you! He'll be back tomorrow and... (*Sneezes. The same roar of blessings. Loudest are:*)

POLICE CAPTAIN. Best of health, Your Honor!

BOBCHINSKY. May you live a hundred years!

DOBCHINSKY. A hundred and fifty!

DIRECTOR OF CHARITIES. Choke, you bastard!

KOROBKIN'S WIFE. Go to hell!

MAYOR. Thank you very much! I wish you the same.

ANNA. We're planning to live in the capital. The atmosphere here is too... too provincial. I must say, it's most distasteful. As for my husband, he will be promoted to the rank of general.

MAYOR. Yes, ladies and gentlemen, I, I, dammit, I'd really love to be a general.

SUPERINTENDENT OF SCHOOLS. May God grant it then.

RASTAKOVSKY. With God all things are possible.

JUDGE. A great ship travels far.

DIRECTOR OF CHARITIES. Honors according to merit.

JUDGE, *aside*. A neat trick, making him a general! Like putting a saddle on a cow! No, old man, not by a long shot. There are better men than you around.

DIRECTOR OF CHARITIES, *aside*. So now he's worming his way in among the generals. What's worse, he may even make it. God knows but the son-of-a-bitch swaggers enough. (*Addressing the* MAYOR.) You won't forget your old friends, will you Anton Antonovich?

JUDGE. If something turns up, I mean if we should require your assistance, you won't refuse us your patronage?

KOROBKIN. Next year I'll be taking my son to the capital to enter him in the government service. Please, Anton Antonovich, help the poor boy out, be his protector.

MAYOR. I'm prepared to do whatever is possible.

ANNA. Antosha! You're always making promises. There won't be time for that sort of thing. And why in the world should you burden yourself with such obligations?

MAYOR. Why not, my dear? Sometimes a man can arrange things.

ANNA. I don't doubt it. But one simply doesn't take every nonentity under his wing.

KOROBKIN'S WIFE. Did you hear how she talks about us?

A WOMAN GUEST. She's always been like that. Seat a peasant at the table and she'll stick her feet on it.

The POSTMASTER *bursts in, breathless, with an unsealed letter in his hand.*

POSTMASTER. Ladies and gentlemen! Prepare yourselves for a shock! The man we took for the government inspector wasn't the government inspector.

ALL. Not the government inspector?

POSTMASTER. Not in the slightest. I found it out from this letter.

MAYOR. Letter? Letter? What letter?

POSTMASTER. *His* letter! Someone handed me a letter at the post office. I couldn't help noticing the address—Post Street! It bowled me over. My first thought was, "He's reporting me for some irregularity in our postal system." Naturally, I opened it.

MAYOR. How could you?

POSTMASTER. I don't know myself. A mysterious force urged me on. I was about to send it off express when my curiosity got the better of me. It was incredible. Something irresistible kept tugging at me, drawing me on. In one ear I heard, "Don't open it or you're a dead duck," while in the other a devil whispered, "Go ahead, open it, open it!" I touched the seal—and fire ran through my veins. I opened it—and turned to ice . . . yes, ice! My hands shook and everything went black.

MAYOR. How dare you open the letter of such an important personage!

POSTMASTER. That's just it. He's not powerful and he's not even a personage.

MAYOR. Then what is he in your opinion?

POSTMASTER. He's a nobody, a nothing. The devil knows what he is.

MAYOR, *furious.* What do you mean, a nobody and a nothing? How dare you call him a nobody and a nothing! I'll have you arrested.

POSTMASTER. Who? You?

MAYOR. Yes, me!

POSTMASTER. You don't have the authority.

MAYOR. Are you aware that he's marrying my daughter, that I'm to be an important person myself, and that I'm about to pack you off to Siberia?

POSTMASTER. What's this about Siberia, Anton Antonovich? Before running on about Siberia you'd better let me read this letter. Gentlemen! Do I have your permission?

ALL. Read it! Read it!

POSTMASTER, *reads.* "My dear Tryapichkin, some amazing things have been happening to me. On my way here, an infantry officer cleaned me out of my last kopeck. The innkeeper was set to have me thrown into jail, when suddenly the whole town took me for a government inspector. It must have been my Petersburg clothes and manners. I'm staying at the mayor's, living it up, flirting like mad with his wife and daughter. I haven't decided who to start with. Probably the mother—she looks ready to go all the way at a wink. . . .

"Remember how hard up we were, the meals we sponged, and the time the waiter threw me out on my ear for charging our dinner to the king of England? Now the tables are turned. They're falling all over themselves to lend me money. What oddballs! You'd die laughing. Why not put them into some of those sketches you write for the papers? Take the mayor—as dumb as an ox. . ."

MAYOR. Impossible! He couldn't have said that.

POSTMASTER, *showing him the letter.* Here! Read!

MAYOR, *reads.* "Dumb as an ox." It can't be! You wrote it yourself.

POSTMASTER. How could I?

DIRECTOR OF CHARITIES. Read on!

SUPERINTENDENT OF SCHOOLS. Read!

POSTMASTER, *reads.* "The mayor's as dumb as an ox. . ."

MAYOR. Oh hell! Do you have to repeat it? The letter's bad enough as is.

POSTMASTER, *reading.* Hm. . .hm. . .hmmmmm. . ."as an ox. The postmaster's a decent fellow but. . ." (*Stops.*) Uh, there's something rude about me, too.

MAYOR. No! Read it!

POSTMASTER. But what for?

MAYOR. Dammit, if you're going to read, then read! All of it!

DIRECTOR OF CHARITIES. Here, let me have it. (*Puts on his eyeglasses and reads.*) "The postmaster is the spitting image of that half-wit watchman in my office. The son-of-a-bitch must drink like a fish."

POSTMASTER, *addressing the audience.* The miserable brat! He ought to be whipped!

DIRECTOR OF CHARITIES, *reading.* "The director of chari-ti-ti-ti. . ."

KOROBKIN. Why did you stop?

DIRECTOR OF CHARITIES. The handwriting's unclear. Besides,

anyone can see he's a scoundrel.

KOROBKIN. Give it here! My eyesight's better than yours.

DIRECTOR OF CHARITIES, *holding on to the letter*. We can skip that part. Further on it's legible.

POSTMASTER. Read it all! We didn't omit anything before.

ALL. Let him have it, Artemy Filippovich! Give him the letter. (*To* KOROBKIN.) Read it.

DIRECTOR OF CHARITIES. Just a minute. (*Hands over the letter, covering the passage with his finger.*) Here . . . start from here. (*All crowd around.*)

KOROBKIN, *reads*. "The director of charities is a pig in trousers."

DIRECTOR OF CHARITIES, *to audience*. It's not even witty. Where do you find a pig in trousers?

KOROBKIN, *reading*. "The superintendent of schools reeks of onions."

SUPERINTENDENT OF SCHOOLS, *to audience*. So help me God, I never touch onions.

JUDGE, *aside*. Thank heavens, there's nothing about me.

KOROBKIN. "The judge . . ."

JUDGE, *aside*. Uh oh! Here it comes! (*Aloud.*) Gentlemen, this letter is far too long. What's the sense of reading such rubbish?

SUPERINTENDENT OF SCHOOLS. No!

POSTMASTER. Read on!

DIRECTOR OF CHARITIES. Every word!

KOROBKIN. "Judge Lyapkin-Tyapkin is the ultimate in *mauvais ton* . . ." (*Stops.*) Hm, must be French.

JUDGE. God knows what it means. If it means "crook," well, all right. But it might be worse.

KOROBKIN, *reading*. "On the whole, though, they're a good-natured bunch. Very hospitable. So long, Tryapichkin, old pal. I intend to follow your example and take up literature. Life's dreary, my friend. In the long run a man hungers for spiritual nourishment. I'll just have to devote myself to the higher things in life. Write me in Saratov." It's addressed, "Ivan Vasílyevich Tryapichkin, Esq., St. Petersburg, 97 Post Street, courtyard entrance, third floor, on the right."

ONE OF THE LADIES. How shocking! It's a slap in the face!

MAYOR. He's slit my throat, slit it from ear to ear. I'm finished, played out, dead!... I can't see straight. Pig snouts everywhere —no faces! Nothing!... Bring him back! Bring him back! (*Waves his arms.*)

POSTMASTER. It's hopeless! As luck would have it, I ordered the stable man to give him the fastest horses available.

KOROBKIN'S WIFE. This is simply...! I've never seen such confusion!

JUDGE. But dammit, gentlemen, he borrowed three-hundred rubles from me.

DIRECTOR OF CHARITIES. And three hundred from me, too.

POSTMASTER, *sighing*. And three hundred from me.

BOBCHINSKY. From me and Pyotr Ivanovich—sixty-five. Yes, sir!

JUDGE, *spreading his arms in perplexity*. How could we have been so mistaken, gentlemen!

MAYOR, *striking his forehead*. How could I? How could I? I'm an old fool, an ass! My brains have gone soft with age!... Thirty years of service, and not a single merchant, not a single contractor put one over on me. I've cheated the cheats and swindled the swindlers. Thieves and frauds willing to steal from their own mothers fell into my clutches. Three governors in a row—I hoodwinked every one of them! What the hell are governors! (*With a wave of the hand.*) Governors aren't worth a damn!

ANNA. I just can't believe it, Antosha. He's engaged to our Mashenka.

MAYOR, *furious*. Engaged! Engaged! Stuff your engagement!... (*In a frenzy.*) Look at me, look at me, I want the whole world, every Christian man and woman, to look at me. See what a fool he's made of the mayor. Call him fool, fool, the old son-of-a-bitch! (*Shakes his fist at himself.*) Oh you thick-nosed idiot! Taking that squirt, that worm, for an important person! And now he's bouncing along the road, carriage bells jingling, spreading the story everywhere. He'll turn you into the laughingstock of all Russia. What's worse, some cheap hack will stick you into a comedy. That's what hurts. He won't show respect for your position. And they'll all grin and clap. (*Addressing the audience.*) What are you laughing at? Laugh at yourselves! (*Stamping in fury.*) I'd love to get my hands on those writers! Oooooh! You pen pushers! Sniveling liberals! Devil's seed! I'd tie you into knots, pound you into jelly, kick the lot of you down to hell! (*Strikes out with his fist and stamps on the floor. A pause.*) . . . I still can't get over it. What they say is true, "Those who God wishes to destroy, He first deprives of reason." What was there about that birdbrain to make us take him for a government inspector? Nothing! Not that much! (*Shows his little finger.*) And yet everyone was suddenly yapping: "It's the inspector! The inspector!" Who started the rumor? Answer me! Who?

DIRECTOR OF CHARITIES, *spreading his arms.* For the life of me, I can't explain it. We were in a fog. The devil blinded us.

JUDGE. You want to know who started it? I'll tell you who—these two geniuses! (*Points at* DOBCHINSKY *and* BOBCHINSKY.)

BOBCHINSKY. Not me, honestly, not me. It never crossed my mind.

DOBCHINSKY. Not me either. I had nothing to do with it.

DIRECTOR OF CHARITIES. Of course it was you!

SUPERINTENDENT OF SCHOOLS. No question about it. They came running from the inn, raving like lunatics. "He's here, he's here, and he won't pay his bill." Some prize you found!

MAYOR. It must have been you! Damned liars, town gossips!

DIRECTOR OF CHARITIES. Go to hell! And take your inspector and your tales along!

MAYOR. Snooping around town, making trouble—that's all you're good for. Windbags, rumor mongers, twittering magpies!

JUDGE. Bunglers!

SUPERINTENDENT OF SCHOOLS. Dunces!

DIRECTOR OF CHARITIES. Potbellied runts!

All crowd around them.

BOBCHINSKY. I swear to God, it wasn't me. It was Pyotr Ivanovich.

DOBCHINSKY. Oh no, Pyotr Ivanovich. You said it first.

BOBCHINSKY. No, Pyotr Ivanovich. You said it first.

A GENDARME *enters.*

GENDARME. His Excellency the government inspector has arrived from the capital. In the name of the emperor he demands your immediate presence at the inn.

The words strike everyone like a thunderbolt. The ladies let out a simultaneous cry of consternation. The entire group changes its position suddenly and remains frozen.

Dumb Scene

The MAYOR *stands in the middle like a post, his arms extended and his head thrown back. On his right, his wife and daughter, their bodies straining to reach him. Behind them, the* POSTMASTER *transformed into the shape of a question mark addressed to the audience. Behind him, the* SUPERINTENDENT OF SCHOOLS *in a state of innocent bewilderment. Behind him, at the far end of the stage, three* LADIES *leaning toward each other and directing very satirical looks at the* MAYOR'S *family. On the* MAYOR'S *left, the* DIRECTOR OF CHARITIES, *his head inclined slightly to the side as if listening for something. Behind him, the* JUDGE, *his arms extended, squatting almost to the floor, and moving his lips as if about to whistle or mutter,* "We're in for it now, my friends!" *Behind him,* KOROBKIN, *turned to the audience, winking and making a sarcastic allusion to the* MAYOR. *Behind him, at the far end of the stage,* BOBCHINSKY *and* DOBCHINSKY, *arms straining toward one another, mouths gaping, and eyes popping. The other* GUESTS *simply stand like posts. The frozen group holds its position for almost a minute and a half. Curtain.*

The Gamblers

An Incident out of the Remote Past

Characters

ÍKHAREV
GAVRYÚSHKA   His servant
ALEXÉY   A waiter
KRÚGEL
SHVÓKHNEV
UTESHÍTELNY
GLOV, MIKHÁL ALEXÁNDROVICH
GLOV, ALEXÁNDER MIKHÁLYCH [GLOV, JR.]
ZAMUKHRÝSHKIN

The Gamblers

A room in a provincial inn.

IKHAREV *enters, accompanied by his servant* GAVRYUSHKA
and ALEXEY, *a waiter.*

ALEXEY. Please step in, Your Honor! Here we are! The quietest
room in the house. You won't be bothered by noise.

IKHAREV. No noise but swarms of cavalry? Eh?

ALEXEY. Cavalry, sir? Oh, fleas. No problem, Your Honor. If a flea
or a bed bug bites a guest, we assume full responsibility.

IKHAREV, *to* GAVRYUSHKA. Bring my things from the carriage.
(GAVRYUSKHA *goes out. To* ALEXEY.) What do they call you?

ALEXEY. Alexey, sir.

IKHAREV, *meaningfully.* Now listen, Alexey, you can tell me, who's
staying here?

ALEXEY. Oh, lots of people. Almost all the rooms are taken.

IKHAREV. Who in particular?

ALEXEY. There's Mr. Shvokhnev, Colonel Krugel, Mr.
Uteshitelny...

IKHAREV. Do they play cards?

ALEXEY. They've been at it for six nights running.

IKHAREV. Here's a couple of rubles for you! (*Thrusts them into his
hand.*)

ALEXEY, *bowing.* Much obliged, Your Honor.

IKHAREV. There's more where that came from.

ALEXEY. Only too glad to be of service.

IKHAREV. Do they just play among themselves?

ALEXEY. Oh, no. The other day they cleaned out Lieutenant

Artunóvsky and took Prince Shénkin for thirty-six thousand.

IKHAREV. Here's another ten rubles! Play ball with me, and you'll get even more. Now own up—you've been buying the decks for them, haven't you?

ALEXEY. No, sir. They bring their own.

IKHAREV. Where do they get them?

ALEXEY. The store in town.

IKHAREV. You're lying, you thief.

ALEXEY. Honestly, sir. It's true.

IKHAREV. All right. I'll be speaking to you later. (GAVRYUSHKA *brings in a box.*) Put it down here. Now go and get my things ready. I want to wash up and shave. (ALEXEY *and* GAVRYUSHKA *go out.* IKHAREV, *alone, opens the box, which is crammed with decks of cards.*) A lovely sight! Every pack a gem. And it took work, good clean sweat. My eyes are still blurred from putting the damn markings on them. But they're money in the bank. An inheritance for my children. Look at this beauty—a treasure, a pearl! That's why I gave her a name. Adelaide Ivanovna. Be good to me, love, the way your sister was. Win me another eighty thousand, and I'll erect a marble monument to your blessed memory. (*Hears a noise and quickly closes the box.* ALEXEY *and* GAVRYUSHKA *enter, carrying a washbasin, a jug of water, and a towel.*)

IKHAREV. Are those gentlemen in?

ALEXEY. Yes, sir. Downstairs.

IKHAREV. I'll just look them over and see what they're like. (*Goes out.*)

ALEXEY. You come a long way?

GAVRYUSHKA. From Ryazán.

ALEXEY. Is that where your master's from?

GAVRYUSHKA. No, Smolénsk.

ALEXEY. So your master's estate is in Smolensk?

GAVRYUSHKA. No, he's got one hundred serfs in Smolensk and eighty in Kalúga.

ALEXEY. I get it. He's from two provinces.

GAVRYUSHKA. That's right. Two provinces. In the house alone there's Ignáty, the butler; Pavlúshka, who used to travel with

the master; Gerásim, the footman; Ivan, the other footman;
Ivan, the kennel boy; Ivan who plays the fiddle; then there's
Grigóry, the cook; Semyón, the cook; Varúkh, the gardener;
Deménty, the coachman; and that's all. (KRUGEL *and*
SHVOKHNEV *enter cautiously*.)

KRUGEL. I'm nervous. He might walk in on us.

SHVOKHNEV. Don't worry. Uteshitelny will keep him busy. (*To*
ALEXEY.) Run along, pal. They want you downstairs. (ALEXEY
goes out. SHVOKHNEV *rushes up to* GAVRYUSHKA.) Where's
your master from?

GAVRYUSHKA. Now he's from Ryazan.

SHVOKHNEV. Landowner?

GAVRYUSHKA. Yes, sir.

SHVOKHNEV. Gambles?

GAVRYUSHKA. Yes, sir.

SHVOKHNEV. Here's fifty rubles! Now spill it!

GAVRYUSHKA. But . . . you won't tell my master?

BOTH. Not a word.
    Don't be scared!

SHVOKHNEV. Well, has he won much lately?

GAVRYUSHKA. You know Colonel Chebotaryóv?

SHVOKHNEV. What about him?

GAVRYUSHKA. Three weeks ago we wiped him out. Eighty
thousand rubles, a brand-new carriage, a Persian rug, even the
epaulets off his shoulders. The gold on them went for sixty
rubles.

SHVOKHNEV, *looking at* KRUGEL *meaningfully*. How about that,
Krugel? Eighty thousand! (KRUGEL *shakes his head*.) Think he's
on the up and up? We'll find out soon enough. (*To* GAVR-
YUSHKA.) Look here, what does your master do when he's by
himself?

GAVRYUSHKA. What does he do? That's as plain as day. He's a
gentleman. He doesn't do anything.

SHVOKHNEV. You're lying. I'll bet he's never without a deck in his
hands.

GAVRYUSHKA. I can't rightly say, Your Honor. It's only my second
week with the master. Before, Pavlushka traveled with him.

We've also got Gerasim, the footman; Ivan, the other footman; Ivan, the kennel boy; Ivan who plays the fiddle; Dementy, the coachman; and the other day they brought in a new fellow.

SHVOKHNEV, *to* KRUGEL. What do you make of it? A cardsharp?

KRUGEL. I'd lay odds on it.

SHVOKHNEV. Let's give him a try anyhow. (*Both go out.*)

GAVRYUSHKA, *alone.* Those gentlemen sure move fast! But the money'll come in handy. A kerchief for Matryóna, some candy for the kids. Ah, it's the open road for me! Always a chance to pick up a bit of change. The master sends you to the store—well, out of every ruble, a kopeck finds its way into your pocket. . . . But what a life the masters have! The mood hits them and away they go! Tired of Smolensk? It's off to Ryazan. Don't care for Ryazan? Try Kazán. If Kazan's no better, then there's always Yarosláv. I still haven't figured out what's more classy—Ryazan or Kazan. Must be Kazan, since Ryazan's . . .

IKHAREV *enters.*

IKHAREV. Nothing special about them. Yet I'd better keep an eye . . . Oh, how I'd love to clean them out! God, I'm bursting to have a crack at them! Just thinking about it makes my heart skip a beat. (*Sits before a mirror and starts to shave.*) The way my hand's shaking, I can barely shave.

ALEXEY *enters.*

ALEXEY. Will you be ordering, sir?

IKHAREV. Yes. Lunch for four. Caviar, salmon, four bottles of wine. And take care of him. (*Points to* GAVRYUSHKA.)

ALEXEY, *to* GAVRYUSHKA. Yours is in the kitchen. (GAVRYUSHKA *goes out.*)

IKHAREV, *shaving.* Well? Did they slip you much?

ALEXEY. Who, sir?

IKHAREV. Don't play games with me! Out with it!

ALEXEY. They did give me a little something. For serving them, Your Honor.

IKHAREV. How much? Fifty rubles?

ALEXEY. Yes, sir. Fifty.

IKHAREV. It won't be fifty from me. See that hundred-ruble bill on the table? It's yours. What are you afraid of? It won't bite. All I ask is that everything be on the level. Is that clear? The cards can come from the store in town or any damn place—that's not my concern. But on top of those, here, take my personal decks. Do you follow me?

ALEXEY. You can count on me, Your Honor. We're used to this sort of thing around here.

IKHAREV. And stash the cards carefully. They might search you. (*Puts away his brush and soap and wipes his face with a towel.*) Oh, how I'd love to hook them. It would be grand, just grand! (SHVOKHNEV, KRUGEL, *and* UTESHITELNY *enter, bowing.*)

IKHAREV, *greeting them with a bow.* You'll have to excuse me, gentlemen. The room isn't exactly luxurious. Four chairs are all I've got.

UTESHITELNY. The gracious hospitality of our host means more to us than mere comfort.

SHVOKHNEV. It isn't the room but who's in it.

UTESHITELNY. How true! Life would be unbearable if not for congenial company. (*To* KRUGEL.) Do you recall, dear fellow, my circumstances when I arrived—all alone, not knowing a soul, an old bitch for a landlady, a chambermaid who was an absolute horror. Before my eyes some sweaty soldier was drooling over her, hungry for what he could get. In a word—I was bored stiff. Suddenly fate sent Mr. Krugel. You can imagine my delight. No, I couldn't survive an hour without good friends. I simply must open my heart to one and all.

KRUGEL. That's a vice, my good man, not a virtue. Overdoing it is always harmful. You've probably been taken in more than once.

UTESHITELNY. Yes, I've been deceived and cheated, and always shall be. Yet it's my nature to be trusting.

KRUGEL. Well, that's incomprehensible to me. How can you open yourself up to everybody? Now, friends are another matter.

UTESHITELNY. But man belongs to society.

KRUGEL. Yes, but not entirely.

UTESHITELNY. No, entirely.

KRUGEL. No, not entirely.

UTESHITELNY. Yes!

KRUGEL. No!

UTESHITELNY. Yes!

SHVOKHNEV, *to* UTESHITELNY. Don't argue. You're wrong.

UTESHITELNY, *heatedly*. I can prove it. It's an obligation...it's...
it's...it's...a moral duty! It's...it's...

SHVOKHNEV. He's gotten carried away. The man's a hothead. His
first few words make sense, but then it's anybody's guess.

UTESHITELNY. I can't help it! On a question of principle, I
completely forget myself. I usually warn others in advance:
"Touch upon a point of honor, gentlemen, and I won't be
responsible." Something comes over me. My blood simply boils
with indignation!

IKHAREV, *to himself*. Oh no, my friend! I've known people who get
hot under the collar at the word *duty*. You may be boiling, but
not on account of that. (*Aloud*.) Well, gentlemen, since we're
discussing sacred duty, how about a little game of bank. (*During
the remainder of the conversation, lunch is served*.)

UTESHITELNY. If the stakes aren't too high, why not?

KRUGEL. I've nothing against innocent pastimes.

IKHAREV. I suppose they have cards in the inn?

SHVOKHNEV. You only have to ask.

IKHAREV. Cards! (ALEXEY *prepares the card table*.) Be my guests,
gentlemen! (*Stepping up to the table and pointing*.) The
salmon's not up to scratch, but the caviar's satisfactory.

SHVOKHNEV, *trying a piece*. No, the salmon's fine.

KRUGEL, *also sampling*. And the cheese is excellent. The caviar
isn't half bad either.

SHVOKHNEV. Remember the superb cheese we had the other week?

KRUGEL. I'll never forget the cheese I had at Alexandrov's.

UTESHITELNY. Do you know when cheese is especially savory,
gentlemen? Between courses of dinner—then it acquires its true
significance. At such moments cheese is like a maître d'hôtel
telling us, "Welcome, gentlemen, there's room for more."

IKHAREV. Welcome, gentlemen, the cards are on the table.

UTESHITELNY, *advancing to the card table*. Look, Shvokhnev—
cards. Ah the days of yesteryear, where have they fled? How long

it's been!

IKHAREV, *aside.* Enough of your bluffing!

UTESHITELNY. Would you like to hold the bank, sir?

IKHAREV. Fine. Let's start small. Five hundred rubles. Will you
cut? (*Deals.*)

The game begins. Exclamations.

SHVOKHNEV. A four, an ace. Ten on each.

UTESHITELNY. A card for the governor's wife! May the old girl
bring me luck.

KRUGEL. Allow me to play a nine.

UTESHITELNY. Shvokhnev, hand me the chalk. I'll keep score.

SHVOKHNEV. What the heck, I double!

UTESHITELNY. And another five rubles for me!

KRUGEL. One moment, please. Let's see what we have here. There
should be two threes left.

UTESHITELNY, *jumps up, aside.* What the hell! Something's fishy.
These aren't our cards. (*The game continues.*)

IKHAREV, *to* KRUGEL. May I ask, do both of them ride?

KRUGEL. Both.

IKHAREV. You're not raising?

KRUGEL. No.

IKHAREV, *to* SHVOKHNEV. How about you? Are you betting?

SHVOKHNEV. With your permission, I'll sit out this round. (*Rushes
over to* UTESHITELNY *and whispers quickly.*) Damn it! He's
switching cards. He's pulling every trick in the book. The man's
a cardsharp!

UTESHITELNY, *agitated.* What do you want us to do? Give up on
the eighty thousand?

SHVOKHNEV. What else if we can't chisel it out of him?

UTESHITELNY. Well, that's still on open question. For now, we'll
lay our cards on the table.

SHVOKHNEV. What?

UTESHITELNY. Make a clean breast of it.

SHVOKHNEV. What the hell for?

UTESHITELNY. I'll tell you later. Come. (*They step over to*
IKHAREV; *each slaps him on a shoulder.*) Let's call it quits.

You've been shooting blanks, my friend.

IKHAREV, *startled.* How so?

UTESHITELNY. What's the point of arguing? It takes one to know one.

IKHAREV, *courteously.* Permit me to inquire, in what sense am I to understand . . .

UTESHITELNY. Oh, come off it. Why stand on ceremony? We've witnessed your considerable skills and readily acknowledge your talent. Speaking for my companions, I'd like to suggest an alliance. Our combined knowledge and capital should guarantee us enormous success.

IKHAREV. How far can I trust you?

UTESHITELNY. Completely. Be aboveboard with us, and we'll pay in kind. Frankly, we were planning to milk you dry. But only because we took you for an amateur. Now it's apparent that you've been initiated into the higher mysteries of our profession. So, will you join us?

IKHAREV. How could I refuse such a generous offer?

UTESHITELNY. Well then, let's shake hands on it. (*They take turns in shaking* IKHAREV'S *hands.*) From this moment we share everything. No pretense, no formalities! Tell me, how long have you studied the secrets of our art?

IKHAREV. Since childhood. It's been an obsession. While my teachers were explaining arithmetic, I held bank under my desk.

UTESHITELNY. I might have known. Skill like yours cannot be attained without constant practice from one's impressionable years. Shvokhnev, do you remember that child?

SHVOKHNEV. I'll never forget him. One day Mr. Uteshitelny's brother-in-law asked me: "Shvokhnev, how would you like to observe a marvel? A kid of eleven and he can switch cards with the best of them. Go down to Tetyushi and see for yourself!" Naturally I made a beeline for the boy's home. A middle-aged gentleman came out to meet me, and I introduced myself. "Excuse me, sir, but I hear God has blessed you with an extraordinary son." It cheered me to hear him reply simply and unpretentiously. "Yes," he said, "that's so. It's inappropriate for a father to brag about his children, but the boy's one of a

kind. Misha!'''he calls. ''We have a guest. Come and show your
stuff.'' The kid turned out to be a little tyke, no higher than my
waist, not much to look at. But when he began to deal, I was
dumbfounded.

IKHAREV. You couldn't notice anything?

SHVOKHNEV. Not a trace! I kept my eyes peeled.

IKHAREV. Incredible!

UTESHITELNY. A child prodigy!

IKHAREV. And to think what it takes—experience, keen sight,
careful study of the markings.

UTESHITELNY. That's been made much easier nowadays. Marked
cards are out of date. Gamblers try to figure out the key.

IKHAREV. The key to the pattern?

UTESHITELNY. That's right. The pattern on the reverse side. In one
town—I won't mention which—a highly respected gentleman
does nothing else. He receives a few hundred decks a year from
Moscow. The sender's name is shrouded in secrecy. His duties
consist in deciphering the designs and sending out the keys. A
deuce may have one pattern, an ace another. For that alone he
gets five thousand a year.

IKHAREV. But it's an important service.

UTESHITELNY. It has to be done that way. The economists call it
''division of labor.'' Take a carriage maker. He doesn't build the
carriage himself. Part of the job is assigned to the blacksmith
and the upholsterer. Otherwise it would take a lifetime.

IKHAREV. May I ask you a question? How do you arrange to put
your decks into play? It's not always possible to bribe a servant.

UTESHITELNY. We wouldn't dream of it! Besides, it's risky. You
can give yourself away. We have other means. We'll send an
agent, posing as a merchant, to a country fair. He puts up at the
best hotel in town, drops off his baggage, runs up a bill on
food and drink, and vanishes without paying. When the
manager ransacks his room, he notices one bundle's been left
behind. He opens it—a hundred decks drop out. Of course, the
cards are immediately sold at public auction for a ruble under
cost, and the storekeepers grab them up. In four days the town is
picked clean.

IKHAREV. Very neat.

SHVOKHNEV. What about the job we did on the landowner?

IKHAREV. What about him?

UTESHITELNY. That wasn't bad either. You wouldn't happen to know a landowner by name of Arkády Dergunóv? Very rich, and a splendid player. As honest as the day is long. We just couldn't find a way to get at him. The sort who looks after everything himself—his servants are well-trained, a palace for a home, gardens in the English style, butlers. . . a Russian gentleman in the full sense of the word. How were we to tackle him? It seemed impossible. Finally we hit upon a plan. One morning a cab, crammed with young fellows, roaring drunk and bawling songs, flies past the servants' quarters. As expected, the servants come scrambling out, gaping and laughing at the spectacle. They see something's fallen from the cab, dash up, and find—a suitcase. Hands wave, voices shout: "Stop! Stop!" Useless! The cart's flown off, leaving only a cloud of dust. Well, they open the suitcase and discover—clothing, underwear, two-hundred rubles in cash, and forty packs of cards. Naturally, they wouldn't turn their backs on the money, the cards found their way to the master's tables, and by the following evening our host was left without a kopeck in his pockets.

IKHAREV. Very sharp. They call it stealing, but it's the product of subtle intelligence and maturity.

UTESHITELNY. People have no appreciation of gambling. A game of chance doesn't take persons into account. A game is indifferent. If my own father were to sit down to cards with me— I'd skin my father. At the card table all men are equal.

IKHAREV. Precisely what they fail to understand. A gambler may be the most virtuous of men. I know a player who's fond of dealing from the bottom of the deck, but he'd give his last kopeck to a beggar. And yet there's no holding him back from joining with two friends to wipe out a third. . . . Gentlemen, since we're leveling with each other, I'll show you something that will knock you off your feet. Have you ever seen a stacked deck where every card can be deciphered from the other end of the room?

UTESHITELNY. We have, but perhaps not the same type.

IKHAREV. I can safely boast, you won't find another like mine. Almost a half year of work went into the markings. For weeks I couldn't stand sunlight. The doctor feared damage to my eyes. (*Takes a deck out of a box.*) Here she is. You'll forgive me, gentlemen, but I've christened her.

UTESHITELNY. What?

IKHAREV. That's right. She's Adelaide Ivanovna.

UTESHITELNY, *laughing*. Do you hear, Shvokhnev? That's a new one—calling a deck of cards Adelaide Ivanovna. I even find it rather witty.

SHVOKHNEV. Beautiful! Adelaide Ivanovna! Very charming.

UTESHITELNY. Adelaide Ivanovna! A German! Hey, Krugel, we've got a wife for you.

KRUGEL. Me a German? My grandfather was German, but even he spoke Russian.

UTESHITELNY, *examining the deck*. A treasure! Absolutely no sign. Can you really spot a card at a distance?

IKHAREV. Try me. I'll step off five paces and call every card. Two-thousand rubles if I trip up.

UTESHITELNY. All right, what card is this?

IKHAREV. A seven.

UTESHITELNY. Precisely. And this?

IKHAREV. The jack.

UTESHITELNY. Well I'll be!... And this?

IKHAREV. A three.

UTESHITELNY. Incredible!

KRUGEL. Unbelievable!

SHVOKHNEV. Fantastic!

UTESHITELNY. May I have another look, sir. (*Examines the deck.*) Marvelous. Truly deserving of a name. But permit me to remark, except with the most amateurish players, there would be difficulties. After all, you'd have to slip it into play yourself.

IKHAREV. Of course, you can only pull it off in the heat of play, when the stakes are so high even the experienced player becomes uneasy. If a man's only slightly off his guard, he's yours for the taking. The top gamblers get stale. Two days and nights without a wink of sleep, and they've played themselves out. Once the action heats up, I switch decks. The trick is to stay cool while the other fellow's excited. There are thousands of ways to distract his attention. Pick a quarrel, accuse someone of putting down the wrong score. All eyes will turn—and in a flash, your cards are in the game.

UTESHITELNY. I see that in addition to skill, you possess a talent for keeping a cool head. That's an important asset. Our association should prove all the more valuable. But enough of ceremony and formality. May we speak as friends?

IKHAREV. High time, gentlemen.

UTESHITELNY. Waiter! Champagne! To the success of our alliance!

IKHAREV. I'll drink to that!

SHVOKHNEV. Well, here we are, united for battle, weapons in hand, troops ready. Only one thing's missing. . . .

IKHAREV. Precisely. A fortress to storm.

UTESHITELNY. Yes, we haven't sighted the enemy yet. (*Looking intently at* SHVOKHNEV.) Well, Shvokhnev? Your face is an open book. You must have a target in mind.

SHVOKHNEV. There is someone, but. . .

UTESHITELNY. I know who you're aiming at.

IKHAREV, *eagerly*. Who? Who is it?

UTESHITELNY. Oh, it's nonsense, sheer nonsense. Nothing to it. You see, there's a landowner named Glov staying here. But it's pointless—he doesn't gamble. We've already worked on him. . . . I've been after him for a month, won his friendship, his confidence—all to no avail.

IKHAREV. Listen, let me have a crack at him. You never can tell.

UTESHITELNY. I assure you, it's not worth the trouble.

IKHAREV. No harm trying.

SHVOKHNEV. At least invite him. If we don't succeed, we'll just chat. Why not?

UTESHITELNY. All right, if you insist. It makes no difference to me.

IKHAREV. Get him right away. By all means.

UTESHITELNY. Very well. (*Goes out.*)

IKHAREV. Yes, you never can tell. Sometimes a job seems impossible and . . .

SHVOKHNEV. I'm of the same opinion. After all, we're not dealing with God here, but man. And a man's only a man. It might be "No" today, "No" tomorrow, the same the day after; but if you keep pressing him, he'll come around. Some people put on a face that says, "We're unapproachable." Take a closer look— you'll find they were easy marks all along.

KRUGEL. But this one isn't that sort.

IKHAREV. I only hope he is! I'm dying for some action. My last winnings were a month ago. Eight thousand from a colonel. A month without practice. Can you imagine the boredom? Deadly, just deadly.

SHVOKHNEV. I appreciate the fix you're in. It's like a general without a war. My friend, these things are intermissions between acts, and they can be fatal. I know from experience, they're no laughing matter.

IKHAREV. The way I'm feeling, if someone wanted to play for kopecks, I'd grab a chair and join in.

SHVOKHNEV. That's only natural. Moods like that can be the ruin of the most skillful gamblers. They're idle, bored, and desperation drives them to play with some stinking sharper. Well, that's money down the drain.

IKHAREV. Is this Glov rich?

KRUGEL. Oho! Money to burn. He's got thousands.

IKHAREV. You don't say! Shall we get him drunk? Send for champagne?

SHVOKHNEV. He never touches the stuff.

IKHAREV. What do you propose? How can we get to him? . . . Wait. Gambling is an enormous temptation. Once he sees us play, there'll be no holding him back.

SHVOKHNEV. It's worth a chance. Krugel and I will get up a little game off in the corner. Only don't be too obvious. These old geezers are a suspicious lot. (KRUGEL *and* SHVOKHNEV *sit off to the side with cards.* UTESHITELNY *and* GLOV, *an elderly man, enter.*)

UTESHITELNY. Mr. Ikharev, may I introduce Mikhal Alexandrovich Glov!

IKHAREV. My pleasure. I've been looking forward to meeting you. Seeing we're at the same hotel, I . . .

GLOV. I'm also delighted to make your acquaintance. My only regret is that I'm about to depart.

IKHAREV, *offering him a chair.* Please sit down. Have you been in town long?

> UTESHITELNY, SHVOKHNEV, *and* KRUGEL *whisper among themselves.*

GLOV. Oh, Mr. Ikharev, I'm sick of this town. Nothing would please me more than escaping as soon as possible.

IKHAREV. Are business affairs detaining you?

GLOV. Oh business, business! It's all so wearisome!

IKHAREV. Probably a lawsuit?

GLOV. No, thank heavens, nothing of the sort. But all the same, a very complicated situation. I'm marrying off my daughter. Can you appreciate a father's plight, Mr. Ikharev? I've come to make various purchases, but chiefly to mortgage my estate. Though the arrangements should have been completed, the bank still hasn't processed my papers. Such a waste of time!

IKHAREV. May I inquire, how much do you expect to receive?

GLOV. Two-hundred-thousand rubles, Mr. Ikharev. The payment should arrive any day now, but how it drags on. I'm just sick of lingering here! At home there are things to be done, a daughter who's engaged... everything's up in the air. I've decided not to wait.

IKHAREV. What's that? Not wait for the money?

GLOV. What can I do, Mr. Ikharev? Put yourself in my shoes. I haven't seen my wife and children for a month now. God knows what's going on at home. My son will remain to handle my affairs. I'm fed up with the whole business. (*Addressing* SHVOKHNEV *and* KRUGEL.) Gentlemen, I'm afraid I disturbed you.

KRUGEL. Oh, no. Not at all. Just a little game to kill time.

GLOV. But you're playing for money.

SHVOKHNEV. Who? Us? Only a kopeck or two—for the fun of it.

GLOV. Gentlemen, listen to an old man. There's no harm in amusing yourselves, and you don't stand to lose much playing for kopecks—that's all very true. But just the same...

Gentlemen, I speak from experience. In life things have a
way of starting small and ending big.

SHVOKHNEV, *aside, to* IKHAREV. The old goat's going to give a
lecture! (*To* GLOV.) You're making a mountain out of a
molehill. You old timers are all alike.

GLOV. I'm not that old, sir. It's the voice of experience.

SHVOKHNEV. I didn't have you in mind. But in general that's how
old people are. If they get burned, they're convinced everyone's
bound to stick his fingers into the same fire. Let some old man
absentmindedly slip on ice, and he's all set to pass a law: "No
one is to be permitted to walk along such and such a road." He
won't take into account that the other fellow may not be
absentminded. No, they never consider that. "Dogs bite." "A
dog bit a man." Ergo, "No one is to be allowed out in the
streets."

GLOV. You have a point, sir. Old people do have that fault. But
consider the young! They're much too reckless. The first thing
you know, they're up to their necks in hot water.

SHVOKHNEV. That's all because we have no happy medium. A
young man's so wild, no one can stand him; and in old age he
turns into such a hypocrite, you still can't stand him.

GLOV. You have a low opinion of the elderly.

SHVOKHNEV. Why low? It's the truth, that's all.

IKHAREV. May I make a remark? You're being somewhat harsh...

UTESHITELNY. When it comes to cards, I find myself in complete
agreement with Mikhal Alexandrovich. I also used to play—with
a passion. But thank my lucky stars, I gave it up. Not because I
lost, mind you, or because my luck turned against me. After all,
what is loss of money compared to peace of mind? But the
mere excitement of gambling visibly shortens a man's life.

GLOV. How true, Mr. Uteshitelny! How true! A most wise
observation! Allow me to ask an indiscreet question. I've
enjoyed the privilege of your acquaintance for some time now,
and I still have no idea...

UTESHITELNY. Why, what is it?

GLOV. At the risk of being indelicate, may I ask your age?

UTESHITELNY. Thirty-nine.

GLOV. Thirty-nine! Imagine that! Why you're still young! If we only had more men of such wisdom in Russia. Good heavens! It would mean the Golden Age! How grateful I am that fate has brought us together.

IKHAREV. I share your viewpoint. I'd never allow young people to touch cards. But why deny responsible adults a little fun? Take a man on in years. He can't very well go dancing or horseback riding.

GLOV. True, quite true, Mr. Ikharev. But life holds so many pleasures, so many sacred duties. Yes, gentlemen, heed an old man's words. Our great mission lies in the bosom of the family. Vanity, gentlemen, mere vanity engulfs you, while true bliss remains to be tasted. Believe me, I can't wait to see my dear ones again. My daughter flinging herself on my neck, sweetly mumbling, ''Papa, darling Papa!'' My son home from school, happy to be near me. . . . Ah! Words fail to describe it. After all that, who could think about cards?

IKHAREV. But why mix paternal feelings and cards? Paternal feelings are one thing and cards another.

ALEXEY, *entering, to* GLOV. Should I take out your luggage, sir? The horses are ready.

GLOV. I'll be right there! Excuse me, gentlemen. Just for a moment. (*Steps out.*)

IKHAREV. He's hopeless.

UTESHITELNY. I warned you. Can't you size up a man? One look should tell you who won't play.

IKHAREV. Still, we ought to have pressed him. Why did you back him up?

UTESHITELNY. That's the only way, my friend. With that sort, you have to be subtle. Otherwise he'll catch on you're out to fleece him.

IKHAREV. Well, what came of it? He's still leaving.

UTESHITELNY. Just hold your horses. We're not finished with him yet.

GLOV *returns.*

GLOV. Gentlemen, I'm very grateful to have made your

acquaintance. I'm only sorry it wasn't earlier. But, God willing, we'll meet again.

SHVOKHNEV. Most likely. It's a small world. People meet if it's in the cards.

GLOV. Oh, yes. Very true. Our destinies are in the hands of Providence. Very true. Goodbye, gentlemen! My sincere thanks! Mr. Uteshitelny, I'm very much indebted to you. You eased an old man's loneliness.

UTESHITELNY. Think nothing of it. My pleasure.

GLOV. Since you're so kind, may I impose upon you for another favor.

UTESHITELNY. Just ask! Only too happy to help.

GLOV. Set an old man's mind at rest.

UTESHITELNY. How?

GLOV. I'm leaving my Sasha here. A wonderful boy. Very good-natured. But inexperienced. He's only twenty-two, almost a child. Nothing appeals to him but the cavalry. "Sasha, you've got time," I tell him, "see a bit of the world first. Who knows? Perhaps you have a bent for government work?" Well, you know what young people are like. Gold braid, a splendid uniform—all that dazzles them. What's a father to do? You can't just throttle a boy's whims. . . . Do me this favor, my dear Mr. Uteshitelny. The boy will be here all by himself, taking care of some business for me. Anything can happen—the bank clerks might cheat him. . . . Take him under your wing, Mr. Uteshitelny, keep him out of trouble. Be so kind, my dear friend! (*Takes* UTESHITELNY'S *hands.*)

UTESHITELNY. Certainly. Certainly. I'll be a father to the boy.

GLOV. Oh, my dear fellow! (*They embrace and kiss.*) You can always tell when a man has a warm heart. God bless you! Goodbye, gentlemen. I sincerely wish you a happy stay.

IKHAREV. Goodbye. Have a good trip!

SHVOKHNEV. I hope all's well at home.

GLOV. Thank you, gentlemen!

UTESHITELNY. I'll see you off.

GLOV. Mr. Uteshitelny, you're too kind. (GLOV *and* UTESHITELNY *go out.*)

IKHAREV. Our pigeon has flown the coop!

SHVOKHNEV. And he would have been worth the plucking.

IKHAREV. When I heard two hundred thousand, my heart skipped
a beat.

KRUGEL. Just the thought of it makes my mouth water.

IKHAREV. And to think of the frivolous ways people squander
money. So what if he has two hundred thousand? It'll all go on
rags for his daughter.

SHVOKHNEV. On trash, garbage!

IKHAREV. And how much money never even gets into circulation!
The banks are stuffed with dead capital rotting away like so many
corpses. A shame, a damn shame. The cash going to waste in the
state bank would be more than enough for me.

SHVOKHNEV. I'd settle for half.

KRUGEL. I'd be content with a quarter.

SHVOKHNEV. Don't lie. You Germans are all alike. You'd want
more.

KRUGEL. Honestly, I . . .

SHVOKHNEV. You'd cheat us out of our share.

UTESHITELNY *runs in, beaming.*

UTESHITELNY. Gentlemen, gentlemen, our worries are over! The
old fool's left—and good riddance! We've got the son. His father
has authorized him to receive the money from the bank, and
yours truly is to supervise the transaction. The son's a daredevil.
He's bursting to be a cavalry officer. Easy pickings! I'll run and
bring him immediately. (*Runs off.*)

IKHAREV. Three cheers for Uteshitelny!

SHVOKHNEV. Hip, hip, hooray!

KRUGEL. Hip, hip, hooray!

SHVOKHNEV. Things have worked out beautifully! (*All rub hands
in delight.*)

IKHAREV. A great guy! Hooray, Uteshitelny! Now I understand why
he played up to the old man. And it was all so clever, so subtle!

SHVOKHNEV. Oh, yes. Uteshitelny has a remarkable talent for that
sort of thing.

KRUGEL. He's unbelievable!

IKHAREV. When the old boy said he was leaving his son here, the idea flashed through my head, but only for a moment. And it took him no time to... What a keen mind!

SHVOKHNEV. You haven't seen anything yet.

UTESHITELNY *enters with* GLOV, JR.

UTESHITELNY. Gentlemen! Meet Alexander Mikhalych Glov. A splendid young man. Treat him as you treat me.

SHVOKHNEV. Delighted. (*Shakes hands.*)

IKHAREV. Pleased to meet you.

KRUGEL. We welcome you with open arms.

GLOV, JR. Gentlemen! I...

UTESHITELNY. No, no. Don't stand on ceremony. Equality before all.... Gentlemen! Now that we know each other, to hell with etiquette! Let's speak as old friends.

SHVOKHNEV. As brothers!

GLOV, JR. Brothers to the end! (*Shakes hands with everybody.*)

UTESHITELNY. Atta way! Bravo! Waiter! Champagne!... Gentlemen, have you noticed? Glov already has something of the cavalry officer about him. No offense intended, but your father's an ass. Forgive me—after all, we did agree to be informal. Really, how could he have dreamed of turning such a brave lad into a grubby clerk?... Well, young man, is your sister's wedding to take place soon?

GLOV, JR. She can take her wedding and go to blazes! On account of her, my father has kept me in the sticks for three months.

UTESHITELNY. Is your sister pretty?

GLOV, JR. Very. If she weren't my sister, I'd have a go at her myself.

UTESHITELNY. Bravo! Bravo! Spoken like a true cavalry officer! Tell me, would you give me a hand if I tried to abduct her?

GLOV, JR. Why not? Certainly.

UTESHITELNY. Bravo! A cavalry officer from top to toe! Waiter! Champagne! Glov, you're a man after my own heart. I'm extremely fond of generous people. Here, let me embrace you.

SHVOKHNEV. Let me also.

IKHAREV. And allow me.

KRUGEL. Well, if that's how things stand, I'll embrace him too. (*They embrace.* ALEXEY *brings in a bottle of champagne; the cork pops and flies to the ceiling; he fills their glasses.*)

UTESHITELNY. Gentlemen! A toast to the future cavalry lieutenant! May he be first in war, first in love, first at the bottle, first.... To cut it short, he can be whatever he damn pleases!

ALL. Whatever he damn pleases! (*They drink.*)

GLOV, JR., *raising his glass.* Long live the cavalry!

ALL. Long live the cavalry! (*They drink.*)

UTESHITELNY. Gentlemen! The time has come to initiate our friend into the traditions of the officers' corps. He drinks well enough, but that's a trifle. He must become a gambler to the hilt! Do you play bank?

GLOV, JR. I'm itching to, but I don't have any money.

UTESHITELNY. Money? Ridiculous! All it takes are a few kopecks to sit in. Before you know it, you'll be swimming in money.

GLOV, JR. But I'm flat broke.

UTESHITELNY. Don't worry about a thing—we'll trust you. I know you have a bank draft. We'll wait. The moment they pay you, you pay us. Until then, we'll accept an I.O.U.... But what am I saying? As if you're about to lose! Why, you can win thousands in cold cash.

GLOV, JR. And what if I do lose?

UTESHITELNY. Lose? You ought to be ashamed. Is that a way for a cavalry officer to talk? Naturally, there are only two possibilities —win or lose. But that's the beauty of it. A man shows the stuff he's made of by taking risks. If results were guaranteed, clerks would stand up to their bosses, and Jews would lead armies into battle.

GLOV, JR., *with a wave of the hand.* What the hell, I'll play! Why should I worry about my father!

UTESHITELNY. Bravo, Lieutenant! Waiter! Cards! (*Pours* GLOV, JR., *a drink.*) What does a man need? Daring, heroism, power— that's what!... Gentlemen, I'll hold bank. Twenty-five thousand. (*Deals.*) Your turn, Lieutenant. Shvokhnev, what do you bet? A peculiar run of cards. Extremely interesting. The jack's dead, the nine scores. What do you have there? Your

four's a winner! Oh, Lieutenant! What a splendid cavalry officer
you are! Ikharev, observe how skillfully he raises!. . . The ace still
hasn't turned up. Shvokhnev, why don't you fill our friend's
glass? Ah! There she is, there's the ace! Look at Krugel grab for
it. Those Germans have all the luck! The four scores again.
Bravo, Lieutenant! Bravo! How about that, Shvokhnev? The
lieutenant's already five thousand ahead.

GLOV, JR. Dammit! Double on the four! And the nine rides for
another five hundred!

UTESHITELNY, *dealing.* Atta boy! That's a cavalry man for you! The
seven. . . no, what the. . . a three, an eight, the queen. Oh, the
lieutenant has tripped up. Well, that's how it goes, my friend.
You can't win them all. Krugel, stop calculating! Bet the card
you pulled. Bravo, the lieutenant rakes it in! Gentlemen,
congratulations are in order. Here's to Lieutenant Glov!

SHVOKHNEV. To Lieutenant Glov! Hooray!

IKHAREV. Hip, hip, hooray! (*They all drink.*)

UTESHITELNY. You know, they say the queen of spades brings bad
luck, but I disagree. Shvokhnev, remember the pretty brunette
you nicknamed Queen of Spades? Where's the little sweetheart
now? Probably gone to the dogs. Krugel! Your card's beaten!
(*To* IKHAREV.) And yours! And yours too, Shvokhnev! And the
lieutenant also loses.

GLOV, JR. Dammit! I bet the bank! Twenty-five thousand!

UTESHITELNY. Bravo, Lieutenant! That's the cavalry spirit! Have
you noticed, Shvokhnev, how the true man always reveals
himself? Before, Glov merely showed promise of being a cavalry
officer. Now he *is* a cavalry officer. That's character for you. . . .
You lose, Officer.

GLOV, JR. Double the bet!

UTESHITELNY. Bravo, Lieutenant! Fifty thousand! Now that's what
I call doing it handsomely! Where would you find another
daredevil like our Glov. The boy's a hero. . . . The hero loses.

GLOV, JR. Double, dammit, double it again!

UTESHITELNY. Oho, Lieutenant! A hundred thousand! What a
man! Observe, Shvokhnev—his eyes are blazing. Another
Napoleon! Now that's heroism!. . . The king hasn't shown yet.

The queen of diamonds for you, Shvokhnev. Here, German, take your seven and stuff it! Trash, nothing but trash! Wretched cards. Aren't there any kings in this deck? Very peculiar. Ah, there's the king, there he is. . . . And the lieutenant is busted!

GLOV, JR., *feverishly*. Double, dammit, double!

UTESHITELNY. Hold on, my friend. That makes two hundred thousand you've run through. Pay up first. Otherwise we can't start a new hand. We're unable to trust you for so large a sum.

GLOV, JR. But where am I to get it? I don't have any money now.

UTESHITELNY. Give us an I.O.U. And sign it.

GLOV, JR. Very well. Anything you say. (*Takes a pen.*)

UTESHITELNY. And hand over your bank draft.

GLOV, JR. Here, take it.

UTESHITELNY. Now sign—there, and there.

GLOV, JR. As you wish. I'm prepared to do anything. See, I signed. Now let's play.

UTESHITELNY. Not so fast, my boy. First show us the color of your money.

GLOV, JR. But I promise to pay. You can count on it.

UTESHITELNY. No, my good fellow. Cash on the table!

GLOV, JR. What's going on? You're not. . . This is outrageous!

KRUGEL. No, not at all.

IKHAREV. Nothing of the kind. Our chances wouldn't be even.

SHVOKHNEV. You might cheat us. It's a well-known fact, if a player sits in without money, he'll try any trick to win.

GLOV, JR. Well, what do you want? Fix whatever interest you like. I'll do anything. I'll pay double.

UTESHITELNY. What the hell do we need your interest for? For two hundred thousand we'll gladly pay interest too.

GLOV, JR., *desperate and decisive*. So that's your final word? You won't play?

SHVOKHNEV. Get the cash, and we'll be only too happy to play.

GLOV, JR., *taking a pistol from his pocket*. In that case, goodbye gentlemen. You've seen the last of me. (*Runs off waving his pistol.*)

UTESHITELNY, *alarmed*. Glov! Glov! What are you doing? You're mad! I'd better run after him. He might really harm himself.

(*Runs out.*)

IKHAREV. There'll be a scandal if the crazy fool goes and shoots himself.

SHVOKHNEV. To hell with him. Let him shoot. Only not right now. We haven't got our hands on his money yet. That's what's so annoying!

KRUGEL. The whole business scares me. It's quite possible he'll...

GLOV, JR., *returns with the pistol still in his hand and* UTESHITELNY *restraining him by the arm.*

UTESHITELNY. Are you out of your mind?... Gentlemen, gentlemen, he was on the verge of sticking the barrel into his mouth. Do you hear me, gentlemen?... Really, you ought to be ashamed!

ALL, *pressing around* GLOV, JR. What's wrong with you? What do you think you're doing?

SHVOKHNEV. Shooting himself over a trifle! And an educated man, too.

IKHAREV. At this rate, every Russian ought to kill himself. We've all been losers, or we will be. Otherwise, how could there be winners? Just think about it.

UTESHITELNY. If I may say so, you're a thoroughgoing idiot. You're blind to your good fortune. Don't you see how you've gained by losing?

GLOV, JR., *annoyed.* Do you take me for a fool? Dammit! What gain is there in losing two-hundred-thousand rubles?

UTESHITELNY. Ah, you're a simpleton! Are you aware of the glory waiting for you in the cavalry? Losing two hundred thousand before you're even commissioned! The troops will parade you on their shoulders.

GLOV, JR., *reassured.* Do you think I don't have the guts to laugh it all off? The devil take the money! Long live the cavalry!

UTESHITELNY. Bravo! Long live the cavalry! Hooray! Champagne! (*The* WAITER *brings in several bottles.*)

GLOV, JR., *glass raised.* Hooray for the cavalry!

IKHAREV. Hooray for the cavalry, God damn it!

SHVOKHNEV. Hip, hip, hooray! Hip, hip, hooray!

GLOV, JR. Now I don't give a rap about anything! (*Puts his glass on the table.*) Only...how can I go home? My father!... (*Clutches his head.*)

UTESHITELNY. But what do you want to go home for? No need for that.

GLOV, JR., *astonished.* What did you say?

UTESHITELNY. Head straight for the regiment. We'll take care of your expenses. Shvokhnev, give him two-hundred rubles. Let the lieutenant have some fun! I noticed he has a sweetheart... a dark-eyed beauty, eh?

GLOV, JR. Dammit! I'll dash right over and take her by storm!

UTESHITELNY. That's the spirit, Lieutenant! Shvokhnev, would you happen to have two hundred on you?

IKHAREV. Here, I'll give it to him. Let the kid live it up.

GLOV, JR., *takes the money, waving it in the air.* Champagne!

ALL. Champagne! (*Bottles are brought in.*)

GLOV, JR. To the cavalry!

UTESHITELNY. The cavalry!... Shvokhnev, I have an idea. Why not toss him in the air—the way we used to back in the regiment? Come, everybody, grab him!

They toss him, singing.

For he's a jolly good fellow,
For he's a jolly good fellow,
For he's a jolly good fellow,
Which nobody can deny...

GLOV, JR., *glass raised.* Hooray!

ALL. Hip, hip, hooray! (*They put him down.* GLOV, JR., *smashes his glass, as do the others, some under their heels, some against the floor.*)

GLOV, JR. I'm off to my girl!

UTESHITELNY. And we're not to accompany you, eh?

GLOV, JR. No! Not on your life! If anyone dares...we'll have it out with swords!

UTESHITELNY. Oh, ho! What a desperado! What passion! Gentlemen, you can see he has the makings of a soldier and a lover! Well, run along, Lieutenant, run along. We won't keep you from your lady.

GLOV, JR. Goodbye.

SHVOKHNEV. Come back and tell us how you made out.

GLOV, JR. *goes out.*

UTESHITELNY. We'd better humor him till the cash is in our hands. Then he can drop dead.

SHVOKHNEV. I'm only afraid the bank might drag it out.

UTESHITELNY. Yes. That could mean trouble. But there are ways to speed it up. No matter what, you always have to grease a palm or two to get things running smoothly.

ZAMUKHRYSHKIN, *an official of the state bank, pokes his head through the door. Dressed in a shabby coat.*

ZAMUKHRYSHKIN. Excuse me, gentlemen. Is there a Mr. Glov here?

SHVOKHNEV. No. He just left. What do you want him for?

ZAMUKHRYSHKIN. A business matter, sir. Regarding payment on a bank draft.

UTESHITELNY. And who are you?

ZAMUKHRYSHKIN. An official of the state bank.

UTESHITELNY. Ah, do come in! Please, be seated. My friends and I are taking a lively interest in this affair. Especially as we've just concluded a friendly transaction with Mr. Glov. These gentlemen (*pointing*) are prepared to make their gratitude known in a most tangible way. You follow me, don't you? Only it's urgent that he be paid as quickly as possible.

ZAMUKHRYSHKIN. That's all very well, but less than two weeks is out of the question.

UTESHITELNY. Far too long. You're forgetting our. . .uh, gratitude.

ZAMUKHRYSHKIN. Oh, that goes without saying. We take it for granted. Otherwise you'd be hanging around for months. There isn't a kopeck in the bank, and none's expected for at least ten days. Last week we received one hundred and fifty thousand, but we paid it all out. Three landowners mortgaged their estates in February, and they're still waiting.

UTESHITELNY. Well, that's fine for others, but can't you do
something for your friends?. . . . Look here, we must become
better acquainted. After all, you're among your own kind! What
do they call you? Fenteléy Fenteléich?

ZAMUKHRYSHKIN. No, sir. Krep Krépovich.

UTESHITELNY. Well, it's all the same. Come now, Krep Krepovich,
think of me as an old friend. Tell me, how are you making out?
How's business?

ZAMUKHRYSHKIN. What can I say? A job's a job.

UTESHITELNY. Well, there are all sorts of ways to pick up some
cash. To be blunt, are you taking much under the table?

ZAMUKHRYSHKIN. Of course. A man has to live, doesn't he?

UTESHITELNY. Listen, you can be frank with me. Is everyone in the
bank a crook?

ZAMUKHRYSHKIN. Sir! You're making fun of me. Those gentlemen
who write for the magazines also joke about people who accept
bribes, but take a closer look—our superiors grab their share too.
And what about you, gentlemen? You may sugar the pill by
calling it a donation or a gift, but it all comes down to the same
thing. A bribe's a bribe no matter what name you give it.

SHVOKHNEV. Say, you've hurt Krepovich's feelings. That's what
comes of touching upon a man's honor.

ZAMUKHRYSHKIN. You know for yourselves, honor is a ticklish
business. But it doesn't upset me. I've been around, gentlemen.

UTESHITELNY. Enough of this. Let's have a friendly chat. Well,
Krep Krepovich, how are you getting along? The world treating
you right? Got a wife? Kids?

ZAMUKHRYSHKIN. Oh, yes, thank heavens. God has been good to
me. Two boys already in school, and two little tots. One's still in
diapers, but the other's crawling.

UTESHITELNY. Their chubby fingers already deft at going into the
till? (*Indicates taking money with his hand.*)

ZAMUKHRYSHKIN. You gentlemen will have your little jokes!

UTESHITELNY. Don't take offense, Krep Krepovich. Remember,
you're among friends, your own kind. Waiter! A glass of
champagne for Krep Krepovich. And make it quick! Really, we
must get to know each other better. As soon as we have a chance,

we'll pay you a visit.

ZAMUKHRYSHKIN, *accepting the glass.* Glad to have you, gentlemen! If I may say so, my tea surpasses anything you'll find at the governor's.

UTESHITELNY. A bribe from some storekeeper? Right?

ZAMUKHRYSHKIN. What else? A special order, too.

UTESHITELNY. But Krep Krepovich, the state bank can't be doing business with piddling storekeepers?

ZAMUKHRYSHKIN, *empties his glass; then with fists on his knees.* The storekeeper got into it on account of his stupidity. A landowner by name of Frakásov was mortgaging his estate to go into partnership with him on a factory. Everything was set; Frakasov was to get his money the next day. Now what do we care if the money's for a factory, or if there's a partner. That's none of our business. But the storekeeper was stupid enough to let it slip out. "I'm in partnership with a landowner," he says; "the money's coming any minute." Naturally, we sent word: "Fork over two thousand, or wait till hell freezes over!" Meanwhile the boilers and vats had been delivered; the suppliers were demanding their deposits. Well, he sees there's no squeezing water out of a stone. He hands over the two thousand and throws in three pounds of tea for each of us. Now some people may call that graft, but the man got what was coming to him. Who told the fool to shoot off his mouth?

UTESHITELNY. Listen, Krep Krepovich, about this little business of ours. Please, see what you can do. We'll take care of you, and you can pass on a slice to your superiors. Only, for Christ's sake, make it snappy. What do you say?

ZAMUKHRYSHKIN. I'll do my best. (*Stands.*) But I must be aboveboard. You're asking the impossible. So help me God, there isn't a kopeck left in the bank. I'll try, though.

UTESHITELNY. How will we find you?

ZAMUKHRYSHKIN. Just ask for Krep Krepovich. Goodbye, gentlemen. (*Makes for the door.*)

SHVOKHNEV. Krep Krepovich! Krep Krepovich! Give it a try!

UTESHITELNY. Krep Krepovich! Don't forget! We're pressed for time.

ZAMUKHRYSHKIN. I already told you. I'll do my best. (*Goes out.*)

UTESHITELNY. Oh, hell! How it drags. (*Bangs his forehead.*) I'll run after him. Maybe something can be done. I won't spare the cash. Dammit, I'll give him three thousand out of my own pocket. (*Runs out.*)

IKHAREV. Of course, it would be more convenient to have it right away.

SHVOKHNEV. We could certainly use it!

KRUGEL. If only he finds a way to get around him.

IKHAREV. Can your circumstances really be so . . .

UTESHITELNY *returns.*

UTESHITELNY, *desperate.* God damn it! He can't do it in less than four days. The way things are going, I'm ready to bang my head against the wall.

IKHAREV. But why are you so worked up? Can't you wait four days?

SHVOKHNEV. That's the point. It's extremely urgent.

UTESHITELNY. Did you say ''wait''? Do you realize, we're expected in Nízhny any minute now? We've been meaning to tell you: four days ago we got word to rush down. We're to come up with some cash, no matter what it takes. On Tuesday a contractor is due to sell a load of iron for six-hundred-thousand rubles, and another arrived yesterday with hemp worth a cool million.

IKHAREV. Well, what of it?

UTESHITELNY. What of it? The contractors are staying at home and sending their sons instead.

IKHAREV. Are you certain the sons will play?

UTESHITELNY. Where have you been living? China? Africa? Don't you know what their sons are like? How merchants raise their children? They bring them up so they don't know their noses from their elbows, or they teach them to ape the nobility. Naturally, all they have on their minds is carousing with officers, and going off on a binge. My friend, these are our best customers. The imbeciles don't realize that for every ruble they swindle out of us, they pay us back in thousands. It's our good luck that all a merchant cares about is getting a general for his daughter, and a government job for his son.

IKHAREV. So it's a sure thing?

UTESHITELNY. Of course! Otherwise they wouldn't have notified us. The money's as good as in our hands. But every minute is precious.

IKHAREV. Then why the hell are we twiddling our thumbs! Gentlemen, our agreement was to act as a team!

UTESHITELNY. Yes, that's to our advantage. Listen, I have an idea. There's no reason for you to hurry off now. You've got some money on you, eighty thousand I believe. Let us have it, and take Glov's I.O.U. You'll clear a hundred and fifty thousand, almost double, and you'll be doing us a favor. We need cash so desperately, we're delighted to pay two kopecks for your one.

IKHAREV. Why not? To show you that the ties of friendship are... (*takes out a roll of bills*.) Here you are, eighty thousand!

UTESHITELNY. And here's your I.O.U.! I'll run and get Glov. We have to make it legal. Krugel, take the money to my room. Here's the key to my cashbox. (KRUGEL *goes out*.) Ah, if we could only arrange everything so as to get out of here by evening. (*Goes out*.)

IKHAREV. He's right. No point wasting time.

SHVOKHNEV. I'd advise you not to lose a minute either. As soon as you receive the money, come and join us. With two hundred thousand, we can squeeze the town dry.... Oh, I forgot to tell Krugel something important. Wait here. Be back before you know it. (*Goes out in haste*.)

IKHAREV, *alone*. How things have turned out! The morning saw me with eighty thousand, and now I've over twice that much. For most people that represents a lifetime of work and constant effort, doing without, broken health. And here, in a few hours— in a few minutes!—I've become as rich as Croesus. Two hundred thousand! Where do you find two hundred thousand nowadays? What property or business brings in that kind of money? A fine one I'd be, stuck in the country, bothering with peasants, making my three thousand a year. Yes, there's something to education! That backcountry muck doesn't wash off easily. Give me the company of well-bred people! And now that I've struck it rich, my time is my own. I can try improving my mind. If the mood hits me to visit Petersburg—then Petersburg it is. Ah, the theaters, the Summer Gardens, the palace! Or Moscow and its classy restaurants. Dressed fashionably, I can be anybody's equal. A man of culture! And what opened the doors for me? To what do I owe everything? Fraud, they call it. Ridiculous! That's not it at all. Any fool can become a crook in no time, but my line of work demands practice, study. Well, suppose it is fraud. But how can you get along without it? In a sense it's merely a precaution. If I didn't cheat them, they'd cheat me. Just now Uteshitelny and his pals thought they'd pull the wool over my eyes, but they saw who they were dealing with. Yes, cunning is a great asset. In our world, it's what really counts. I have my own way of looking at life. It's no trick to live like a fool; but to live subtly, artfully, to deceive everybody and not be deceived yourself—now that's a goal worthy of a man.

GLOV, JR., *comes flying in.*

GLOV, JR. Where are they? I tried their room and no one's in.

IKHAREV. You just missed them. They stepped out for a moment.

GLOV, JR. What's that? They left? Did they take any money from you?

IKHAREV. Yes, we came to an arrangement. You're to deal with me now.

The waiter ALEXEY *enters.*

ALEXEY, *addressing* GLOV, JR. You asked about the gentlemen, sir?

GLOV, JR. Yes.

ALEXEY. They checked out.

GLOV, JR. Checked out?

ALEXEY. That's right, Your Honor. Their carriage was at the front door for the last half hour.

GLOV, JR., *wringing his hands.* We've been had!

IKHAREV. What are you blabbering about? I can't make sense of it. Uteshitelny is due back any minute. You're to pay the entire debt to me. It's in my hands now.

GLOV, JR. Oh, sure! You'll receive payment! Like hell! Can't you see, they've played you for a sucker?

IKHAREV. You're ranting. I can see you're still drunk.

GLOV, JR. It seems both of us are. Open your eyes! Do you think I'm Glov? I'm as much Glov as you're the emperor of China.

IKHAREV, *upset.* What are you driving at? It's crazy! What about your father. . . and . . .

GLOV, JR. The old man? First of all, he's not anybody's father, and if he were, he'd have the devil for a son. Second, his name's not Glov, but Krynítsyn, and it's not even Mikhal but Ivan. One of their gang.

IKHAREV. Listen, you! Be serious, this is no joking matter.

GLOV, JR. Some joke! I was one of them and they gulled me too. They promised me three thousand for my efforts.

IKHAREV, *stepping up to him, heatedly.* Don't play games with me! Do you take me for an idiot? What about the bank draft, the official. . . Krep Krepovich? Do you suppose I can't send for him?

GLOV, JR. He's not a bank official, but a retired army officer; and his name's not Krepovich, but Semyonovich; and it's not Krep but Flor.

IKHAREV, *desperate.* And who are you? The devil? Speak! Who are you?

GLOV, JR. Who am I? I was an honest man before they turned me into a scoundrel. They stripped the shirt from my back, skinned me alive. What was I to do? Starve? For three thousand I agreed to take up with them and hoodwink you. There! I've been quite candid. You can see I'm a gentleman.

IKHAREV, *in a fury, seizes him by the collar.* Gentleman! Why you son-of-a-bitch!

ALEXEY, *aside.* Well, it's coming to blows. Time for me to clear out. (*Goes out.*)

IKHAREV, *dragging* GLOV, JR. Come on! Come on!

GLOV, JR. Where to?

IKHAREV, *in a frenzy.* Where to? Where to? To the police! Where else?

GLOV, JR. But you have no case.

IKHAREV. What's that? No case? Robbing left and right, stealing in broad daylight, and you say I have no case? Using cheap tricks,

and I have no case? Tell it to me from your cell in Siberia. No
case! Just wait! They'll catch up with that thieving crew of yours!
I'll teach you to abuse the trust of decent honest people. Justice!
I demand justice! (*Drags* GLOV, JR. *along*.)

GLOV, JR. Call for justice when you're blameless. Remember, you
plotted with them to swindle me. The cards have your markings
on them. Oh, no, my friend! There's the rub. You don't even
have a right to complain!

IKHAREV, *beating his forehead in despair.* He's right, damn it!
(*Sinks to a chair, exhausted. Meanwhile* GLOV, JR., *escapes*.)
Only it's such a dirty trick!

GLOV, JR., *peeking in at the door.* Cheer up! You're not alone.
You've got Adelaide Ivanovna! (*Disappears*.)

IKHAREV, *furious.* To hell with Adelaide Ivanovna! (*Hurls the deck
of cards against the door. The cards fly to the floor.*) Scum like
that are a disgrace to mankind. It's enough to drive me out of my
mind—the way they played their parts! The cunning! Diabolical!
A father, a son, even a bank official! And every track covered! I
can't even complain! (*Leaps up from his chair and paces the
room in agitation.*) You spend your life scheming, using your
wits, refining all the tricks of the trade! Forget it! It's not worth
the effort. Some crook will turn up who's twice the crook you are.
At one stroke the bastard will bring down what you've spent
years building. (*Waves his arms in disgust.*) What a sham this
country is! The only ones to have any luck are brainless nitwits—
clods who don't think, don't act, and play gin rummy for
kopecks!

Appendix
Gogol on the Theater and His Own Plays

Comedy

An ancient rule: someone on the verge of reaching and taking hold of a desired object, when all of a sudden—interference and its removal to an enormous distance. As in...games of chance.

An abrupt and surprising discovery, suddenly giving everything a new twist or placing it in a new light.

Notebooks, 1832-33

Russian Theater in the 1830s

The ballet and the opera are the tsar and tsarina of the Petersburg theater. ... rapt audiences have forgotten the existence of stately tragedy involuntarily inspiring the responsive hearts of its silent auditors to exalted emotions; or of comedy—the true record of society, rigorously planned and producing laughter by the depth of its irony, not laughter born of frivolous impressions, superficial witticisms, puns; nor the laughter of the coarse crowd, which requires convulsions and grimacing caricatures of nature; but electric, life-giving laughter erupting spontaneously, freely, and unexpectedly from a soul struck by the dazzling brilliance of true wit, laughter springing from serene delight and produced only by a great mind. ... Melodramas and vaudevilles have made their appearance on our stage; these foreign guests, who were masters of the French theater, have played an extremely curious role in the Russian. We have long recognized the incongruity of Russian actors representing marquises, viscounts, and barons, just as Frenchmen, taking it into their heads to imitate Russian peasants, would in all likelihood be ridiculous; but what about balls, soirées, fashionable galas in Russian plays? And vaudevilles? It's some time now since vaudevilles have invaded the Russian stage, entertaining the average man who is so easily amused. Who could conceive that not only translated but even original vaudevilles would appear on the Russian stage? Russian vaudeville! The very words sound a bit strange, since this facile, insipid plaything could only originate among the French, a nation lacking a profound and fixed character. But when the still somewhat severe and ponderous Russian is forced to play the fop, I can't help imagining one of our corpulent, shrewd, and thick-bearded merchants, a man who has never worn anything but heavy jackboots, sticking one foot into a slender pump and gossamer stocking, leaving the other in his heavy boot, and dressed so, standing with his partner at the head of a French quadrille.

For five years now melodramas and vaudevilles have dominated the world's theaters. What a sham! Even the Germans—but who would have thought the Germans, a solid people, given to profound esthetic enjoyment, would now be writing and performing vaudevilles, reworking and slapping together overblown and cold melodramas! If only this craze had been a response to the powerful call of genius! When the entire world sang to Byron's lyre, we didn't find it comical; there was even something comforting about it. But the likes of Dumas and Ducange have become legislators to the world!—You have my word, the nineteenth century will come to feel shame for these five years.[1] O Molière, great Molière, you who developed your characters in such breadth and fullness and traced their every shadow with profundity. You, severe and circumspect Lessing. And you, noble, ardent Schiller, who revealed the dignity of man in poetic radiance! Behold what has become of our stage after your passing; look at the strange monstrosities that have infiltrated our theater in the guise of melodrama! Where then is our life? Where are our contemporary passions, our contemporary idiosyncrasies? If we might only see some reflection of our life in our melodramas! But our melodramas lie unconscionably.

It is an unfathomable phenomenon: only a profound and uncommon talent can take note of what surrounds us in our daily lives, what is inseparable from us, the common, while mediocrity clutches with both hands at the rare occurrence, the exceptional, the deformity that stops us short, disharmony in the midst of harmony. . . .

The strange has become the subject of contemporary drama. The whole trick is to narrate an incident indisputably current, indisputably strange, unprecedented and unparalleled: murders, fires, the wildest passions which have no place in contemporary society! It is as if the sons of torrid Africa had dressed themselves in our European frock coats. Hangmen, poisons—a constant straining for effect; not a single character inspires any sympathy whatesoever! No spectator ever leaves the theater touched, in tears; on the contrary, he clambers into his carriage hurriedly, in an anxious state, and is unable to collect his thoughts for a long time. And to think of our refined educated society at such spectacles! There automatically springs to mind those bloody arenas where all Rome assembled in the age of its great empire and criminal indulgence. But, thank God, we are not yet Romans; we are not in the sunset of our existence, but at its dawn! If all the melodramas of our times were collected in one spot, we might think it a museum of curios, where nature's monstrosities and blunders had been deliberately assembled, or better yet, a calendar in which the singular occurrences of the day had been recorded with documentary dispassionateness: today in such and such a place such and such a swindle was perpetrated; today some brigands and arsonists had their heads lopped off; on such and such a day some worker slit his wife's throat, etc. I can imagine the perplexity of our descendents, thinking to discover our society in our melodramas. . . .

The situation of the Russian actor is pitiful. All about him a young nation pulsates and seethes, and they give him characters he has never laid eyes upon. What can he do with these strange heroes, who are neither Frenchmen nor Germans, but bizarre people totally devoid of definite passions and distinct features? Where can he display his art? On what can he develop his talent? For heaven's sake, give us Russian characters, give us ourselves—our scoundrels, our eccentrics! On to the stage with them! Let everybody laugh! Laughter is a great thing: it doesn't deprive us of life or property, but in its presence the guilty individual is like a hare caught in a trap. We have become so accustomed to tame French plays that we are timid about seeing ourselves. . . .

What a pity. Truly, it is high time we learned that only a faithful rendering of characters, not in general stereotyped features, but in national forms so striking in their vitality that we are compelled to exclaim, ''Yes, that person seems familiar to me''—only such a rendering can be of genuine service. We have turned the theater into a plaything, something like a rattle used to entice children, forgetting that it is a rostrum from which a living lesson is spoken to an entire multitude, a place where, in the presence of festive brilliant lighting, thundering music and general laughter, secret vice shows its face and elevated emotions, timidly hidden from view, make themselves known before hushed murmurs of common sympathy.

From ''Petersburg Notes of 1836,'' published in 1837

But what is romanticism? It was constantly discussed as the first quarter of the century drew to a conclusion, and even turned into a genre of works, so that one play was called romantic; another, not romantic. Classicism was opposed to it. . . . But what was the thing they called romanticism? It was nothing other than an urge to come closer to our own society, from which we had been completely estranged by imitations of the societies and characters to be found in the works of the ancient writers. All the states of the ancient and modern world experienced the same urge. The transitional stage of this aspiration, its first explosions and ventures, are made by desperately audacious people of the sort who create rebellions in society. They perceive inappropriate forms, rules that do not correspond to their manners and customs, and they force their way through the breach. They see no limits, continually smash everything without reasoning, and wishing to correct injustice, they inflict as much harm as good. . . . But they have nurtured a chaos from which a great creator, serenely and deliberately, creates a new edifice, his wise double vision embracing the outworn and the novel. . . .

The public and the writers were right in being dissatisfied with previous plays. These plays were indeed pale. Even Molière, a true talent, who, were he to appear today, would drive from the boards our rambling, unruly contemporary drama—even Molière is now long-winded and boring on the stage. His plots are skillfully devised, but according to antiquated rules, to the same unchanging pattern; the action is too decorous; it has been composed independently of the age and the times, and yet many of his characters really belonged to his age. There is not one contemporary story in the exact form in which it occurred, as we find in Shakespeare. On the contrary, he put together his plots according to the schemes of Terence, and had them performed by characters possessing the peculiarities and eccentricities of his age. Later, audiences found this lacked animation; it could only please friends who were able to notice all the small points. . . .

Contemporary drama has attempted to draw its laws of action from our own society. One must be a great talent to notice the common elements of our society, its motivating forces.

From "The Petersburg Stage of 1835-36," written in 1836, published posthumously

Truth and Fury

The idea of a comedy has possessed me. . . . Just the other day its subject began to take shape; I had already jotted down the title in a blank thick notebook, *The Vladimir Order, Third Class,* and what fury, laughter, pungency! But I stopped short, realizing my pen had touched upon things the censor wouldn't dream of passing. What is a play that won't be performed? Drama lives only on the stage. An unperformed play is like a soul without a body. Would any craftsman exhibit an incomplete work? All I can do now is to concoct a subject so innocuous that it couldn't offend even a policeman. But what is comedy without truth and fury! So I can't attempt a comedy. But if I pick up my historical studies—before my eyes the stage comes alive, applause reverberates, faces jut from boxes and galleries, grins appear in the orchestra—and to hell with history.

From a letter to M. P. Pogodin, February 20, 1833

The Government Inspector

Do me a favor; send me some subject, comical or not, but an authentically Russian anecdote. My hand is itching to write a comedy. . . . Give me a subject and I'll knock off a comedy in five acts—I promise, funnier than hell. For God's sake, do it. My mind and stomach are both famished.

From a letter to Pushkin, October 7, 1835

Above all, beware of falling into caricature. Nothing ought to be exaggerated or hackneyed, not even the minor roles. On the contrary, the actor must make a special effort to be more modest, unpretentious, and dignified than the character he is playing. The less the actor thinks about being funny or making the audience laugh, the more the comic elements of his part will come through. The ridiculous will emerge spontaneously through the very seriousness with which each character is occupied with his own affairs. They are all caught up in their own interests, bustling and fussing, even fervent, as if faced with the most important task of their lives. Only the audience, from its detached position, can perceive the vanity of their concerns. But they themselves do not joke at all and have no inkling that anybody is laughing at them. The intelligent actor, before seizing upon the petty oddities and superficial peculiarities of his part, must strive to capture those aspects that are *common to all mankind.* He ought to consider the purpose of his role, the major and predominant concern of each character, what it is that consumes his life and constitutes the perpetual object of his thoughts, his *idée fixe.* Having grasped this major concern, the actor must assimilate it so thoroughly that the thoughts and yearnings of his character seem to be his own and remain constantly in his mind over the course of the performance. He shouldn't worry much about individual scenes or small details. They will come by themselves, successfully and deftly, if only he does not relinquish this *idée fixe* for an instant. Such details and petty accessories can be exploited even by an actor capable of mimicking and catching the walk and movements of a character without creating a role in its entirety; they are no more than colors to be laid on when the design has been composed and drawn faithfully. They are the trappings of a part— not its soul. So, one should first grasp the soul of a part, and not its dress.

The mayor is one of the principal parts. He is a man primarily concerned with not letting a good thing slip through his fingers. Because of this preoccupation, he has never had time to view life rigorously or to examine himself closely. Because of it he has become a tyrant without knowing it, for he has no malicious desire to tyrranize; all he wants is to rake in whatever he lays his eyes on.

He has simply lost sight of the fact that this creates a back-breaking burden for others. He abruptly pardons the merchants, who are scheming to ruin him, when they make a tempting offer, because the temptation of creature comforts has possessed him, coarsening him and dulling his sensitivity to the plight and suffering of others. He senses that he is a sinner, attends church, believes that his faith is firm, and is even planning to repent some day. But the temptation of easy gain is great, and creature comforts are enticing, and to grab everything, not letting anything slip through his fingers, has become a mere habit. He is thunderstruck by the galloping rumor about a government inspector, even more so by the fact that this inspector is travelling *incognito* and that there is no knowing where or when he will show up. From beginning to end he finds himself in a more heightened emotional state than he has ever experienced. His nerves are taut. Shifting from terror to hope and joy excites his senses, and he becomes more susceptible to deception. Though he is a man not easily fooled at other times, it is now possible to do so. Noting that the government inspector is in his clutches, is no longer terrifying, and is even about to become a member of the family, he abandons himself uncontrollably to his delight in the thought of a life spent carousing, drinking with his cronies, handing out jobs, demanding horses at relay stations and forcing mayors to wait, putting on airs and throwing his weight around. That is why the sudden announcement of the arrival of the genuine government inspector is a more earthshaking blow for him than for any of the others, and why his situation becomes truly tragic.

The judge is less guilty of bribe-taking; he is not even particularly interested in wrongdoing; but his passion for hunting with dogs (What can be done? Everyone has some passion) has led him into a multitude of wrongdoings, without even being aware of it. He is self-centered, vain about his intellect, and an atheist only because it gives him scope to show off. Every occurrence, even one that strikes terror in others, is a find for him, since it nourishes his conjectures and observations—he is as content with these as an artist with his work. This self-satisfaction should be conveyed by the actor's mien. While talking, he remarks what effect his words produce on others. He is on the lookout for fine-sounding expressions.

Zemlyanika is physically gross, but a subtle crook—despite his immense girth. There is much that is shifty and fawning in his behavior. In response to Khlestakov's question as to the name of the fish they have eaten, he dashes right up to him with all the nimbleness of a twenty-two-year-old dandy: "Labardan, sir."[2] He belongs to that class of people who, to extricate themselves from trouble, can find no other means except to drown everybody else. He is quick to engage in chicanery and to inform on others, making no exception for friends or relatives, but thinking only about saving his own neck. Despite his clumsiness and obesity, he is always quick on his toes. The intelligent actor will not miss those opportunities where the toadying of a fat man will be particularly funny, though he must avoid any attempt to turn it into caricature.

The superintendent of schools is simply a man frightened out of his wits by frequent inspections and reprimands—for God knows what—and hence deathly afraid of any visit. He quivers like a leaf at the news of the government inspector, although he has no idea how he is at fault. The role presents no difficulties for the actor; all he has to do is to convey perpetual terror.

The postmaster is ingenuous to the point of naïveté. He looks at life as an assembly of interesting anecdotes for whiling away the time, which he reads in letters he unseals. The actor merely has to show him to be as simpleminded as is possible.

However, the two town gossips, Bobchinsky and Dobchinsky, require particularly fine performances. The actor must define them very carefully. These are people whose entire lives consist in racing about town to pay their respects and exchange the latest news. Paying visits absorbs them completely. A passion for telling tales has consumed every other interest and become the motivating passion and endeavor of their lives. In a word, these are men cast aside by fate to live for the needs of others, not their own. Their delight in finally being allowed to relate a morsel of news should be made palpable. Their scurrying and fussiness is solely out of anxiety lest someone interrupt and prevent them from talking. Their curiosity—out of a desire to have something to talk about. As a result, Bobchinsky even stammers a bit. They are both short, squat, have little potbellies, and resemble one another in the extreme. Both are round-faced, neatly dressed, with sleeked hair. Dobchinsky is even blessed with a small bald spot in the middle of his head—it is evident that he is not a bachelor like Bobchinsky, but married. But for all that, Bobchinsky gains the upper hand over him by reason of his greater liveliness; to some extent he even sways his opinions. In a word, the actor must ache with curiosity and be afflicted with a wagging tongue if he wants to play these roles well. He must forget that the character is, as it turns out, a total nonentity, and put aside all its petty features; otherwise he is certain to fall into caricature.

All the other characters—the storekeepers, wedding guests, police, various petitioners—pass before our eyes daily and hence can be easily caught by anyone capable of noticing the peculiarities of speech and manners of people of diverse classes. The same may be said of the servant [Osip], though this role is more significant than the others. The Russian servant getting on in years, who never looks you in the eye, is rude to his master, having sized him up as a bluffer and good-for-nothing, who is fond of lecturing his master under his breath, and is a sly scoundrel, though quite skilled at seizing passing opportunities to fill his pockets— the type is known to one and all. For this reason the role has always been performed well.

Everyone without exception can sense the extent of the impact the arrival of the government inspector can produce on each of these characters.

Only one must not lose sight of the fact that they cannot get the government inspector off their minds. They are all preoccupied with him. Their fears and hopes whirl about him. For some he represents hope of deliverance from the unscrupulous bribe-taking of the mayor and other assorted grafters. Others are panicked at the sight of the top officials and the town's elite gripped by terror. Those who regard the affairs of the world serenely, while picking their noses, feel curiosity, not without an admixture of secret fear, at finally seeing the person who has aroused so much anxiety and hence must inevitably be an extraordinary and extremely important individual.

The most difficult role is that of the man who is taken by the frightened town as the government inspector. Khlestakov himself is a person of no consequence. Even shallow people have labelled him as the most shallow of men. In all his life he has never done anything capable of attracting attention. But the force of general terror has made him into a remarkable comic character. Terror, in clouding everyone's eyes, gives him an arena for his comic role. Snubbed and rebuffed in everything, even in playing the swaggering dandy on the Nevsky Boulevard, he now senses that he has free scope and, to his own astonishment, he lets himself go. Everything about him is surprising, unexpected. For a considerable length of time he cannot even surmise why people are showing him such attention and deference. He merely feels pleased and delighted in seeing that they listen to him, oblige him, cater to his every whim, hang avidly on his every word. He runs off at the mouth, without having any notion at the beginning of a dialogue where it will lead. His interlocutors feed him topics for conversation. It is as if they put the words into his mouth and create the conversation. He merely feels he can cut a fine figure anywhere, provided nothing impedes. He imagines that he is cock of the walk in literature, second to none in the ballroom, that he himself throws lavish parties, and finally that he is an important dignitary. He has no compunctions whatsoever about lying. The lunch, with its various delicacies and wines, has given his tongue a vivid loquacity and eloquence. The further he gets, the more feeling enters his speech. Hence he expresses himself at times almost fervently. Having no intention to deceive, he himself forgets he is lying. By now it seems to him that he has really done all these things. For precisely this reason the scene in which he speaks of himself as an important dignitary is able to confound the town's officials. Especially when he tells of giving a dressing-down to everyone in Petersburg—at that moment his mien becomes pompous, taking on all the attributes appropriate to his position. Having been called on the carpet more than once himself, he ought to play the role masterfully; he experiences special pleasure at finally being in the position to bawl out others, even if it is only a tall tale. He might have even gone further, but his tongue wasn't up to it; consequently the town's officials were compelled to lead him off to his lodgings, respectfully and in terror. Upon awakening he is the same old Khlestakov. He cannot even recall what it was that frightened everybody. He is still uncomprehending and behaves stupidly. He falls for the mother and daughter almost simultaneously. He asks for money because the words escape his lips involuntarily, and also because he asked his first visitor, who readily offered it. Only toward the end of the act does he surmise that he has been taken for someone of higher position. But if not for Osip, who somehow manages to make him see that such a fraud cannot last long, he would have waited imperturbably until he was kicked out the door in disgrace. Although he is a phantasmagorical character, a character who, as the incarnation of lying and deception, flies off in his troika, God knows where, nonetheless the part must be assigned to the best actor available, since it is the most difficult. This shallow and worthless person has an assortment of traits found in worthy people. Above all, the actor must keep in mind that the desire to posture, which infects all people and is reflected by Khlestakov to an extreme, is a childish desire. Nevertheless, many intelligent and elderly people possess it, so that rarely in life does one fail to come across it. In a word, the actor playing this role must have an extremely multifaceted talent, capable of expressing the diverse characteristics of a person and not merely the same unchanging traits. He must put himself in the shoes of a very nimble man-about-town; otherwise he will be unable to convey, simply and naturally, that empty modish flightiness which carries a man, head in the clouds, in all directions, and which has been allotted to Khlestakov in such considerable quantities.

The final scene of *The Government Inspector* must be performed with particular intelligence. Now the joking is over, and the plight of many of the characters is almost tragic. That of the mayor is the most striking of all. Whatever the circumstances, seeing oneself all of a sudden so rudely hoodwinked, and by a featherbrained, insignificant whippersnapper, who did not pull it off by dint of his appearance and stature, since he resembles a matchstick (Khlestakov, it will be remembered, is skinny, all the others fat)—to be tricked by such a person is no laughing matter. Especially not for a man who knew how to dupe clever people and even the most experienced crooks. The announcement of the arrival of the genuine government inspector hits him like a thunderclap. He is petrified. Arms outstretched, head thrown back, he stands stock-still, while the entire group instantaneously forms around him, frozen into varied attitudes.

The whole scene is wordless, and hence must be composed like *tableaux vivants*. Every character should be assigned a pose conforming to his character, the extent of his fear, and the shock the words heralding the arrival of the genuine government inspector must have produced. These poses must not at all coincide, but should be varied and diverse; therefore, everyone should recall his own pose and be ready to assume it the moment the fateful news strikes his ears. At first it will appear forced, the characters will resemble automotons; but after a few rehearsals, as the actor penetrates deeper into his situation, he will assimilate the pose, and it will become natural and part of him. The woodenness and awkwardness of automotons will vanish, and it will seem as if the dumb scene appeared spontaneously.

The gasp that women emit at some surprise may serve as a signal for the change in positions. Some arrive at their assigned positions gradually, starting to shift at the appearance of the messenger with the fateful news; these are less astounded. Others bolt abruptly; they are thunderstruck. It would not be a bad idea for the head actor to leave his position momentarily and check the scene several times from the point of view of the audience, so as to note what has to be relaxed, strengthened, softened, to make the scene more natural.

... For the group to cohere deftly and easily, it would be best to commission an artist capable of composing groups to prepare a sketch, and then keep to it. If each actor has entered, even to some extent, all the circumstances of his role over the course of the play, then he will also convey its striking situation in the dumb scene, thereby crowning the perfection of his performance. If he was cold and tight during the performance, he will remain cold and tight here too, with the difference that in the dumb scene his lack of artistry will be more apparent.

"Advice to Those Who Would Play The Government Inspector *as It Ought To Be Played," written c. 1846, published posthumously*

There remains the most difficult role in the play—that of Khlestakov. I don't know whether you'll be choosing the actor. God spare us if they play him with the farcical mannerisms commonly used for braggarts and theatrical rogues! Khlestakov is just stupid. He runs off at the mouth only because he sees others are willing to listen, tells tall tales because he has had a hearty lunch and drunk his fill of wine, minces solely when approaching the ladies. Pay special attention to the scene in which he lies through his teeth. His every word (that is, phrase or speech) is a totally unexpected improvisation and should be spoken staccato. Keep in mind that toward the end of the scene he gradually gets carried away. But don't have him bouncing about on his chair; he should merely turn red as a beet and hold forth in an even more astounding manner—the more he says, the louder he gets. I am extremely apprehensive about this role. . . .

... One more thing: don't dress Bobchinsky and Dobchinsky as they appeared in the sketches. . . . The one with the light hair should wear a dark coat, and the one with dark hair (that is, Bobchinsky), a light coat. Dark trousers on both. In general, don't force it. But they absolutely must have potbellies, protruding sharply, as on pregnant women.

From a letter to M. S. Shchepkin, May 10, 1836

Don't neglect to prepare the actors by playing Khlestakov for them, a part which no one but you can perform. By doing so you can give them a model once and for all. None of them are capable of grasping the idea that he absolutely must be played as a man-about-town, *comme il faut,* without any desire whatsoever to act the liar or the literary hack, but, on the contrary, with an innocent wish to play a role one rank above his own, but in such a way that in the end the liar, the scum, the coward, the complete literary hack show themselves spontaneously. You can impress this upon them only through your performance; words and instructions will have no effect, no matter how convincingly you speak. Second-rate actors, as you well know, are capable of mimicking but cannot create a character.

From a letter to I. I. Sosnitsky, November 2, 1846 (New Style)

[Gogol told me that] in Khlestakov he wished to portray a man who tells cock-and-bull stories enthusiastically, with gusto, who is unaware how the words spring to his lips, who, at the moment he's lying, has absolutely no idea that he is doing so. He merely relates his perpetual fantasies, what he would like to achieve, as if these fantasies of his imagination had already become reality. But sometimes in a burst of jabber he loses the thread of his conversation, [and] reality merges with dream.... "Khlestakov is a lively fellow," Gogol said; "he should do everything fast, animatedly, without reasoning, almost unconsciously, not reflecting for a moment what will come of his actions, how they will conclude, how his words and actions will be received by others."

From the reminiscences of Lev Arnoldi [3]

Also, don't forget: the mayor expresses himself somewhat ironically even at moments of annoyance; for example, at the words "So far they've been snooping around other towns. Now it's our turn." In the second act, in conversation with Khlestakov, his face ought to be much livelier. Here you have completely varied expressions of sarcasm.

From a letter to M. S. Shchepkin, c. July 10, 1847 (New Style)

Pay particular attention to the final scene. It must by all means be vivid and even astounding. The mayor should be completely nonplussed and not at all comical. His wife and daughter, in absolute fright, should direct their gaze at him alone. The superintendent of schools' knees should shake violently; Zemlyanika's likewise. The judge, as you know, squats. The postmaster, as you also know, stands like a question mark addressed to the audience. Bobchinsky and Dobchinsky look to each other for an explanation of what's going on. Malicious smiles on the female guests, except for Lukanchik's wife, who should be terror incarnate, pale as death, her mouth gaping. This dumb scene absolutely must continue for a minute or two, so that Korobkin, grown bored, might have time to offer Rastakovsky some tobacco, and one of the guests even to sneeze rather loudly into his handkerchief.

From a letter to M. S. Shchepkin, October 24, 1846 (New Style)

The Government Inspector must be performed properly (at least to some degree in compliance with its author's intentions), and that requires time. It is essential that you replay each role, if only in your mind; that you feel the unity of the play and read it through to the actors several times, so that they might involuntarily assimilate the true meaning of every phrase, which, as you know, can suddenly change because of a single shift in emphasis. . . . introduce . . . the actors to the proper essence of their roles, to a dignified and correct measure in their speech—do you understand?— a false note must not be heard. Don't let anyone set off his role and lay on colors, but have them heed its universal accents and maintain human dignity in their speech. In a word, root out caricature entirely and lead them to understand that an actor must not *present* but *transmit*. He must, first of all, transmit ideas, forgetting about the person's oddities and peculiarities. It is easy to lay on colors; one may add them to the part afterwards; for that sort of thing, all you have to do is take the first eccentric to come along and be able to mimic him; but to sense the essential matter for which the character has been invoked is difficult.

From a letter to M. S. Shchepkin, December 16, 1846 (New Style)

The reaction to [*The Government Inspector*] has been extensive and tumultuous. Everybody is against me. Respected officials, middle-aged men, scream that I hold nothing sacred in having had the effrontery to speak of officialdom as I did. The police are against me, the merchants are against me, the literati are against me. They rail at me and run off to the play; it's impossible to get tickets for the fourth performance. If not for the intervention of the emperor, my play would never have remained on the stage, and yet there were people seeking to have it banned. Now I see what it means to be a writer of comedies. The faintest glimmer of truth—and entire classes are up in arms against you.

From a letter to M. S. Shchepkin, April 29, 1836

The pitiful situation of the writer in our country is a melancholy sight. Everyone is against him, and there is no counterbalance whatsoever. "He's an incendiary! A rebel!" And who is saying this? Government officials, experienced people who ought to have enough intelligence to see things in their true light, people who are considered to be educated and whom society, or at least Russian society, calls educated. Crooks appeared on the stage and everyone is indignant: why do you show us crooks? I can understand that the crooks are angry, but why those whom I never regarded as such? This uncultured petulance is very distressing to me; it is a sign of the profound, tenacious ignorance widespread in all classes of our society. The capital's sensitivities have been offended by the manners of six provincial officials, but what would the capital say had its own manners been depicted, even gingerly?.... Whatever enlightened people would greet with loud laughter and sympathy provokes the acrimony of the ignorant, and this ignorance is widespread. Call a crook a crook, and they consider it an undermining of the state apparatus; show a true and living feature, and they translate it to read as a defamation of an entire class and an incitement of other or subordinate classes against it. Consider the plight of the poor author who nevertheless loves his country and his countrymen intensely.

From a letter to M. P. Pogodin, May 15, 1836

The Government Inspector has been performed—and I have such a troubled and strange feeling.... My creation struck me as repellent, bizarre, and not at all mine. The major role was a failure.... Khlestakov ...turned into someone from the ranks of those vaudeville rogues, who have come to us from the theaters of Paris to flit about our stages. He became the conventional bluffer—an insipid figure who has appeared in the same guise over the course of two centuries. Doesn't Khlestakov's part really speak for itself? Khlestakov doesn't at all bluff; he isn't a liar by vocation; he forgets he is lying and almost believes what he says. He has become expansive, is in good spirits, sees that all is going well, people are listening to him—and as a result his speech becomes more fluent, and free and easy. He is sincere, completely frank, and in telling lies he shows the stuff he is made of. As a rule our actors are incapable of lying. They imagine that lying is simply chattering away. To lie, one must speak in a tone so close to the truth, so natural, so naïve as only truth can be spoken— the comedy of lying consists precisely in this. I am almost certain that Khlestakov would have fared better had I assigned the part to the most untalented of actors, telling him only that Khlestakov is a sharp fellow, very *comme il faut*, clever, and perhaps even virtuous, and that he ought to play him as such. Khlestakov doesn't lie with calculation or like a theatrical braggart; he lies with feeling; his eyes convey the pleasure it gives him. It is the finest and most poetic moment of his life—almost a kind of inspiration.... Of course it is incomparably easier to caricature elderly officials in their threadbare uniforms and frayed collars; but to capture those traits that are fairly agreeable and do not markedly differ from what may be found in conventional society is a task for a powerful master. Nothing about Khlestakov should be put in sharp relief. He belongs to a social circle which, apparently, is in no way distinguishable from those of other young people. At times he even conducts himself properly, speaks weightily, and only on occasions requiring presence of mind or character does his somewhat vulgar and paltry nature reveal itself. The mayor's character is more fixed and clear. His immutable, hardened exterior designates him distinctly, and partially attests his character. Khlestakov's character is extremely fluid, more subtle, and hence more difficult to grasp. Actually, who is Khlestakov? A young man, a civil servant, and what we call an empty fellow, but one who possesses many traits belonging to people the world does not call empty.... In a word, he should typify many things that are scattered in various Russian characters, but which have accidentally combined in one, as frequently occurs even in nature. Everyone, if only for a minute, or even several minutes, has been or is a Khlestakov, though, of course, he doesn't care to admit it....

... In general the public was satisfied. Half the audience even received the play sympathetically, while the other half, as usual, railed against it— for reasons having nothing to do with art....

All in all, it seems to have been the mayor who completely won over the audience. I was confident of it even beforehand.... I also counted on the servant [Osip], because I had noticed the actor's great attentiveness to the words and how observant he was. On the other hand, our friends Bobchinsky and Dobchinsky came off worse than one might have expected. Although I anticipated it..., I nevertheless thought their appearance and the situation in which they find themselves would somehow save them from caricature. The opposite occurred—namely, caricature. Even before the performance, seeing their costumes, I gasped. These two chubby little fellows, essentially quite tidy, their hair decorously sleeked, found themselves in high, ungainly wigs, disheveled, untidy, rumpled, wearing enormous elongated dickies. And on the stage they were so affected that it was simply unbearable. In general, for most of the play the costumes were very bad and unconscionably caricatured....

One word about the final scene. It did not at all come across. The curtain fell at a confused moment and the play seemed unfinished. But I'm not to blame. They didn't want to listen to me. I'll say it again: the final scene will not meet with success until they grasp that it is a dumb scene, that a single frozen group is to be represented, that the drama has been concluded and replaced by mute mimicry, that the curtain must not drop for two to three minutes, and that all this is to be accomplished in the manner of so-called *tableaux vivants*. But their answer was that this would restrict the actor; the company would have to be entrusted to a ballet master; it is even somewhat humiliating for the actor, etc., etc., etc. I caught sight of numerous other *etceteras* on their faces even more vexing than the verbal ones. Despite all these etceteras, I stand my ground and say a hundred times: No. It won't restrict the actor in the slightest, it's not humiliating. . . . Limits do not stop true talent, just as granite banks do not hold back a river; on the contrary, when flowing between them, the waves move more rapidly and with greater fullness. And in his assigned pose the sensitive actor can express himself more fully. No one has placed fetters on his countenance; only the grouping has been arranged. His mien is free to express any emotion. This mute condition holds the possibility of infinite variety. The fright of each of the characters is dissimilar, as are their characters and the degree of their fear and terror, which are a consequence of the magnitude of their individual offenses. The mayor is struck dumb one way, his wife and daughter another. The judge takes fright in his unique way, as do the director of charities, the postmaster, etc., etc.... Only the guests may come to a dead stop in an identical manner, but they form the background of a picture which is outlined by one stroke of the brush, and overlaid with a single color.

"Fragment of a Letter to a Man of Letters, Written by the Author Shortly after the First Performance of The Government Inspector,*" May 25, 1836*[4]

AUTHOR OF THE PLAY [*The Government Inspector*]. . . . I would like to be transported suddenly to the boxes, galleries, orchestra, to be everywhere. Then I might hear all their views and impressions while they are still fresh and innocent, while they have not yet been submitted to the opinions and judgments of experts and journalists, while each individual is still under the influence of his personal judgment. I need to know these things because I'm a writer of comedies. All other works and genres are subject to the judgment of the few; only the writer of comedies is subject to the judgment of all. Everybody has a claim to him; all men, whatever their positions, are his judges. . . . I'll remain here in the lobby, where I'm sure to hear interpretations of the new play. A man under the influence of his first impression is always animated and quick to share it with others.

. . . .

Two Lovers of Art

THE FIRST. I'm not at all one of those whose sole recourse is to the words *filthy, disgusting, bad form,* and so on. . . . I'm merely saying that the play has no plot.

THE SECOND. Yes, if you take plot in the usual sense of a love intrigue, then there actually isn't any. But it's time we stopped relying on that timeworn plot. It's worth our while to look more attentively about us. The world changed some time ago. Today the urge to obtain a profitable position, to dazzle and outshine others at all costs, to take revenge for slights and ridicule give the drama greater coherence. Don't rank, capital, an advantageous marriage possess more electricity than love in our times?

FIRST. That's all very well, but even in this respect I fail to see a plot in the play.

SECOND. I won't affirm or deny the existence of a plot. All I'll say is that, as a rule, people look for a plot centered on private life and prefer not to see the general. Simplemindedly, they have become accustomed to these incessant lovers and their marriages, without which no play can conceivably end. Of course, you have a plot here, but of what sort—something resembling a precise little knot at the corner of a handkerchief. No, comedy should cohere spontaneously, in all its mass, into one great, inclusive knot. The plot should embrace all the characters, not one or two—and touch upon the things that stir all of them, to whatever degree. In this conception, everyone is a hero; the flow and progress of the play transmit vibrations to the entire mechanism—not a single wheel should remain idle and rusty.

FIRST. But they all can't be heroes; one or two ought to govern the others?

SECOND. Not at all, though perhaps, predominate. In a machine also some wheels are more obvious and move with greater force—we may call them the most important. But it is an idea, a thought that governs a play. Without it, a play has no unity. And anything can tie things together: horror, terrified anticipation, the threat of law looming on the horizon.

FIRST. But you're attaching a universal significance to comedy.

SECOND. Isn't that its true significance? In its very beginnings comedy was a social and national creation. At least its father, Aristophanes, showed it to be such. Later it fell into the narrow rut of plots concerned with private life, introduced love stories, and the same indispensable plot. And how feeble a plot it is in the work of the best writers of comedy, how contemptible are these theatrical lovers with their cardboard amours!

A THIRD, *approaching*.... You're wrong; love has a place in comedy, just like other emotions.

SECOND. I don't deny it. But love and all other elevated emotions make a great impression only when realized in all their profundity. If you concentrate upon them, you must inevitably sacrifice everything else. All that constitutes the comic aspect will grow weak, and the social significance of comedy is bound to be lost.

THIRD. In that case, must the subject of comedy necessarily be base? If that's true, comedy would turn into a low genre.

SECOND. It is—for those who attend to the words but fail to penetrate to the meaning. But aren't the positive and negative capable of serving the same end? Cannot comedy and tragedy express the same lofty idea? Doesn't the thoroughly contorted soul of a base and dishonest man potentially convey an image of an honest man? Doesn't that aggregation of moral turpitude, of deviations from justice and law enable us to perceive clearly the demands of justice, duty, and law? In the hands of the skilled physician, cold and hot water cure the same illnesses with equal success. In the hands of the gifted, everything can serve as an instrument of the beautiful, provided it is guided by the great idea of serving the beautiful.

A FOURTH, *approaching*. What can serve the beautiful? And what are you discussing?

FIRST. Comedy. We've been talking about it in general terms, but no one has yet said anything about the new comedy. What do you think?

FOURTH. Here's what I think: it evinces talent, accurate observations of life, much that is funny, true, and taken from nature. But all in all the play lacks something. You can't make out a plot or a denouement. It's odd that our writers of comedy can't get by without the government. Without it, not one of our comedies would have a denouement.

THIRD. That's true. But on the other hand, it's quite natural. We all belong to the government. Most of us are in the government service; the interests of each of us are, more or less, linked to the government. It's no wonder that this is reflected in the works of our writers.

FOURTH. Correct. By all means, let us hear about this link. Only I find it ludicrous that no play can end without the intervention of the government. It's bound to make an appearance, just like inevitable fate in ancient tragedies.

SECOND. Well, by now this is something involuntary for our writers of comedy. It has come to constitute a distinguishing feature of our comedy. Our hearts contain a hidden trust in the government. What of it? There's nothing wrong in that. May God help the government heed its calling at all times and in all places—and act as the representative of Providence on earth. May we trust in it as the ancients trusted in a fate that overtakes crimes.

A FIFTH. Good evening, gentlemen! All I hear is the word *government*. The comedy has raised a hue and cry . . .

SECOND. We'd better speak about this hue and cry at my place, and not here, in the lobby of a theater.

. . . .

Two members of the audience come out.

THE FIRST. Explain this to me: Why is it that each action and character, taken separately, is true, alive, lifted from nature, while all in all it seems monstrous, exaggerated, caricatured, so that leaving the theater you involuntarily ask yourself, "Do such people really exist?" And yet it's not that they're villains.

THE SECOND. Not at all. They are precisely what the saying describes: "Not bad at heart, merely a swindler."

FIRST. And one more thing: the way the author piles it on, the excess— aren't they a fault in the comedy? Where do you find a society consisting of such people, a society lacking, if not a fair share, at least some portion of decent people? If comedy is to be a portrait and mirror of our social life, then it must reflect it with complete faithfulness.

SECOND. In my opinion, this comedy is not a portrait at all. . . . As you can see, the scene and place of action are ideal. . . . What we have here is a place of assembly. From all over, from the four corners of Russia, what has been excluded from the truth, moral failings and abuses, have flocked together to serve a single idea: to produce in the audience an intense, noble disdain for whatever is ignoble. The fact that not one of the characters has lost his human image makes the impact that much stronger. The human spirit can be sensed everywhere. For this reason the viewer shudders in the depths of his being. While laughing, he involuntarily draws back, as if sensing the object of his laughter standing nearby, and knowing that he must be constantly on guard lest it burst into his soul. I find it most amusing to hear the author reproached because his heroes and characters aren't attractive, when he employed all his powers to make them repellent. Had even one honest character been put into the comedy and made fully appealing, everyone would have favored him and completely forgotten those who had been so terrifying. Upon the completion of the performance, the latter images would not incessantly haunt the imagination; the audience would not carry away a melancholy impression nor ask, "Do such people really exist?"

. . . .

AUTHOR OF THE PLAY, *stepping out.* I heard more than I had anticipated. What a variety of opinion! Fortunate is the writer of comedies born into a nation where society hasn't yet been moulded into a single inert mass, where it hasn't become enveloped in the crust of ancient prejudice, conforming everyone's thoughts to the same mold, and where each person has his own viewpoint and is the creator of his own character. What a diversity of viewpoints, and how the firm, clear Russian intelligence sparkled throughout!. . . But why then is my heart so heavy? It is a strange thing: I regret that no one noticed the honorable character who is present in my play. Yes, there is an honorable, noble character acting over its course. This honorable, noble character is—*laughter.* He is noble because he dared to make an appearance despite the slight importance the world attaches to him. He is noble because he dared to appear despite the offensive appellation of cold egoist he brought upon the writer of comedies, and despite provoking doubts as to the existence of tender emotions in his soul. No one stood up for laughter. As a writer of comedies, I have served it honestly and therefore must be its defender. Yes, laughter is more significant and profound than men imagine. Not the laughter engendered by temporary agitation, by a bilious, sickly disposition. Not superficial laughter serving as idle diversion and amusement. But the kind of laughter that soars from man's bright nature, from the depths that contain its eternally surging spring. The kind of laughter that brings out the profundity of its subject, makes vivid what would otherwise go unnoticed, and without whose penetrating power the trivia and emptiness of life would not terrify man so. All that is contemptible and worthless, that man passes with indifference in his daily life, would not be magnified before his eyes to such a terrible, almost grotesque power, and he would not cry out, shuddering, "Can there really be such people?" when his consciousness informs him there are worse. Unjust are those who say laughter is disturbing. Only what is somber disturbs, and laughter is luminous. Many things shown in their nakedness would rouse a man to indignation, but when illuminated by the power of laughter, they bring reconciliation to his soul. He who would avenge himself upon a wicked man is brought to the verge of making peace in seeing his enemy's base impulses turned to ridicule. Unjust are those who say laughter has no effect upon its targets, that a scoundrel is the first to laugh at a scoundrel depicted on the stage—the scoundrel's progeny will laugh, but the contemporary scoundrel cannot! He senses that everyone has been left with an indelible image, that one wrong move on his part is enough to make this image his eternal designation. And even he who fears nothing in the world, is afraid of ridicule. No, only a profoundly magnanimous soul can burst into good-natured, bright laughter. But the world does not heed the mighty power of such laughter. "The comical is base," it says; only what is enunciated in a severe, strained voice is favored with the title "sublime." But my God! How many people pass us daily for whom nothing on earth is sublime. All the products of inspiration are trifles and bagatelles for them. . . . My soul could not remain indifferent when the most perfect creations were abused with the epithets "trifle" and "bagatelle," when all the luminaries of this world were said to be no more than creators of bagatelles and trifles! It pained me seeing how many, in the very midst of life, are dead, mute, terrible in the still coldness of their souls and the barren deserts of their hearts. It pained me when not even a shadow of expression quivered on their faces from what has plunged the profoundly loving soul into divine tears, that they did not become tongue-tied in pronouncing their eternal, "Bagatelles!". . .Bagatelles! Balconies and railings of theaters tremble; from floor to ceiling everything quakes, transformed into a single emotion, a single instant, a single human being. All men are come together, like brothers, in a single spiritual motion, and a hymn of gratitude rings out in a burst of applause. . . . And lo! Into this astounded multitude there came one weighed down by the sorrow and unbearable oppressiveness of life, prepared to raise his hand against himself in his despair; and suddenly refreshing tears fell from his eyes, and he left reconciled to life, imploring the heavens anew for sorrow and suffering, so that he might only live and shed tears again at such bagatelles. Bagatelles!—The world would slumber without such bagatelles, life would grow shallow, the soul moldy and slimy. Bagatelles!—O, may the names of those heeding such bagatelles with good will be eternally sanctified; the miraculous hand of Providence rested continually upon the brows of their creators. Even in moments of disaster and oppression, all that was most noble in the state stood, above all, as their defender; the Crowned Monarch guarded them with his royal shield from the heights of his inaccessible throne.

Onward then and with good cheer! And may my soul not be troubled by censure but gratefully accept criticism of shortcomings. May it not darken even when men deny its lofty impulses and sacred love for humanity! The world resembles a whirlpool; opinions and doctrines are in perpetual flux, but time threshes everything. False teachings fall away like husks, and fixed truths remain like hard seeds. Things considered groundless may afterwards appear armed with rigorous meaning. At the heart of cold laughter one may find fiery sparks of an eternal and mighty love. And who can tell? Perhaps everyone will then recognize why, by the force of the same laws, the proud and powerful appear weak and pitiful in misfortune, while the weak grow into giants, and why, by the force of the same laws, whoever often sheds heartfelt tears also laughs the most in this world!

From "Leaving the Theater after a Performance of a New Comedy [The Government Inspector]," *written probably in 1836, published in 1842*

PYOTR PETROVICH [*a man of society*]. . . . Allow me, however, . . . a remark about the play itself. . . : I fail to see any real benefit to society in *The Government Inspector*. . . that would entitle one to say society is in need of this play.

SEMYON SEMYONYCH [*also rather well-placed in society*]. I even detect harm. The play shows us our degradation; I can't discern any love for the fatherland in its author. Besides, what disrespect, even impudence! It completely escapes me how he dare tell everyone to his face: "What are you laughing at? Laugh at yourselves!"

. . . .

PYOTR PETROVICH. . . . I'll tell you what I personally felt: it was as if at that instant I was confronted by a man mocking everything that is ours, our manners, customs, way of life, and after provoking us to laugh, saying to our faces, "You're laughing at yourselves." . . . I see neither a great idea nor a purpose in this comedy; at least they don't come to light in the work itself.

NIKOLAY NIKOLAICH [*a man of letters*]. What other purpose can you wish, Pyotr Petrovich? Art, by its very nature, contains a purpose. An aspiration toward the beautiful and the sublime is precisely what art is. This is an indispensable law of art; without it art ceases to be art. Hence art can never be immoral. It necessarily aspires to the good, whether by positive or negative means: it shows us the beauty of whatever is best in man, or ridicules the worst. If you expose all the filth in man so that each member of the audience experiences total revulsion—well, I ask you, isn't that in itself praise of the good?

. . . .

PYOTR PETROVICH. ... Nikolay Nikolaich spoke profoundly.... But it doesn't answer my question. What you just said, namely, that virtue ought to be shown in its magical power, captivating the bad man as well as the good, and that evil ought to be portrayed so contemptuously that the audience not only feels no desire to be reconciled to the characters, but, on the contrary, wishes to repel them unhesitatingly—all that... is an indispensable condition of every literary work. It's not even a purpose. In addition, every work should make a unique, personal statement,... otherwise its originality vanishes.... That's why I fail to see the great significance others ascribe to *The Government Inspector*. It ought to have been made palpably clear why such a work was undertaken, what it's after, what it's driving at, what new idea it hopes to demonstrate....

NIKOLAY NIKOLAICH. Pyotr Petrovich, what can you possibly have in mind? Why—why, it's plain as day.

PYOTR PETROVICH. No, Nikolay Nikolaich, not at all. I can't see any particular purpose to this comedy.... *The Government Inspector* doesn't at all produce an impression that would raise the spirits of an audience; on the contrary,... some felt futile irritation, others even hostility, and everyone was left with an oppressive emotion. In spite of the pleasure aroused by adroitly contrived scenes, the comical circumstances of many of the characters, and the masterful treatment of some of them, as a whole it leaves one with something—I can't even explain it—something monstrously dismal, a kind of terror at our social chaos. The appearance of the gendarme, emerging in the doorway as if he were an executioner, the numbing effect of his words heralding the arrival of the true inspector, who is to destroy them all, obliterate them completely, wipe them from the face of the earth—all this is inexplicably terrifying. I mean it literally, *à la lettre;* no tragedy has ever made me feel so melancholy, pained, and desolate. I'm even prepared to suspect the author of intending just such an effect in the final scene of his comedy....

THE FIRST COMIC ACTOR [MIKHAYLO SEMYONOVICH SHCHEPKIN]. But haven't you noticed that *The Government Inspector* has no ending?

NIKOLAY NIKOLAICH. What do you mean, no ending?

SEMYON SEMYONYCH. What other conclusion could it have? There are five acts; comedies in six acts don't exist....

PYOTR PETROVICH. Permit me to remark, Mikhaylo Semyonych, what is a play without an end? Can the laws of art account for that too, Nikolay

Nikolaich? In my opinion, what you're doing is placing a locked casket before everybody, and asking what's in it.

FIRST COMIC ACTOR. But if it were put before you just so that you might make the effort to open it yourselves?

PYOTR PETROVICH. In that case you might at least apprise us of the fact, or simply give us the key.

. . . .

NIKOLAY NIKOLAICH. Stop speaking in riddles! You know something. The author must have given you the key, and you're keeping it a secret. . . . Give us the key. That's all!

SEMYON SEMYONYCH. The key, Mikhaylo Semyonych!

FYODOR FYODORYCH [*an enthusiast of the theater*]. The key!

PYOTR PETROVICH. The key!

ALL THE ACTORS AND ACTRESSES. The key, Mikhaylo Semyonych!

. . . .

FIRST COMIC ACTOR. Very well. . . . Take a close look at the town depicted in the play. Everyone agrees that no such town exists in all of Russia; a town in our country where all the officials are monsters is unheard of. You can always find two or three who are honest, but here—not one. In a word, there is no such town. Do you agree? Now suppose this town is actually our spiritual city and is to be found in each of us? No, let's not look at ourselves through the eyes of a man of the world (after all, it's not he who will pronounce judgment upon us); let us look, as well as we can, with the eyes of Him Who will call all men to account, before Whom the best of us—mark it well—will cast down their eyes in shame. Let us see who will then have enough courage to ask, "Is my face crooked?" Pray we are not alarmed by our own crookedness, just as we felt no fear upon seeing the crookedness of those officials. . . . No, Semyon Semyonych, it's not our beauty that ought to concern us but the fact that our lives, which we are in the habit of regarding as comedies, might very well end in the same sort of tragedy that concluded this comedy. Say what you will, the inspector who awaits us at the portals of the grave is terrible. Can you really be ignorant of this inspector's identity? Why deceive ourselves? He is our awakening conscience, who will force us, once and for all, to take a long hard look at ourselves. Nothing will remain hidden from this inspector, for he is sent by command of the Almighty. There will be no turning back when his coming is heralded. Suddenly horrors to make a man's hair stand on end will be revealed about and within us. Far better to examine ourselves at the beginning of our lives than at the end. Instead of engaging in idle self-centered chatter and self-congratulation, let us now visit our deformed spiritual city, a city several times worse than any other, where our passions run amuck like hideous officials plundering the treasury of our souls! At the beginning of our lives, let us take an inspector by the hand and examine all that lies within us—a true inspector and not a counterfeit! Not Khlestakov! Khlestakov is a mediocrity; he is the frivolous conscience of the world, venal and deceitful. The passions residing in our souls will buy him off in an instant. Arm in arm with Khlestakov, we will see nothing of our spiritual city. Note how in conversing with him, each official cleverly wriggled out of his difficulties and justified himself. They emerged almost sanctified. Don't you think our every passion, or even a trivial vulgar habit, has more cunning to it than does a swindling official?... No, you will not discern anything in yourselves with the superficial conscience of the world: [our passions] will deceive it, and it will deceive them, as Khlestakov duped the officials, and then it will vanish without leaving a trace. You will be in the position of the mayor turned fool, who let his imagination run away with him, began worming his way into a general's rank, announcing he was certain to be top man in the capital, promising positions to others, when he suddenly saw that he had been hoodwinked and played for a fool by a young whippersnapper, a featherbrain bearing no resemblance to the true inspector. No... gentlemen,...fling aside your worldly conscience. Examine yourselves, not through the eyes of Khlestakov, but those of the true inspector! I vow, our spiritual city is worth the same thought a good ruler gives to his realm. As he banishes corrupt officials from his land sternly and with dignity, let us banish corruption from our souls! There exists a weapon, a scourge, that can drive it out. Laughter, my worthy countrymen! Laughter, which our base passions fear so! Laughter, created so that we might deride whatever dishonors the true beauty of man. Let us restore to laughter its true significance! Let us wrest it from those who have turned it into a frivolous worldly blasphemy that does not distinguish between good and evil! Just as we laughed at the abominations of others, let us laugh at those abominations we uncover in ourselves! Not only this comedy, but everything that ridicules the ignoble and depraved, no matter who the author, must be understood as referring to ourselves, as if written about us personally.... Let us not swell with indignation if some infuriated mayor or, more correctly, the devil himself whispers: "What are you laughing at? Laugh at yourselves!" Proudly we shall answer him: "Yes, we are laughing at ourselves, because we sense our noble Russian heritage, because we hear a command from on high to be better than others!'' Countrymen! Russian blood flows in my veins, as in yours. Behold: I'm weeping. As a comic actor, I made you laugh earlier, and now I weep. Allow me to think that my calling is as honest as yours, that I serve my country as you do, that I'm not a light-headed jester created for the amusement of frivolous people, but an honorable functionary of God's great kingdom, and that I awakened laughter in you— not that dissolute laughter stemming from the empty vanity of idle hours by which man mocks man, but laughter born of love for man. Together we shall prove to the world that everything in the Russian land, from small to great, strives to serve Him Whom all things should serve, and that whatever exists in our land is surging upwards (*glancing up*) to the Supreme Eternal Beauty!

From ''The Denouement of The Government Inspector,'' *written in 1846, published posthumously*

I handled that play [*The Denouement of ''The Government Inspector''*] so clumsily that the audience must conclude I wish to turn *The Government Inspector* into an allegory. I don't have that in mind. *The Government Inspector* is what it is, and every viewer must of necessity apply to himself, not even *The Government Inspector,* but whatever suits him apropos of *The Government Inspector.* That's what I ought to have shown regarding the words ''Can it be my face that's crooked?''

From a letter to M. S. Shchepkin, c. July 10, 1847 (New Style)

It's not up to me to determine to what extent I'm a poet; all I know is that even before I grasped the significance and purpose of art, I felt with all my heart that it must be sacred. . . . I wasn't yet aware (and how could I have been in those days?) what the subject of my writings should be, but my creative powers were stirring, and the circumstances of my personal life pressed subjects upon me. Everything seemed to happen independently of my personal (free) will. For example, I never conceived of becoming a satirist or making my readers laugh. It's true that while still in school a playful mood at times took hold of me, and I wearied my classmates with inappropriate wisecracks. But these were temporary fits; basically I was of a melancholic disposition, given to reflection. Subsequently, illness and depression combined with the above. Illness and depression were the reasons for the gaiety that appeared in my early works; without any ulterior goal and plan, but merely to divert myself, I concocted characters and placed them in comical situations—there you have the origin of my stories! A passion for observation of people, nurtured since childhood, gave them a

measure of naturalness; people even started calling them faithful repro-
ductions of nature. One more consideration: my laughter was at first
good-natured; I never thought of ridiculing anything for any purpose, and
when I heard that entire groups and classes of society were taking offense
and were even angry at me, it amazed me to such a degree that I finally
began to reflect, "If the power of laughter is so great as to be feared,
then one ought not waste it purposelessly." I decided to assemble all the
evils I knew, and deride them once and for all—there's the origin of *The
Government Inspector.* It was my first work specifically intended to produce a good influence upon society, which, by the way, didn't work out;
people detected an intention to ridicule the legitimate order of things and
the forms of government, when I only intended to ridicule arbitrary
deviations on the part of some individuals from these forms and from the
legitimate order. The performance of *The Government Inspector* made a
painful impression upon me. I was angry at the audience, who failed to
understand me, and at myself for being at fault in not making myself
understood. I wanted to run away from it all.

From a letter to V. A. Zhukovsky, December 29, 1847-January 10, 1848

Notes

The plays have been translated from N. V. Gogol', *Sobraniye khudozhestvennykh proizvedeniy v pyati tomakh*, 2d ed. (Moscow: AN SSSR, 1960), vol. 4. Material in the Appendix has been translated from that source or from the edition of the complete works on which it is based, *Polnoye sobraniye sochineniy* (Moscow: AN SSSR, 1940–52), henceforth referred to as *PSS*. Quotations from Gogol's writings in the Introduction, the sources of which are not given in the notes, are taken from the Appendix. Dates throughout are according to the above and are in the Old Style unless specified otherwise.

Introduction

1. P. A. Pletněv to V. A. Zhukovsky, February 17, 1833, in *N. V. Gogol' v pis'makh i vospominaniyakh*, comp. Vasily Gippius (Moscow: Federatsiya, 1931), p. 70. Gogol reworked parts of the play and published them, along with *The Gamblers*, under the heading "Dramatic Fragments and Individual Scenes" in the first edition of his collected works of 1842. *An Official's Morning* had previously appeared in Pushkin's *Contemporary* in 1836. The other titles are *A Law Suit*, *The Servants' Quarter*, and *Fragment*. They may be found in Nikolay Gogol, *The Government Inspector and Other Plays*, trans. Constance Garnett (London: Chatto & Windus, 1926; New York: A. A. Knopf, 1927).

2. M. S. Shchepkin to I. I. Sosnitsky, June 3, 1836, in *Mikhail Semĕnovich Shchepkin*, comp. M. A. Shchepkin (St. Petersburg: Novoye vremya, 1914), p. 163. A. I. Gertsen [Herzen], *Du développement des idées révolutionnaires en Russie*, in *Sobraniye sochineniy*, vol. 7 (Moscow: AN SSSR, 1956), p. 98.

3. To M. S. Shchepkin, December 3, 1842 [New Style], *PSS*, 12:129.

4. Quoted in G. P. Makogonenko, ed., *Russkiye dramaturgi*, vol. 1, *XVIII vek* (Leningrad-Moscow: Iskusstvo, 1959), p. 52.

5. From "Epistola o stikhotvorstve" [Epistle on the writing of poetry]; and "O blagorodstve" [On nobility].

6. From Sumarokov's *Chudovishchi* [The monsters].

7. V. V. Gippius, "Nikolay Vasil'yevich Gogol'," in *Klassiki russkoy dramy*, ed. V. A. Desnitsky (Leningrad-Moscow: Iskusstvo, 1940), p. 129.

8. *PSS*, 5:154.

9. Vladimir Nabokov, *Nikolai Gogol* (New York: New Directions, 1944), p. 42.

10. *PSS*, 8:109.

11. Ibid., p. 293.

12. S. T. Aksakov, *Istoriya moyego znakomstva s Gogolem* (Moscow: AN SSSR, 1960), pp. 17, 21–22.

13. Cited by Nick Worrall, "Meyerhold Directs Gogol's *Government Inspector*," *Theatre Quarterly* 2, no. 7 (July–September 1972): 80.

14. V. Ye. Meyerkhol'd, *Stat'i, pis'ma, rechi, besedy*, pt. 2 (Moscow: Iskusstvo, 1968), pp. 143–45.

15. To M. A. Maksimovich, April 20, 1834, *PSS*, 10:311.

Marriage

Written 1833–35. Final revision in 1841. Published and first performed in 1842.

Characters. Gogol often chooses or concocts descriptive or comical names. Some meanings are

AGAFYA (Agatha). From Greek *agathē* 'good'. Tikhonovna would suggest *tikhiy* 'quiet' 'gentle', or *tikhonya* 'a meek person', though that is not the etymology.

PODKOLYOSIN. From *pod koleso* 'under the wheel'.

KOCHKARYOV. *Kochkar'* in the dialect of Astrakhan meant 'a pedigreed ram that has not been neutered'.

ANUCHKIN. An earlier version had Onuchkin from *onucha*, leggings worn by peasants. In dialects, derivative forms had pejorative meanings of 'tramp' and 'a beggar who is tediously importunate'.

ZHEVAKIN. From *zhevat'* 'chew'; figuratively, 'to repeat with tiresome monotony'. "Baltazar Baltazarovich" is almost as exotic to Russians as it is to Americans.

STARIKOV. From *starik* 'old man'.

4   **a court councilor is equal to a colonel.**   The titles court councilor,

collegiate assessor, titular councilor, and so on, which recur in the plays, indicated ranks in the civil service, not actual occupations. The Table of Ranks, instituted by Peter the Great in 1722, was intended to furnish incentives for service to the state. Ranks in the civil service paralleled military ranks. A court councilor was equal to a lieutenant colonel. Until 1845 the lowest rank (fourteenth) gave its owner personal nobility; the eighth, hereditary nobility. Podkolyosin holds the seventh, which makes him a nobleman. Since *nobility* and *aristocracy* carry various connotations, it should be reiterated (see Introduction) that the majority of the Russian nobility were poorly educated and of modest means.

6   **She's the daughter of a respectable merchant.** Literally, "a merchant of the third guild"—the lowest of the three guilds into which merchants were organized. Merchants had an inferior social status in Russia. The more ambitious sought entry into the nobility by enrolling in the government service. Women might acquire noble status for themselves and their children by marrying into the nobility.

8   **Brandakhlýstova?** From *brandakhlyst* 'watery soup' or 'watery beer.' Also 'a good-for-nothing' 'a loafer'.

8   **Kuperdyágina.** Gogol may have had in mind the dialect word *skuperdyaga* 'miser' 'skinflint'. The suffix *yag-a* is pejorative.

16   **Akínf Stepanovich Panteléyev.** Pantaleyev, absent from the final version, made an appearance in the first draft to stammer the line: "Miss, I, on this third of January, ask your ha..., ha..., ha...nd. ..." (*PSS,* 5:258–59). He was used in at least one Russian production of the play.

17   **senator. governor.** The senate was established by Peter I in 1711 to supervise judicial, financial, and administrative activities of the state. Senators were appointed. Never able to contravene the tsar's will, the senate lost much of its authority in later years. By Gogol's time it had become primarily a judicial institution, acting as a supreme court of appeal, but without the power to establish precedents. Governors, also appointed, administered provinces of the Empire.

20   **"Dateci del pane" "portate vino!"** "Give me some bread," "bring wine," of course in Italian, not French.

41   **The festival** A public outing on the first of May at Ekaterinhof outside of Petersburg, where there was a park and a palace built by Peter for his wife.

The Government Inspector

Written in 1835. First published and performed in 1836. Second revised edition published in 1841; revised again for the collected *Works of Nikolay Gogol* in 1842.

Epigraph. Gogol added it to the 1842 edition, no doubt as a response to his critics.

Characters

SKVOZNIK-DMUKHANOVSKY (the mayor). *Skvoznik* 'a draft'; figuratively, 'a sly penetrating old fox' 'an experienced swindler'. *Dmukhnuti* (Ukrainian) 'to blow', with secondary colloquial usages suggesting rapid motions, including 'to whack'. Also *dmit'* (Church Slavic), 'to puff out' and 'to swindle'. The suggestion is, so to speak, of 'a bag of wind' and 'a crook' squared.

KHLOPOV (superintendent of schools). From *khlop* (*kholop*), 'slave' 'serf'; *kholop* has a secondary meaning of 'a grovelling servile person'. The name also suggests the etymologically unrelated *khlopat'* 'to slap, smack', with dialectal usages of 'to lie, chatter idly, speak nonsensical rumors'; also *khlopotat'* 'to bustle, fuss'; and *khlopoty* 'trouble' 'cares'. His first name and patronymic suggest *luk* 'onion', of which he reeks.

LYAPKIN-TYAPKIN (the judge). From *lyapat'* 'to botch'; *tyapat'* 'to hit' 'to snatch' (figuratively, 'to steal'). Cf. *tyap-lyap*, a colloquial expression meaning 'in a slipshod way'.

ZEMLYANIKA (director of charities). The name means 'wild strawberries', a delicacy that contrasts with his grossness.

KHLESTAKOV. From *khlestat'* 'to lash, whip', with secondary meanings of 'to abuse, insult, swear, chatter idly'. Nabokov writes: "Khlestakov's very name is a stroke of genius, for it conveys to the Russian reader an effect of lightness and rashness, a prattling tongue, the swish of a slim walking cane, the slapping sound of playing cards, the braggadocio of a nincompoop and the dashing ways of a lady-killer." (*Nikolai Gogol*, p. 55.)

DR. HÜBNER. The Russian version of the name of the good doctor in whose hospital patients "recover like flies" is Gibner, suggesting *gibnut'* 'to perish'.

LYULYUKOV. From *lyulyukat'* 'to lull, rock to sleep'. Cf. *lyul'ka* 'a cradle'.

RASTAKOVSKY. From *rastakat'sya* (*takat'*) 'to agree out of servility' 'to be a yes-man'.

KOROBKIN. From *korobka* 'a box'.

POLICEMEN.

UKHOVYORTOV. From *ukho* 'ear' and *vertet'* 'twist'.

SVISTUNOV. *Svistun* 'a whistler'.

PUGOVITSYN. *Pugovitsa* 'a button'. He is actually very tall.

DERZHIMORDA. From *derzhat'* 'to hold' and *morda* 'snout' 'mug'. The implication is that he will take hold of his victim's face in a violent manner. The name has come into the language to describe someone with the inclinations of a brutal cop.

POSHLYOPKINA. From *poshlëpat'* 'to slap, spank'.

The town's officials. Until the reforms of the 1860s, Russian law made little allowance for local autonomy. Officials, whether appointed, like the mayor, or elected by the nobility, like the judge, were subject to the authority of appointed provincial governors, the various ministries, and ultimately, of course, to the autocratic tsar. The mayor, judge, director of charities, and the superintendent of schools held ranks in the Table of Ranks (see note to p. 4) and were members of the civil service. In Russia power always had a personal, extralegal character, and in addition to their subordinate status in a governmental hierarchy, officials were exposed to the intervention of "important personages." Because positions in provincial administration paid poorly and offered few opportunities for initiative and ambition, they were shunned by the more prosperous and better educated. If law gave local functionaries small scope, Russian reality had its compensations. Distances to centers of authority were often enormous, communication was difficult, and the bureaucracy, though growing, was undermanned. "Mayors," who were essentially policemen, and their confreres came to regard their bailiwicks as personal fiefdoms where they might do pretty well as they pleased. Corruption, abuses of power, and plain incompetence were staggering. Nicholas I, determined to remedy the situation, had government inspectors dispatched to the provinces with frequency. Tales of men mistaken for such inspectors were common in the literature and gossip of the period. A second-rate play by Grigory Kvitka-Osnovyanenko, *Visitor from the Capital, or a Commotion in a District Town,* bears resemblances of plot and incident to Gogol's. Though it was not published until 1840, copies of the manuscript (written in 1827) circulated widely. Gogol denied having read it.

Did Pushkin give Gogol the plot of *The Government Inspector* in response to Gogol's letter of October 7, 1835 (see Appendix)? He may very well have. Pushkin himself was taken for a government inspector on a trip to Nizhny Novgorod in 1833. Among Pushkin's papers there was the following plan of a work, probably jotted down the same year: "Krispin arrives in the Province...to a fair—he is taken for [illegible]...[dots in original]. The governor is an honest fool—the governor's wife flirts with him—Krispin woos the daughter." (A. S. Pushkin, *Polnoye sobraniye sochineniy*, vol. 8, bk. 1 [Moscow-Leningrad: AN SSSR, 1948], p. 431.) (The sexual rivalry of a mother and daughter is not uncommon in comedy; it had been used by Sumarokov in *Mother—Rival of her Daughter* [1772].) Where Gogol diverges from his predecessors—we do not know what Pushkin would have made of the anecdote—is in turning Khlestakov into an unwitting imposter.

58   **freethinkers** . Or, "disciples of Voltaire."

59   **marshall of the nobility** An official elected by the nobility of districts and provinces to represent them to the monarch.

60   *Moscow News*! A dry official newspaper, founded by Moscow University in 1756 and later leased to private publishers.

63   **Two weeks** Omitted: "He arrived on St. Basil of Egypt's Day."

63   **the town council** The reference is to another official, the *golova*, also commonly translated as "mayor," who was elected by the townspeople—merchants, tradesmen, journeymen, professionals, etc. He and the town council (*duma*) were technically responsible for the running of the town, but in practice the *gorodnichiy* (the "mayor" of the play) and other officials appointed by the central government held the reins of administration. The structure of municipal government had been established by Catherine II's Charter of the Towns of 1785, which remained the law of the land until the Reforms of Alexander II (1855-81).

63   **a book on protocol.** Actually, "in the book: *The Deeds of John Mason*." Gogol is probably alluding to John Mason (1706-63), an English nonconformist minister, whose *Self Knowledge*... (London: J. Waugh, 1745) had wide currency in Russia, especially among Masonic circles. Freemasonry, like any organization independent of the government, was mistrusted in Russia. Masonic lodges were at times loci for independent and liberal thought. Many of the Decembrists, who rose against autocracy in 1825, had been associated with the Masonic movement. Thus the reference is to the judge's "freethinking."

68   **the bottom of the heap.** Khlestakov is a collegiate registrar, the

lowest rank in the Table of Ranks of the civil service.

71 *"Robert le diable,"* An opera by Meyerbeer (1831).

71 *"Red Sarafan,"* A Russian folk song.

71 **nobody would rent me a carriage.** It was Iokhim, the most fashionable carriage dealer in Petersburg, who refused Khlestakov.

75 **Reliable dealers** Dealers from Kholmogory, who were renowned for the quality of their beef.

77 **a medal on your lapel.** The reference is to the Order of St. Vladimir, which was a ribbon.

79 **a couple of bottles.** Literally, "a fat-bellied bottle." "Fatbelly" (*tolstobryukhiy*) was a nickname for tax-farmers, who held the state liquor monopoly. Worral claims that it is a pun on the name of a distillery, "Tolstooriucha [sic]," but I have been unable to find it in lists of nineteenth-century firms that were accessible to me (Worrall, "Meyerhold Directs Gogol's *Government Inspector,*" p. 87).

85 **Filet of sole,** *Labardan* (from the Dutch *labberdaan*) is actually salted cod, which had recently become a fashionable delicacy. Khlestakov (p. 91) is enraptured by the sound of the word. "Salted cod" just won't do.

87 **the country also has its hillocks, its rivulets.** *Prigorki, rucheyki.* Khlestakov, here and elsewhere, appropriates the diction of Russian sentimental poetry in conversing with the ladies.

88 **to promote me,** Literally, "to make me a collegiate assessor," the eighth rank in the table (see note to p. 4).

88-89 We have substituted the more familiar **Don Giovanni** for Meyerbeer's *Robert le diable.* **Norma** (1831) is an opera by Bellini. Beaumarchais' **The Marriage of Figaro** (1784) was very popular in Russia in the 1820s; *Robert le diable* in the 1830s. "**The Frigate Hope**" (1833) was not by Baron Brambeus but by Alexander Bestuzhev (pseudonym, Marlinsky), a romantic poet and novelist in vogue in the 1830s. **The Moscow Telegraph** was of course not a work but a journal which had a run of approximately ten years (1825-34). **Baron Brambeus** was the nom de plume of Osip Senkovsky (1800-58), a hack journalist and humorist of the time who was hostile to Gogol and whom Gogol in turn despised. As editor of the middlebrow magazine *Library for Reading,* Senkovsky, like Khlestakov, "corrected" manuscripts indiscriminately, which infuriated writers, Gogol among them. Gogol also wrote approvingly of an article that accused Senkovsky of plagiarism (*PSS,* 8:162, 530). The publisher who pays Khlestakov forty thousand (per poem?) was the highly respected Alexander Smirdin. The full title of the popular historical novel by Mikhail Zagoskin, one of Walter Scott's numerous Russian imitators, referred to here as *The War of 1612,* was *Yury Miloslavsky, or the Russians in the War of 1612* (1829). In an earlier variant, Khlestakov wrote vaudevilles also.

89 **My mind works with extraordinary speed.** A word by word rendering would be: "I have an extraordinary lightness in my thoughts." The expression has become part of the language, designating a light-headed individual.

90 **the cabinet** Actually the State Council, a legislative body established by Alexander I in 1810, composed of appointed members, whose decisions were not binding on the crown.

91 Khlestakov here retires for what is apparently a nap after lunch; in the Russian he awakens the following morning. Following the earlier cue, we have compressed the action into a single day.

97 **Collegiate Assessor,** etc. See note to p. 4.

102 **a flaming radical.** Literally, "worse than a Jacobin."

102 **Petunia.** Perepetuya in the original, an unusual name chosen for its comic effect.

103 **state bank.** Actually, the Board of Public Charity, which was authorized to perform many of the functions of banks. Russian banking institutions in Gogol's time were supervised by the government, which furnished the bulk of their funds. Though the so-called state bank did not exist until the 1860s, we have used the terms *bank* or *state bank* throughout.

104 **senators** See note to p. 17.

107 **A STOREKEEPER.** We may assume this is the Abdulin mentioned earlier. Gogol either forgot to insert his name, or, more likely, wanted to emphasize a collective group of storekeepers, literally, "merchants."

111 In the original, Khlestakov, of course, does not quote Robert Burns but the opening lines of Mikhail Lomonosov's "Ode, Adapted from *Job*" (1751): "Oh man who in thy sorrow/ Vainly murmur against thy God." Lomonosov (1711-65) was the outstanding figure of the Russian Enlightenment. Khlestakov is apparently grasping at lines he heard as a schoolboy.

113 **as the poet says,** The poet is Nikolay Karamzin; what he says is in "Bornholm Island" (1794). Karamzin (1766-1826) was the most prominent figure of Russian sentimentalism; also an influential historian.

118   **the red or the blue?** The blue was the Order of St. Andrew the Apostle; the red, of St. Alexander Nevsky. The blue was higher.

124   **With God all things are possible.** Matt. 19:26.

125   **Post Street!** The Postmaster is bowled over because Post Street was the address of the central administration of the Russian postal system.

127   **pig in trousers.** "Pig in a skull cap" in the original.

127   **97 Post Street, etc.** Except for the substitution of "Post" for "Malaya Morskaya" (now, Gogol Street), all the details of Trya-pichkin's address are identical to those of Gogol's at the time he wrote the play. Author and character also share the same patro-nymic: Vasilyevich. Tryapichkin, from *tryapka* 'rag' or 'a spineless person'.

128-29   **Engaged!...down to hell!** This entire section was added to the final edition of 1842, probably, like the Epigraph, as a reaction to hostile criticism of the play.

129   **GENDARME** An officer of the dreaded Section Three of His Majesty's Own Chancery, a secret police force established in 1826 by Nicholas I.

The Gamblers

Begun apparently in 1836. Completed and published in 1842. First per-formed in 1843.

Characters

  KRUGEL. Though intended to suggest a German name, perhaps from *kruglyak,* a gambling term meaning 'a stacked deck'

  UTESHITELNY. An unmodified adjective meaning 'consoling' 'comforting'.

  GLOV. From *golova* 'head' 'brains'.

  ZAMUKHRYSHKIN. *Zamukhryshka* 'a plain, insignificant, poorly dressed, slovenly individual'.

138   **bank.** Bank (or *Shtoss*) is a simplified version of faro. Each player, as well as the banker (or dealer), has his own deck. The player draws one or more cards from his deck and places a bet on each. He may continue to bet, or "raise," during the course of a deal. The dealer deals cards face up, first to the right, then to the left. When a card equal to the player's card turns up on the right, the dealer wins. If it

turns up on the left, the dealer loses and the player wins. If both right and left match, the dealer wins. We have eliminated the technical terms of the original. Card playing, long a favorite pastime of the Russian gentry, became the rage in the 1830s. In Pushkin's classic *Queen of Spades* (1834), *Shtoss* is also played.

146   **the bank**   See note to p. 103.

149   **the cavalry.**   In the original, "the Hussars."

153   **Another Napoleon!**   Napoleon has been substituted for Barclay de Tolly, who was a prominent Russian army commander in the War of 1812.

156   **he has the makings of a soldier and a lover!**   A paraphrase of the opening line of Denis Davydov's poem, "Burtsovu" (1804): "Burtsov, yëra, zabiyaka."

158   **Krep Krépovich.**   In the Russian, Psoy Stakhich. The quaintness of the original might be missed by non-Russians. Also, Perpentich has been changed to Fenteleich.

164   **gin rummy**   In the original, boston.

Appendix

1. Melodramas by Alexandre Dumas (1802-70) and Victor Henri Ducange (1783-1833) had been running frequently on the Petersburg stage. Gogol borrowed from the latter's *Trente ans, ou la vie d'un joueur* (1827) for *The Gamblers.*

2. See note to p. 85.

3. *Russkiy vestnik,* no. 1 (1862), pp. 91-93.

4. Gogol dated the letter May 25, 1836, and described it as a shortened version of a letter intended for Pushkin but never sent. Doubt has been cast on both the date and whether it was really intended as a letter. The surviving manuscript was written in 1840-41.

Bibliography

Russian titles have been omitted. Those who read Russian should start with Vasily Gippius, *Gogol'* (Leningrad: Mysl', 1924), still the best book in any language on Gogol; and Yury Mann, *Komediya Gogolya "Revizor"* (Moscow: Khudozhestvennaya literatura, 1966), the best study of the plays. A more extensive bibliography may be found in Proffer (see below).

Čiževskij, Dmitrij (Chizhevsky). "Gogol: Artist and Thinker." *Annals of the Ukrainian Academy of Arts and Sciences in the U. S.* 2 (Summer 1952): 261-78. Reprinted in *Gogol', Turgenev, Dostoevskij, Tolstoj.* Forum Slavicum, edited by Dmitrij Tschiževskij, vol. 12. Munich: Wilhelm Fink, 1966.
Sees Gogol, artist and thinker, whole. Indispensable.
———. *History of Nineteenth-Century Russian Literature.* Translated by Richard Noel Porter. Edited by Serge A. Zenkovsky. Nashville: Vanderbilt University Press, 1974.
An excellent account of the literary movements and changing styles.
———. "The Unknown Gogol." *Slavonic and Eastern European Review* 30 (1952): 476-93.
Coleman, Arthur Prudden. *Humour in the Russian Comedy from Catherine to Gogol.* New York: Columbia University Press, 1925.
Debreczeny, Paul. *Nikolay Gogol and His Contemporary Critics.* Transactions of the American Philosophical Society, 56, pt. 3 (new series). Philadelphia, 1966.
Erlich, Victor. *Gogol.* New Haven: Yale University Press, 1969.
A lively, often illuminating study.
Evreinoff, Nicolas. *Histoire du théâtre russe.* Paris: Editions du Chêne, 1947.
A view of a prominent Russian director and dramatist.
Fanger, Donald. *The Creation of Nikolai Gogol.* Cambridge, Mass.:

Harvard University Press, 1979.

Not in print at time of preparation of this volume. Fanger is a knowledgeable and discerning scholar.

Fülöp-Miller, René, and Gregor, Joseph. *The Russian Theatre: Its Character and History*. Translated by Paul England. London: George G. Harrap, 1930.

A short history supplemented by gorgeous illustrations. A lovely book to look at.

Gourfinkel, Nina. *Gogol*. Les grands dramaturges, vol. 14. Paris: L'Arche, 1956.

Karlinsky, Simon. *The Sexual Labyrinth of Nikolai Gogol*. Cambridge, Mass.: Harvard University Press, 1976.

Besides exploring the sexual motives of Gogol's art, the book contains much valuable material, including an informed discussion of Russian comedy (pp. 144-50).

Leiste, Hans Walter. *Gogol und Molière*. Nuremberg: H. Karl, 1958.

McLean, Hugh. "Gogol and the Whirling Telescope." In *Russia: Essays in History and Literature*. Edited by Lyman H. Legters. Leiden: E. J. Brill, 1972.

A thoughtful discussion of "artistic distancing" in Gogol's works.

Magarshack, David. *Gogol: A Life*. London: Faber and Faber, 1957.

A useful introduction. Allows Gogol to speak for himself through ample quotations.

Maguire, Robert A., ed. and trans. *Gogol from the Twentieth Century: Eleven Essays*. Princeton, N.J.: Princeton University Press, 1974.

A wide ranging collection of modern Russian views of Gogol, some of them extremely influential. Highly recommended.

Marshall, Herbert. *The Pictorial History of the Russian Theatre*. New York: Crown, 1977.

Mirsky, D. S. *A History of Russian Literature*. Edited by Francis J. Whitfield. New York: Alfred A. Knopf, 1949.

Still unsurpassed. Alive and consistently intelligent.

Nabokov, Vladimir. *Nikolai Gogol*. Norfolk, Conn.: New Directions, 1944.

Demonstrates that literary biography and criticism can be fun, even if the fun is sometimes at the expense of the subject matter. One-sided. Also scintillating.

Patouillet, Jules. *Le théâtre de mœurs russes des origines à Ostrovski (1672-1850)*. Paris: H. Champion, 1912.

Dated but still usable.

Pollok, Karl Heinz. "Zur dramatischen Form von Gogol's *Spielern.*" *Die Welt der Slaven* 4 (1959): 169-80.

Proffer, Carl R., ed. *Letters of Nikolai Gogol.* Translated by Carl R. Proffer in collaboration with Vera Krivoshein. Ann Arbor: University of Michigan Press, 1967.

Includes an extensive bibliography.

Rahv, Philip. "Gogol as a Modern Instance." In *Image and Idea.* New York: New Directions, 1958.

A balanced essay, describing Gogol as a prototype of the modern artist without losing sight of the nineteenth-century context.

Setschkareff, Vsevolod. *Gogol: His Life and Works.* Translated by Robert Kramer. London: Peter Owen, 1965.

A thorough and reliable presentation of the facts.

Slonim, Mark. *Russian Theater: From the Empire to the Soviets.* Cleveland: World, 1961.

Readable and informative.

Thiess, Frank. *Nikolaus W. Gogol und seine Bühnenwerke.* Berlin: F. Scheider, 1922.

Troyat, Henri. *Divided Soul: The Life of Gogol.* Translated by Nancy Amphoux. Garden City, N.Y.: Doubleday, 1973.

A readable popular biography.

Varneke, Boris. *History of the Russian Theatre: Seventeenth Century through Nineteenth Century.* Translated by Boris Brasol. Revised and edited by Belle Martin. New York: Macmillan, 1951.

Detailed and ponderous.

Welsh, David J. *Russian Comedy, 1765-1823.* The Hague: Mouton, 1966.

A competent survey of the major trends.

Wilson, Edmund. "Gogol: The Demon in the Overgrown Garden." *The Nation* 175 (1952): 520-24.

An astute appraisal by one of our greatest critics. Takes issue with Nabokov.

Worrall, Nick. "Meyerhold Directs Gogol's *Government Inspector.*" *Theatre Quarterly* 2, no. 7 (July–September 1972): 75-95.

A detailed reconstruction of one of the most famous productions of the Russian and modern stage. Excellent photographs.

Zeldin, Jesse. *Nikolai Gogol's Quest for Beauty.* Lawrence, Kan.: Regents Press, 1978.

Has the virtue of taking Gogol's ideas seriously. A handy table giving dates of composition, publication, and production of the plays (pp. 63-64).